SOILING THE HANDS

The journey of the Canon of Scripture

by
Michael Mahony

The *One of Us* Collection - Book Three

Published by:

SA Catholic Online Books
59 Tom Brown Boulevard
St Francis Bay, 6312
frank@sacatholiconline.org
www.sacatholiconline.org

Edited By Frank Nunan
Cover Design: Frank Nunan

© Copyright 2014 - Michael Mahony
All rights reserved - no part of the publication may be reproduced, stored in a retrieval system, or transmitted in any form or by any means electronic, mechanical, photocopying, recording or otherwise, without the prior permission of the publisher.

ISBN: 978-0-620-60467-3

June 2014

Printed & Bound by Print on Demand, Cape Town.

About the Author

Michael ("Mike") Mahony was born in Ireland in 1944 and has lived in South Africa since 1975, having previously worked in Nigeria, Dublin, and London.

Mike holds an honours degree in physics from University College Dublin, and a Master's degree in business from The University of South Africa, as well as a Master's degree in Catholic Theology from the University of KwaZulu-Natal.

His life-occupation has been primarily in IT (software development) in banking, from which he retired in 2002.

Since his conversion to Christ in 1978 he has been actively engaged in Christian ministry as a lay person, both in Catholic and Evangelical churches, and is currently a member of St. Charles Catholic Church, Victory Park, Johannesburg.

Mike has been married to his wife, Mary, since 1967. They have been blessed with three sons and three daughters, and a wonderful multinational clan of grandchildren.

This collection of seven books, (*One of Us*) is Mike's first venture into 'doing theology' and expressing it in writing. If he had known that it was going to be such fun, he would have undertaken it years ago.

for *Conor*

iconoclast of secular gods

Dedication

To the self-effacing person of יהוה: **The Holy Spirit**

εἰς τὸν κόσμον λέγει· θυσίαν καὶ προσφορὰν οὐκ
into the world he says, sacrifice and offering not
ἠθέλησας, σῶμα δὲ κατηρτίσω μοι·
you did desire a body but you have prepared for me

[When coming] into the world he [Christ] said: "Sacrifice and offering you did not desire, but a body you have prepared for me."

Manuscript: papyrus 46 [P^{46}]

Dated: Approx. 200AD

Source: Chester Beatty Library, Dublin.

Disclaimer

If one wanted to be admitted to a college of the National University of Ireland in the 1960s one had to pass Latin in the entrance (i.e. matriculation) examination.

Most aspiring university students didn't bother to sit such an examination since a pass in the Government's national examination system (the "Leaving Cert") qualified as a matriculation exemption. As a founding member of the Sandycove Lawn Tennis Club Poker School I had long appreciated the strategy of hedging one's bets, and since I had never grasped what Messrs Caesar, Livy, Virgil and Cicero were all about I thought that I should sit both examinations. Given that in all my school years I had never once passed Latin, one can regard this as a prudent act, a futile strategy, or the wishful thinking of a fool.

In 1962 I failed the Latin matriculation examination for entrance to University College Dublin (UCD); I did however pass the Leaving Cert Latin test, and so was admitted to the Science Faculty of UCD.

There is no logical explanation for this strange occurrence. Other than the lines (somewhere) in Caesar's Gallic Wars, "his rebus cognitis, Caesar..." (meaning "these things having been considered, Caesar did something or other..."), I really hadn't a clue what was going on in that test.

At the time I gave all the credit to the Guinness. I didn't drink the stuff myself; but I became convinced that the examiner had consumed a large quantity of that particular beverage prior to marking my test paper. I took peculiar delight at the time in concluding that perhaps I was one of those rare individuals who could expect to get away with it – to live a charmed life to some extent. This sentiment was reinforced when I discovered that none other than the young Winston Churchill had failed the Latin examination required to enter Harrow, and yet – somehow – had got away with it and had been admitted. I actually felt somewhat more justified than Churchill; I, at least, had attempted to answer the questions[1].

It was only many years later that I came to see that this was one of the many instances of "Someone" coming after me with a dustpan and brush; cleaning up the mess that I was leaving in my wake...

I mention all this about the Latin just to say that I later developed a great love for the Bible and became sufficiently interested to do an elementary course in New Testament Greek, along with a fascination with the Old Testament Hebrew, although I have never actually studied the latter. The (selective) use of Greek terms in this little project, is only resorted to when it is germane to the journey (particularly in Book Two), and is clearly not in any way a claim to scholarship on my part: It would take much more Guinness than the River Liffey could supply for any contemporary examiner to grant me a pass in classical languages.

As for the other playthings mentioned in this little project - rugby, physics, mathematics, jazz, Information Technology, etc. – sojourners must not be deluded. My only claims to notoriety on the rugby field are the broken bones (arm; ankle; nose - twice) earned on the schoolboy playing fields of Lansdowne Road (Marian College had the use of the practice fields) and on the hazardous surfaces enjoyed by the Plateau Rugby Club of Northern Nigeria. I distinguished myself in the Science Faculty of UCD by getting a "Third" in my Honours examination in 1966. It would be dishonest to attribute such a mediocre academic performance to the Friday nights spent with Flan at the Green Lounge Jazz Club in Stephen's Green, or to the girls who broke my adolescent heart at Saturday night dances at Palmerstone, Bective, and other rugby clubs. But in spite of my limited abilities, one could still experience the excitement of what was Theoretical Physics in the 1960s, and I loved every minute of it. I just wish that I had had the capability of enjoying it more. As for IT, I confess that the problem-solving character of maths-physics found its fun outlet in the debugging of computer programmes; the "buzz" of the first thirty years of computing was indeed exhilarating.

What, you may be thinking, has any of this got to do with the subject matter of this little project?

It was once suggested to me that in the telling of each of our stories it may well be possible to hear something of God's own story. So, my journey of life is the natural "container" within which to try and articulate my own searching, grappling with issues, and personal experiences of God – albeit undertaken alongside fellow travellers. Such "theologizing" is by definition (in my case) an amateur endeavour, but even so, I found the comments by Thomas O'Loughlin on **real** theologians encouraging with respect to my choice of "container:"

> Many people can read theology books, and indeed write them, but the creative theologian is above all someone who is grappling with his or her own religious questions and passions... the history of theology is punctuated by great religious figures whose personal quests, engagements with the world, their individual make-up – and indeed hang-ups – have shaped what they have done and written. These, in turn, raised the questions to be answered, and laid out the directions to be taken, for generations after them. We have only to think of the lives of Augustine, Aquinas and Luther to note how their personal questions inspired their works and moved theology in one way rather than another. Theology is activity: one does it, one theologises, and the way

one does theology says much about the theologian. So...to have an overview of a theology we have to situate the works within the life, and be attuned to noting the impact of the life in the works. Theology, therefore, can be seen as the results of the searches of individuals – aware of the community of Christians[2] and giving weight to the results of others' searches – for understanding. The individual who searched and the account of the searching are interdependent[3].

* * *

---

1 In '*My Early Life*', Churchill describes his performance on the Harrow Latin entrance exam: "I wrote my name at the top of the page. I wrote down the number of the question, '1'. After much reflection I put a bracket around it, thus, '(1)'. But thereafter I could not think of anything connected with it that was either relevant or true. Incidentally, there arrived from nowhere in particular a blot and several smudges. I gazed for two whole hours at this sad spectacle; and then merciful ushers collected up my piece of foolscap and carried it up to the Headmaster's table." [Quoted in Keegan Churchill p.23].

2 [Own Note]; O'Loughlin's limitation (to Christians) is understandable given the context and scope of his particular study, but generally one is keenly aware of the theologians of other faiths (not least the Jewish faith) as members also of such a 'community'. Cf. Pope Benedict XVI's own stated acknowledgment in this regard to the Jewish scholar Jacob Neusner and his book: A Rabbi Talks with Jesus in Benedict XVI Jesus of Nazareth Part One (2007), p.103-127.

3 O'Loughlin (Celtic Theology – 2003) p.68.

* * *

Acknowledgements

To the many people who have contributed to the journey, I am sincerely grateful. Your presence is evident within this little collection of seven books, albeit that, on occasion, some detective work may be required to verify this claim. The venture of bringing this seven-volume collection to birth could not have been completed without the sterling work undertaken by Frank Nunan of SA Catholic Online [Publishing]. Thank you, Frank

Thank you all

CONTENTS

A. A paradoxical designation
1. Who Rules? — 3
2. The Bible & The Canon: Content & Process — 15

B. The Journeys of the Biblical Canons
3. The journey of the Old Testament Canon — 21
4. The journey of the New Testament Canon (Introduction) — 35

C. Responsibility and Authority
5. The *Apostolic Kerygma* and Apostolic Authority — 47
6. The journey of the New Testament Canon (Resumed) — 51
7. "Discovering" the Scriptures — 63
8. The Canonization journey tells us more about the Church than it does about the Scriptures — 83

Appendices A-F

Appendix A – New Advent article (Catholic): Canon of the Old Testament (1908) — 97

Appendix B – New Advent article (Catholic): Canon of the New Testament (1908) — 117

Appendix C – The Muratorian Fragment — 135

Appendix D – Article: Evangelicals and the Canon of the New Testament [M. James Sawyer (2004)] — 147

Appendix E – Apostolic Succession: An Orthodox Essay [Fr. John Behr (2007)] — 169

Appendix F – Vatican II: Dogmatic Constitution on Divine Revelation — 173

***

The Collection: One of us – an overview — 187

Bibliography — 190

PREFACE

This present volume is one in a set of seven books collectively entitled "One of Us" – a reference to the incarnational reality that God the Son, in the person of Jesus of Nazareth, truly became one of us.

The seven books consist of a trilogy on the Word of God, one volume on some of the characteristics of the early church prior to 100 AD, and a trilogy on the Eucharist. Each of the seven books can be read in its own right without requiring reference to any of the others. The seven titles (along with their subtitles) are as follows:

Book One
The Dependent God [*God's journey in our journey*]
Book Two
The Great Collaboration [*The journey with God's Written Word*]
Book Three
Soiling the Hands [*The journey of the Canon of Scripture*]
Book Four
The Jigsaw Puzzle Church [*The journey of the Apostolic (AD 33-67) and Sub-Apostolic Church (AD 67-100)*]
Book Five
The Act of Sustainable Covenant [*The Framework & Theology of the Eucharist*]
Book Six
The Worship of All Nations [*The Cotemporaneous Eucharist of Bishop John Moore (Nigeria 2010), Moél Caích (Ireland 793 AD), & Polycarp (Smyrna 155 AD)*]
Book Seven
From Bruised Reeds to Patmos Island [*The length, breadth, and depth of Scripture in the Eucharist*]

Further details on each of the seven books are given at the end of this book, immediately prior to the Bibliography.

The books also catalogue my personal journey of Faith, and the opinions and conclusions reached in them are purely my own.

Michael Mahony
Johannesburg 2014

Of periscopes and pericopes

Since 'journeys' feature in much of what will be addressed herein, it is beholden of me to introduce two journey 'markers' which shall be encountered periodically.

Periscopes

Every once in while in the course of our journey we will pause and take stock of where we are – not unlike what a submarine does when it suspends its normal path and its direct line of vision for just a moment, in order to 'look above the surface'.

Pericopes

In our travels, we will also find it necessary to periodically pause for a moment and bring other elements into our vision in order to better continue the journey. And the things which we shall be on the lookout for will vary considerably. Some relate to methodologies (including insights into biblical authorship and textural criticism).

Others, parable-like, will add colour to our landscape by way of illustrations from fellow sojourners (some contemporary, some historical, some metaphorical, some in an incomplete state...) while little signposts will also be noted from parallels and encounters with others on their journeys. We must also not be too surprised to find – as indeed we also do in the Scriptures – a variety of literary forms included in these pericopes: a fragment of a poem here, a little playlet there, a long-lost personal letter encountered bobbing up and down 'in a bottle' as our craft proceeds...

...and yes, since this little project was dedicated to the Holy Spirit, keeping one's seat-belt on is recommended, but loosely... any irruptions we experience are there to remind us as to – ultimately – whose journey we are undertaking. Where I have sensed his word I have endeavoured to faithfully record it; when he has "spoken" in the silence, that too...

***

A.

A paradoxical designation

In Israel, around the BC/AD transition, the Rabbis used the (paradoxical) term "Soiling the Hands" as a technical expression denoting those books which were the product of prophetic inspiration.

The thinking seems to have been that amongst the corpus of the Hebrew writings which had developed within Israel throughout their long history, certain distinctions were made between the different "books". Some of the books (presumably the majority) were regarded as so sacred that they left their marks on the hands that touched them. Those hands required a ritual purification after reading them.[1] These were the books which were considered to be divinely inspired.

1. Who Rules?

In our present age, and adopting a Christian perspective, the set of documents ("books") which are accepted as having met the criteria of Authorship, Inspiration, Inerrancy, and Authority, are those which make up the corpus of what is termed the Bible, the one Written Word of God in its Old and New Testament constituents.[2] This collection of books is what is termed the Canon[3] of Scripture. However, the word "accepted" immediately begs the question, "accepted by whom?"

Canons of the Old Testament (OT) and of the New Testament (NT) emerged in history and are now established realities. These Canons are, to use the accepted expression, closed; no more books can be added and no books can be deleted. This historical fact implies – more than implies – that by some process or other a distinction was made between those writings which were considered divinely inspired and those which were not. This is true both of the writings of the ancient Hebrew people and of the various writings of the early Christians.

There are complications. While, within the Christian community of today, there is consensus as to what books constitute the NT Canon (all Churches agree upon the 27 books which make up the NT Canon), unfortunately, that is not the case with respect to the OT Canon. Leaving aside for the moment, the posture adopted by contemporary Judaism,[4] we note that the Roman Catholic and Orthodox[5] Churches recognise an OT Canon of 46 books, while the Churches emerging from the Reformation of the sixteenth century recognise 39 books.

Catholic and Orthodox Bibles (OT and NT combined) accordingly contain a total of 73 books while those of other Churches contain 66 books.

Are there doctrinal consequences arising from these different Canons? It would seem so, and the degree to which such doctrinal issues can be regarded as major or minor can be debated, but that shall not be undertaken in this particular book, since that is not the focus of our attention. Our focus is on the responsibility and authority of the Church which, by definition, is raised by the very notion of a "Canon" of Scripture.

As explained elsewhere,[6] this collection of seven books (the *One of Us* collection) owes its origin to a particular challenge which the present narrator was presented with by the Lord. The challenge related to two issues: the authority of the Church, and the Eucharist, and as claimed above, the issue of such authority emerges, by definition, from the existence of a "canon".

But is such a claim – such an assumption – valid? Does such an issue emerge "by definition?" What is the connection? Where is the connection? In what specific way does the existence of a Canon of Scripture oblige us to look at the subject of the authority of the Church?

In introducing this topic, reference was made to the role played by criteria such as Authorship, Inspiration, Inerrancy, and Authority, in arriving at the Canon. But a fundamental question arises: On what basis are these criteria applied and who does the applying? Who decides what books are "in" the Canon, and which ones are "out"?

Even more fundamentally, who says that we need a Canon in the first place? Or taking the question even further, do mature human societies actually need canons at all? Have we not become too sophisticated for such external objectively determined values and standards to be prescribed for us?

Vacuums get filled

> "Over the past two hundred years the influence of intellectuals has grown steadily. Indeed, the rise of the secular intellectual has been a key factor in shaping the modern world. Seen against the long perspective of history it is in many ways a new phenomenon. It is true that in their earlier incarnations as priests, scribes, and soothsayers, intellectuals have laid claim to guide society from the very beginning. But as guardians of hieratic cultures, whether primitive or sophisticated, their moral and ideological innovations were limited by the canons of external authority and the inheritance of tradition. They were not, and could not be, free spirits, adventurers of the mind."[7]

In 1988, with these words, Paul Johnson introduced his highly provocative book, "Intellectuals." That such a prolific and respected writer of history, including histories of major religions, should refer to "canons of external authority" is not surprising. What is intriguing is that he believes that such canons do achieve their purpose of constraint.

Johnson is acutely aware that vacuums get filled, not least power vacuums. The question so often boils down to: "Who rules?" In his seminal work, "A History of the Modern World," he convincingly demonstrated how the Relativistic Age of the 19th/20th centuries allowed vacuums to emerge that were filled by dictatorships from both sides of the political spectrum, Communism and Fascism. Dictatorships rule. And as we all know to our cost, they rule with an authority that is absolute and personal; one that does not defer to any external canons.

To rule without a Canon, should be an oxymoron. The English word Canon means, at its heart, a rule or a standard.[8] Its Greek root is so used by Paul in the NT:

> ...but what matters is a new creation. Peace and mercy to all who follow this as their rule and to the Israel of God...[9]

[Peterson has "standard" in place of "rule"; Philips and other translators speak of those "who live by this principle."]

"Canon" therefore implies some principle-based rules or standards by which individuals may live well and societies be governed on a defined value-basis.

In "Intellectuals," Johnson is concerned with issues of authority more pervasive than just the political:

> "With the decline of clerical power in the eighteenth century, a new kind of mentor emerged to fill the vacuum and capture the ear of society. The secular intellectual might be deist, skeptic, or atheist. But he was just as ready as any pontiff or presbyter to tell mankind how to conduct its affairs. He proclaimed, from the start, a special devotion to the interests of humanity and an evangelical duty to advance them by his teaching. He brought to this self-appointed task a far more radical approach than his clerical predecessors. He felt himself bound by no corpus of revealed religion. The collective wisdom of the past, the legacy of tradition, the prescriptive codes of ancestral experience, existed to be selectively followed or wholly rejected entirely as his own good sense might decide. For the first time in human history, and with growing confidence and audacity, men arose to assert that they could diagnose the ills of society and cure them with their own unaided intellects: more, that they could devise formulae whereby not merely the structure of society but the fundamental habits of human beings could be transformed for the better. Unlike their sacerdotal predecessors, they were not servants and interpreters of the gods but substitutes. Their hero was Prometheus, who stole celestial fire and brought it to earth.[10]
>
> One of the most marked characteristics of the new secular intellectuals was the relish with which they subjected religion and its protagonists to critical scrutiny. How far had they benefited or harmed humanity, these great systems of faith? To what extent had these popes and pastors lived up to their precepts, of purity and truthfulness, of charity and benevolence? The verdicts pronounced on both Churches and clergy were harsh..."[11]

In a merciless *tour de force*, Johnson subjects the lives of many of these societal oligarchs to clinical scrutiny; and he does so on the basis of a number of objective canons:

> "...Now, after two centuries during which the influence of religion has continued to decline, and secular intellectuals have played an ever-growing role in shaping our attitudes and institutions, it is time to examine their record, both public and personal. In particular, I want to focus on the moral and judgmental credentials of intellectuals to tell mankind how to conduct itself. How did they

run their own lives? With what degree of rectitude did they behave to family, friends, and associates? Were they just in their sexual and financial dealings? Did they tell, and write, the truth? And how have their own systems stood up to the test of time and praxis?"[12]

From Jean-Jacques Rousseau and Percy Bysshe Shelley through to Noam Chomsky, Johnson exposes the groundlessness of the authority claimed and audaciously exercised by these secular intellectuals. The field of investigation is broad: Marx, Ibsen, Tolstoy and Hemingway are all indicted. The polymath Bertrand Russell is included in this unenviable *Who's Who*. Over his exceptionally long life, Russell offered advice to humanity in 70 books and voluminous articles across a variety of domains, including morals, mathematics, mysticism, and even marriage - but left in his wake a massive legacy of misery in terms of human relationships, particularly women and how he had exploited them.[13] Brecht, Sartre, Edmond Wilson, Gollancz, and Lillian Hellman find themselves as uncomfortable bedfellows, and in his final chapter, which for a book on intellectuals has the ironic title "The Flight of Reason," the roll-call is embarrassing, starting with Orwell, Waugh, and Cyril Connolly.

But more than being named and shamed on an embarrassing list is at issue here. Johnson links the phenomenon of supposedly liberal-minded, supposedly tolerant intellectuals, supposedly models of society, supposed pacifists – to the cult of violence. His thesis on this is original and masterful. When I read "Intellectuals" in 1988, I was not surprised by the link between such egoistical intellectuals and hedonism and the whole phenomenon of the permissive society, but the symbiotic relationship with violence was unexpected. "The Flight of Reason" is a clinical series of case studies inter-connected by a common seam of violence and the inter-threading of permissiveness with violence which characterized the 1960s and 1970s.[14] And not just the facts of violence (personal and societal) but the re-definition in subtle, and not so subtle ways, of "Violence": once abhorrent, then acceptable, then desirable, then admirable. Johnson traces its metamorphosis via Connolly, Sartre, Norman Mailer, and the German film director Rainer Werner Fassbinder. I find, alas, that Johnson was more truly prophetic than even the insightful Milton:

> The mind is its own place, and in itself
> Can make a heav'n of hell, a hell of heav'n.[15]

More than twenty years after the publication of "Intellectuals" we have the well established movie genre of Torture Porn included in our shopping mall cinemas. Even Evil has now been redefined, our minds indeed invaded by τοῖς πνεύμασι τοῖς ἀκαθάρτοις [evil/unclean spirits]. But the Hell of all of this is not just in the mind; it is a real world...[16]

Johnson was a contemporary of many of these intellectuals; in some instances moving in parallel worlds or in the same world. He was a freshman in Oxford when Kenneth Peacock Tynan made one of his grand entrances to Magdalen College lodge in 1946, and I sensed a tone of real sadness in Johnson's chronicle of vulgarity, self-abasement, self-destruction, and the same repeated sad pattern of destructive relationships – not to mention societal destruction – of a man of such enormous talent in journalism and the theatre:

> Tynan's last years, a sinister counterpoint of sexual obsession and physical debility are movingly told by his widow and make appalling reading to those who knew and admired the man. They recall Shakespeare's arresting phrase, "the expense of spirit in a waste of shame."[17]

Johnson concludes his analysis with a caution:

> Beware intellectuals...Beware committees, conferences and leagues of intellectuals...For intellectuals, far from being highly individualist and non-conformist people, follow certain regular patterns of behaviour. Taken as a group, they are often ultra-conformist within the circles formed by those whose approval they seek and value. That is what makes them, *en masse*, so dangerous, for it enables them to create climates of opinion and prevailing orthodoxies, which themselves often generate irrational and destructive courses of action. Above all, we must at all times remember what intellectuals habitually forget: that people matter more than concepts and must come first. The worst of all despotisms is the heartless tyranny of ideas.[18]

"Intellectuals" was, understandably, much criticised at the time on the selectivity of Johnson's targets (they were essentially all left-wing). And ten years after the publication of "Intellectuals," Johnson was criticised again (and justifiably so), triggered by the revelation of his own personal failings.[19]

The personal and very public failings over recent decades of people who did claim to adhere to "external canons", has also caused considerable human suffering, and such individuals are in no position to point the finger at others. However, the answer to such hypocrisy is (rather obviously) not to abandon the canons but to ensure that there are processes in place to enforce them. There are canons which define and identify what sin is, and when these canons have been violated, corrective action is required.

In contrast, what Johnson pointed out about the canon-free domain of "Intellectuals" was that the notion of sin had disappeared. Indeed the societal norms had, by the 1980s, moved so radically that not only had "sin" been dropped from the conversation, it had been elevated (e.g., in the case of violence) to an acceptable norm.

The distinction between societies accepting objective external canons and those which are canon-free is not a subtle one. The two result in very different models of society and how society is lead and ultimately ruled. The "Intellectuals" of Paul Johnson's book insisted upon the autonomous individual having the right to live life "free" of constraints to a degree that has led us to societies of massive vacuums. But, as already posited, and as history has demonstrated, vacuums get filled; someone always rules.

A 21st century *free* of canons?

In South Africa we are suffering in this regard, and much that is evil has filled our particular vacuums.

The trappings of a canon-free Western permissive society, when combined with the male-domination of our African/South-African culture, have made for a pernicious cocktail that our women and children are having forced down their throats. It is destroying them: it is killing them.

South Africa experienced an extraordinary Grace in 1994. We got what we had never deserved, and we never went through what we had deserved. Seldom in the history of nations has such a level of mercy been so publicly demonstrated and globally witnessed. The terrible tragedy of contemporary South Africa is that instead of humbly acknowledging God's mercy towards us, and in response living lives of compassion, selflessness, and justice, we have presumed upon his grace – (presumption is always an extremely foolish thing to do when it comes to God)[20] - and taken the downward path of nations who have declared not just independence, but wilful independence from God, despising his grace.

So, this Easter of 2008, as I have meditated afresh on the Via Crucis[21] of Jesus, I hear the broken heart of the Father weeping over us again, and imploring us to show him what else he could have done for us that he has not done.

Our 14 years of freedom have become 14 Stations of the Cross which was borne by his Son, and the Church recalls every Good Friday at each Station the Father's cry calling to us from the prophet Micah, calling to us from Calvary: *Oh! My people, what have I done to you? And how have I wearied you? Answer Me!*[22]

fourteen steps to freedom day

27th April 1994-2008
(for Michael Cassidy)

Villanelle [Micah 6:3]

South Africa, what have I done to thee?
Your shame My Via Crucis; insults hurled
How have I wearied thee? Answer Me!

Weep now the beloved country; free? flee?
The Fall, your falls, My falls do three times hold
Beloved land, what have I done to thee?

Redeemed, forgiven; the pain-filled TRC
wipes Africa's bloodied face - Veronica furled
How have I burdened thee? Answer Me!

I thirst! I'm naked! shamed! the world to see
"two planks, a kaffir, a bag of nails," lips curled
Beloved land, what have I done to thee?

A mid-day darkness; silent tomb - tomb free
The soldiers' duty done; three renegades furled
How have I saddened thee? Answer Me!

We adore thee Oh Christ; in silence, worship Thee
The Cross through which you have redeemed the world
South Africa, what have I done to thee?
How have I wearied thee? Answer Me!

The word "anarchy" is derived from the Greek *arkhein* [to rule]: "anarchism" being a doctrine in political theory advocating the abolition of government. It is a deception; vacuums get filled. Again, looking at our own continent of Africa, even in the shambles of Somalia, there are those who rule. Someone always rules. The only question is: Who rules? We can be ruled with or without canons, but ruled we will be. Someone is always "god".

The nature of Canons

From our contemporary world view, it may surprise us to hear that even as societies in times past became more literate, the transition from oral traditions to ones expressed in writing were not always initially seen as giving more assurance or more clarity in matters related to truth, values, and canons. With the explosion of Christian communities throughout the Gentile world in the first century, the demand for apostolic teachings and personal eye-witness testimony to the life, death and resurrection of Jesus, could no longer be met by a Church whose initial confines had been within a short travelling distance of Jerusalem.

This need was first addressed by epistles such as those of Paul. With the passing of time, and the corresponding dispersion and death of apostles, together with the growing geographic spread of the early communities, reliance on written records developed. These were eventually assembled into the Gospels, but it is to be noted that such documents were regarded as of secondary value compared with "the real thing" – oral witness – as we hear from Eusebius who recorded that Papias, in the 2nd century, was still seeking oral testimony even though he knew of written records.[23]

On the other hand, I personally do not find it all that surprising. One of the criticisms that one comes across from within some contemporary democracies is that we have over-legislated and under-enacted. We are much into writing laws and less effective in the living thereof.

Furthermore, there is even sometimes in society a real disconnect between what is on the written statutes and what communities actually hold dear as values; and when the chips are down it is often the latter set of values that effectively hold sway in practice – sometimes for good, oft-times for ill. I would not want to imply that such issues are always, if ever, easy to resolve: the dynamic between the populous and our leaders/rulers, particularly in democracies, is a complex one. But I raise it at this point because the issue of what constitutes the Canon of Scripture has a similar dynamic within it – firstly in its origins, and secondly in its position in the Church today. The point is: a Canon can be oral and/or written.[24]

If we are surprised at this it may be because we look at things with a 21st Century worldview. We live in an age – and in a world – of written legislation recorded "on the statute books". This is the case whether we are dealing with international affairs (e.g. The UN Declaration of Human Rights), agreements between nations, constitutions and laws within a nation-state (at various levels of government) constitutions and rules governing everything from the responsibilities of business corporations to those of the local Church or the university chess club, or employment conditions which are enshrined in formal contracts, etc. And it is no surprise – and a very good thing – that when a nation which has freed itself from oppression of one kind or another, one of the first actions it undertakes is the formulation of its national constitution, amounting to a written definition of what it values and what it is determined to defend in terms of its rights as a nation and the rights[25] of its citizens.

It is even assumed in most people's minds today that every modern nation state has a constitution and would indeed be unable to function without one. The reality is that some of our most mature and enduring states do not. Britain is a case in point. They had a go at a "constitution" many centuries ago, in the form of the Magna Carta; a charter granted by King John at Runnymede in 1215 which recognised the rights and privileges of the barons, Church, and freemen. But they made no serious attempts to "keep it up to date" and instead down the centuries – (particularly since the political developments around the establishment of Parliament and its relationship with the monarchy after the Restoration) - have formulated and maintained their values and the rule of law in their society by making and adapting the rules of the game[26] "as they went along".

The actual name for this process is called Common Law, i.e. that body of law based upon judicial decisions (precedent) compared with those which over time became enshrined in statute. This approach has served them very well,[27] and one has only to point to the "law" applicable to a common law marriage to witness how effective such an approach can be, even where the definition of what is so constituted is loosely or vaguely defined.[28]

This unwritten value-system also gives us some insight why considerable latitude is given – is admired actually – in England to a chap "breaking the rules", providing, of course, that he does so in the (naturally unspecified) acceptable manner. How do you think that notion of the eccentric Englishman came about? He is, first of all, genetically-obliged to break the "silly rules" that other upstart nations wrap up in massive tombs of red-tape or convention; then secondly – and symbiotically - he is driven by unconscious forces to challenge his own home-grown and unwritten ones. It is the *unwritten* element of the latter that makes for such visual humour in British Society; typified by examples such as the following from Gerald Hoffnung's classic "Guide to Tourists when visiting Britain":

> "Upon entering a railway carriage be sure to shake hands with all the passengers..."

And my all-time favourite:

> "Do try out the famous echo in the Reading Room of the British Museum..."

The point being that for an Englishman to do either of these in a thoroughly (of course undefined but terribly) English way would pass unnoticed and, of necessity, would remain un-remarked upon – being inherently unremarkable, but for a French person or an Austrian yodeller to do either would constitute an outrage, resulting in letters to *The Times*, and most certainly a question in the House of Commons.[29]

In spite of the historical injustices inflicted by the English upon my ancestors, I still hold many British institutions in high regard. I have a particular affection for the House of Commons; mainly because of the "Commons" component. It is where the voice of the common people of Britain is heard; and where their representatives own, on their behalf, the values, policies, and actions taken by Parliament. It is not a passive ownership either; it is active. The

House of Commons is where the common people, having received the body of legislation enacted therein, then judge the voice of their patricians, and having judged, then decide and act...and demote or elect.

This fluid concept of what might constitute a Canon, will be helpful to us going forward because it has introduced the element of **process** in addition to that of **content** into the notion of a Canon.

* * *

---

1   Smith (1968) 66:9 p501 in the Jerome Biblical Commentary. Alternatively, "Defiling the hands" - Downers Grove, IL: InterVarsity Press, 1988, pg.34.
2   Cf. Book Two, Chapters 26 and 27, in this collection.
3   **G2583** κανών, kanōn, *kan-ohn"*. From κάνη kanē (a straight *reed*, that is, *rod*); a *rule* ("canon"), that is, (figuratively) a *standard* (of faith and practice); by implication a *boundary*, that is, (figuratively) a *sphere* (of activity): - line, rule. There are more generic contemporary applications of the word *canon*: e.g. one can speak of the Canon of English literary works – a topic of considerable dispute. Cf. Canon Fighting p27-34 in Stevenson (2007).
4   The role of Judaism in regards to the Canon of their Scriptures in the years subsequent to the destruction of the Jerusalem Temple in 70AD, is discussed later in this book, in Chapter 3.
5   Cf. https://oca.org/questions/scripture/canon-of-scripture. From this point onwards, and apart from Appendix E, no further reference shall be made to the Orthodox Church's position. This is to be regretted, but extending the scope of this present volume to include the perspective of Orthodoxy was not possible at this time.
6   Cf. Chapter 8 in Book One (*The Dependent God*), of this collection of seven books. Cf. the Overview of this Collection (One of Us), at the end of this book, immediately preceding the Bibliography.
7   Johnson (Intellectuals) (1988) p1. Johnson's insightful comment, (about the rise and influence of the secular intellectual in the perspective of history being a completely new phenomenon), is a key theme in Charles Taylor's magisterial work , "A Secular Age".
8   Old English, from Latin, from Greek *kanōn* rule, rod for measuring, standard; related to *kanna* reed.
9   Gal 6:15b-16
10 [Own Note]: Cf. For a succinct exposé of the terror-filled impoverishment underlying such Promethean "heroism" see Merton (The New Man – 1962) pp15-34
11 Johnson (1988) (Intellectuals) p1-2.
12 Ibid. p2.
13 Johnson (1988) (Intellectuals) p212-219.
14 C.f. Johnson (1988) (Intellectuals) p324.
15 John Milton, "Paradise Lost", Book I lines 254-5.
16 Cf. Book One, Chapter 7, of this collection.
17 Johnson (1988) (Intellectuals) p330. cf. Shakespeare, *Sonnets*, 129.
18 Johnson (1988) (Intellectuals) p342
19 In 1998 Johnson's former mistress, Gloria Stewart, told the papers of her 11-year affair

with Johnson. When challenged on this in a 2010 interview, his response was described in these terms: "After a moment of diplomatic amnesia, he growls: 'If you acquire any kind of fame, that's the kind of thing that's liable to happen. You just put it out of your mind. It's what Shakespeare called 'the dark backward and abysm' of the past'". Elizabeth Grice, 04 Jun 2010 in: http://www.telegraph.co.uk/lifestyle/7800902/Paul-Johnson-After-70-you-begin-to-mellow.html

The quote is from Prospero:

"Thou hadst, and more, Miranda. But how is it
That this lives in thy mind? What seest thou else
In the dark backward and abysm of time?
If thou remember'st aught ere thou camest here,
How thou camest here thou mayst." [The Tempest, Act 1, Scene 2.]

20 ...and keep Your servant back from presumptuous sins; do not let them have dominion over me; then I shall be upright, and I shall be innocent of great transgression. [Ps 19:13]. But the person who acts presumptuously – defiantly - be he citizen or alien, that one commits an outrage against YHWH, and such a man will be cut off from among his people. Since he has treated YHWH's word with contempt and has disobeyed his order, such a man will be completely cut off, and he will bear the consequences of his guilt. [Num 15:30-31]. Cf. also 1Sm 15:23: Mathew Henry's comment on Samuel's words to Saul: He reads his doom: in short, "*Because thou has rejected the word of the Lord,* hast *despised it* (so the Chaldee), hast *made nothing of it* (so the Septuagint), hast cast off the government of it, therefore he has *rejected thee,* despised and made nothing of thee, but cast thee off *from being king.*

21 The Way of the Cross.

22 Micah 6:3

23 Turro & Brown (1968) 67:50 p525

24 Turro & Brown (1968) 67:5 p516

25 And, let it be noted, that it is **rights** that are emphasised in such nation-state constitutions whereas in the constitutions of many other bodies (e.g. Church organisations, professional societies, clubs, NGOs etc.) it is the **responsibilities** and **obligations** of such bodies that are (quite correctly of course) emphasised.

26 I also don't use the word *game* here in a frivolous manner. If one wants to really understand the English it is essential to understand that they see it all really as one great big *game*, and they delight in letting the rules of the game develop on a trial and error basis – whether that is in the serious transition from the common game of football to the noble game of Rugby, or in descriptions by the contending parties in real wars (not war-games) of empire, such as the battle over Spionkop where the British and Afrikaner generals communicated with one another across battle-lines using Cricket terminology. The only non-negotiable rule (it is never stated of course and absolutely never put in writing) is that it is a given that the English are the ones who make and change the rules as one goes along. The emphasis is on the English, not the British. They have utilised their better educated Scottish subjects most particularly to administer their rules throughout the Empire and their rough & ready Welsh youngsters to enforce them in their infantry, but they are rules of Englishmen, of that there is no question – and no questioning.

27 Not to mention what it has saved them in terms of the cost such as that experienced in the USA for example which has an industry engaged in Constitutional Law, its amendments, its management, and its deployment.

28 If any sojourner doubts the presumed Anglo-centricity of all of this, I merely refer thee to

the name of any significant sporting competition in Britain; that for Football (the FA Cup - contrast the Scottish FA Cup), and that for golf (The Open); the absence of adjectives go unnoticed. I mean, you've just got to hand it to them; one has the US Open, the Irish Open, the SA Open, etc. but the premier open golfing competition that is played in Britain (frequently, by the way, in Scotland) is just called "The Open". No appellatives need apply...

29   Given this brief profile of the English *game*, is it really so hard to understand Britain's difficulty in coming to grips with a nonsense like an EU Constitution/"Revised Treaty", etc.? An edifice, furthermore, enshrined in all the double-figure official languages of the EU, including, adding insult to injury, that of the Irish language, (Gaeilge), which they had practically eliminated by their linguacide of the Irish tongue in the nineteenth century.

* * *

2. The Bible & The Canon: Content & Process

With all of that in mind, let us address the issue of the formation of the biblical Canon. It is a **process** issue that I wish to deal with here. The Bible as we now have it is a **content** issue;[1] we are interested in what it contains, what it says. The Canon is a process issue: we are interested in how we arrived at it. The two issues are related but they are not the same. The content of the Bible contributes much to the revelation of God, but equally (yes equally) answering this process question will also contribute significantly to the revelation of God, both in terms of how God interacts with us, and to the end result emerging from such interaction.

Question: Why is it that the gospel written by Luke (who was a person, as we have noted, of relatively minor significance) is part of the Canon of Scripture and why is the gospel of Thomas (one of the Twelve, the inner circle disciples of Jesus) excluded from the canon? Similarly, why is the very personal letter of Paul to Philemon concerning a runaway slave "in" and Clement's pastoral letter from Rome (dated around 97AD) to the Church of Corinth "out"?

Answer: God decided. The Holy Spirit, who is the author of Scripture and the one who inspired the human authors, is the One who gave us the Canon. The Bible is (simply) the collected corpus of all of the inspired books. Such an answer is true but, of course, is not helpful in that it still does not explain how it came about that Luke is "in" and Thomas is "out". In other words, it is not helpful because it does not address the issue of how this in/out selection was made; i.e. it does not address the issue of the process.

It is also not helpful to list the reasons which I think/you think/he-she thinks why one book is "in" and another book is "out". Such opinions may be valid/invalid or somewhere in between. Ultimately though, they are just that – "opinions". They are not a record of the process which did actually lead to the formation of the Canon of Scripture.

Because, in my experience, many Christians have not given this issue a moment's thought, let us start by isolating those processes which God could have followed but chose not to in the formulation of the Canon.

What God did *not* do:

God did not give a list of books to certain trustworthy individuals and tell them that that was **it**. He could have done so under the OT dispensation[2] and/or the New. One could envisage a situation, for example, where in the NT Gospels a canonical list of Old Testament books could have been recorded – e.g. if Jesus had given such a list. And we could trust such a "list" to the degree that we could trust the gospels in which they appeared, not unlike the way in which the names of the twelve apostles in Jesus' initial inner circle have come down to us.[3] Such a basis would, of course, still have presupposed some process for accepting the testimony of those who wrote the gospels in the first place.

But God chose not to do it that way.

In the very earliest days of the Church (e.g. prior to the writing of Acts[4]) God could have had the apostles raise the question of what constituted the Canon of the Old Testament Scriptures (e.g. let us imagine, for the benefit of the Gentiles) and have it resolved by a process similar to that reported in Acts[5] over the contentious issue of Gentile/Jewish believers in Jesus and their relationship with the Torah. He could then have had the list "published" (e.g. by Luke in Acts) and (again in so far as such a NT record was trusted and accepted) that would have pretty well settled the scope of the OT Canon.

But he chose not to do it that way.

Here is another possibility, one that could have addressed both the OT and the NT canon: Since the Book of Revelation seems to have been the last book of the NT that was written (and for the purposes of this "argument" let so assume so) Jesus, who in glory appeared to John as recorded in that book, could have "closed" the Canon of both the OT and the NT for once and for all by giving John such a list, and (again, subject to such a testimony by John being trusted) that would have been (or at least could have been) the end of the matter.

But God chose not to do it that way.

I dare say that other speculative ways of arriving at the Canon could be explored but let us rather now focus on how the Canon actually did come about.

What God *did* do:

He involved us in the selection process. He involved the Church in the process; that is what he did.

This, of course, is consistent with what I described earlier on our journey as the partnership processes that God seems to deliberately employ – and enjoy![6] Just as he involved us in the authorship process, he involved us in the selection process (i.e. in the canonization process); highly consistent behaviour on the part of our God.

In looking first at the formulation of the OT Canon, (the NT Canon will follow) we recognise the historical reality that a number of journeys are involved, and since I dealt earlier on our journey, in a metaphorical way, with the journey of the OT Scriptures from Abraham to Ezra,[7] it is probably sufficient, in looking at the concept of a Canon of the OT Scriptures, to look at the journey from the time of Ezra onwards. To that topic we now turn.

* * *

---

1 Clearly, as covered in quite some detail in Book Two of this collection, arriving at the "accurate" contents of the various books and letters of the Hebrew people and of the early Church, also involved much in the way of process. The point that is now of issue is the further process of distinguishing between those documents which were divinely inspired and which were not.

2 There are actually examples of types of such lists: e.g. in the apocryphal book the *Apocalypse of Ezra [4-Ezra]*, written between AD 100-200, God is portrayed as speaking to Ezra of 24 sacred books that are available to all the people, as distinct from the 70 books that are to be kept secret. Turro & Brown (Canonicity) (1968) 67:33 p521, and Brown (Apocrypha) (1968) 68:41 p542.

3 But, let it be noted, that even this is not as definitive as one may presume, since one of the Twelve is named variously, *James of Alphaeus, Thaddeus, Lebbaeu*s, or *Judas (Jude) of James*. [Stanley & Brown (Aspects of New Testament Thought 1968) 78:163 p796].

4 The *Acts of the Apostles* is variously dated: most likely in the 80s; some have it as early as the 60s. cf. Turro & Brown (1968) 67:66 p528

5 The Jerusalem Council of Acts 15: "...For it seemed good to the Holy Spirit and to us... etc." (Acts 15:28).

6 Extensively in Book Two, Chapter 27, *Deliberate Divine Disharmonies*.

7 Culminating with Ezra: cf. Book One, Chapters 18-25.

* * *

B.

The Journeys of the Biblical Canons

3. The journey of the Old Testament Canon

I have divided this journey into three constituent journeys, labelled in **Fig 3.1** as OT1, OT2, and OT3:[1]

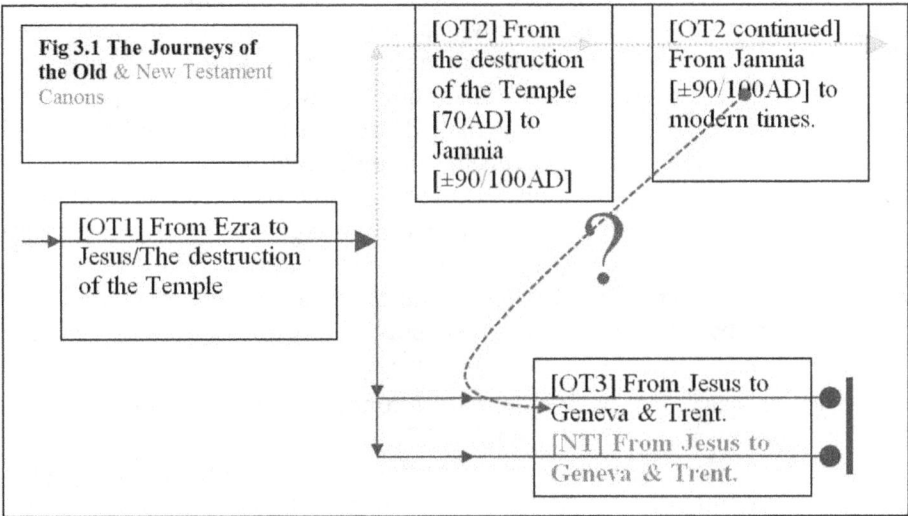

Fig 3.1 The Journeys of the Old & New Testament Canons

A clarification of terms

The name **Trent** in this context refers to the Council of Trent, which was a part of the process in the Catholic Church for the formal stabilization of the Canon of Scripture in the Sixteenth Century.

The name **Geneva**, on the other hand, could perhaps have been better written as **"Geneva"**, since it is being used as a metonym for the events leading up to the emergence of the Canon of Scripture settled upon by the Reformers in the same century.

[OT1] *No mad rush*: the journey of the Old Testament Canon from Ezra to Jesus/The destruction of the Temple

Let it be noted that under the Old Covenant (and, as we shall see, also under the New) the issue of the Canon did not seem to be a contentious issue for many years, certainly not contentious enough to bring it to a head in those communities living under them.[2]

Now, in our journey so far, we have met, and had much reason to appreciate, the role played by the common people of Israel (the *am ha-arez*) in the relating of "God's journey in our journey".[3] For them, the words of Torah, etc., constituted a given, and received, body of truth, which had been tried, tested, and accepted (almost one might say by osmosis) over the evolving centuries by hierarchy and the common people alike.

The Holy Spirit worked, let us say, on a default basis. Those words of Torah, of the Prophets, of (generally speaking) the Writings, which remained alive and vibrant in the life, including the liturgical life of his people – both in their oral and written traditions - those which were copied again and again; these ended up being in the Canon – in a partnership between God and his people. He gave; they received – active tense, not passive tense. He spoke; they responded and took ownership of their destiny. Their very life became the "incarnation" of YHWH's [יהוה] revelation; enfleshed in their language. The Word which had called them into being as a people - his people - and which then sustained them, and the Word which they expressed and endeavoured to live, were inseparable. The "canon" by the time that John the Baptiser appeared was known; well "defined" at its core, but loosely defined in scope "at the edges" by different groups or schools. There was not a single written list; there does not seem to have been a desperately felt need for one.

Particularly as far as *The Writings* were concerned there are various "lists" that contend. By end of the 1st century AD there were in Judaism two lists, a shorter Palestinian Canon drawn up by the rabbis at Jamnia,[4] and a longer Alexandrian Canon represented by the Septuagint (LXX).[5] Josephus knows of the 5 law books of Moses, the 13 books of the Prophets, and 4 books containing "hymns to God and precepts for the conduct of human life." The last mentioned are thought to have been Psalms, Songs of Songs, Proverbs and Ecclesiastes.[6] This total of 22 "books" is possibly (with different enumeration) the same list of 24 books eventually settled upon by Judaism.[7]

[OT2] The journey of the Old Testament Canon from the destruction of the Temple (70AD) to Jamnia (±90/100AD) and from Jamnia to modern times...

Here (in OT2) we are looking exclusively at a journey within Judaism,[8] and it is intriguing that a need by the OT People of God to more formally enshrine a "canon" of what constituted their Scriptures only arose well into the Christian era. The destruction of the Temple in Jerusalem (in 70AD) must surely have been a major catalyst.

Although there are different traditions in Judaism with various suggestions as to when the "final" collection of OT books was made,[9] it is generally recognised by critical scholars today that the OT Canon was not completed until the Christian era when various factors gave the necessary impetus to such a "closing" of the Canon. These factors included rivalry between Christian and Jewish books, as well as disputes within Judaism itself, particularly between Pharisees and some of the more apocalyptically minded Jewish sects.

On the "closure" of the OT Canon... (and here I quote directly and extensively from Turro & Brown):

> ...it is often suggested that the Canon was closed at Jamnia (Jabneh or Jabneel, a town near the Mediterranean, West of Jerusalem) where Rabbi Johanan ben Zakkai re-established his school at the time of the fall of Jerusalem. After a decade, Gamaliel II became the head of the school, and in the period AD 80-117 he and Eleazar Ben Azariah were the predominant teachers. It has been proposed that about AD 90-100 the council of the rabbis at Jamnia settled once and for all time the definitive list of inspired books, namely, "the Palestinian Canon", consisting of the books now called protocanonical. Recently[10] this thesis has been subjected to much-needed criticism (J.P. Lewis, JBR 32 [1964] 125-32.
>
> Four points of caution should be noted: (1) Although Christian authors seem to think in terms of a formal Church-type[11] council at Jamnia, there was no "council of Jamnia". At Jamnia there was a school for studying the Law, and the Jamnia rabbis exercised legal function in the Jewish community. (2) There is no evidence that any list of books was drawn up at Jamnia. The rabbis, of course, recognized that certain books were uniquely sacred and "soiled the hands," so that purification was necessary after using them (Mishnah,[12] *Yadaim* 3.2). But this attitude may represent the popular acceptance of 22 or 24 books that we saw in Josephus and in *4-Ezra* at roughly the same period. It is no proof that a definite list had been drawn up. (3) A specific discussion of acceptance at Jamnia is attested only for Eccl and Ct [Songs], and even in these instances arguments persisted in Judaism decades after the Jamnia period. There were also subsequent debates about Est. (4) We know of no books that were excluded at Jamnia. A book like Sirach, which did not eventually become part of the Standard Hebrew Bible (based on the putative Jamnia Canon), was read and copied by Jews after the Jamnia period. Tosephta, *Yadaim* 2:13, records that Sirach was declared as not soiling the hands, but does not say where or when this was decided.
>
> Perhaps the safest statement about the closing of the Jewish Canon is one which recognizes that although in the 1st century AD there was popular acceptance of 22 or 24 books as sacred, there was no rigidly fixed Hebrew Canon until the end of the 2nd century or the early 3rd century. In this period various Jewish groups continued to read as sacred, books that were not included in the 22/24 count.[13]

The Mishnah has been referred to in this important comment on Jamnia, and to give it some context, I show, in **Fig 3.2,** the origin and dating of the Mishnah as well as its relationship with the broader body of Jewish writings.

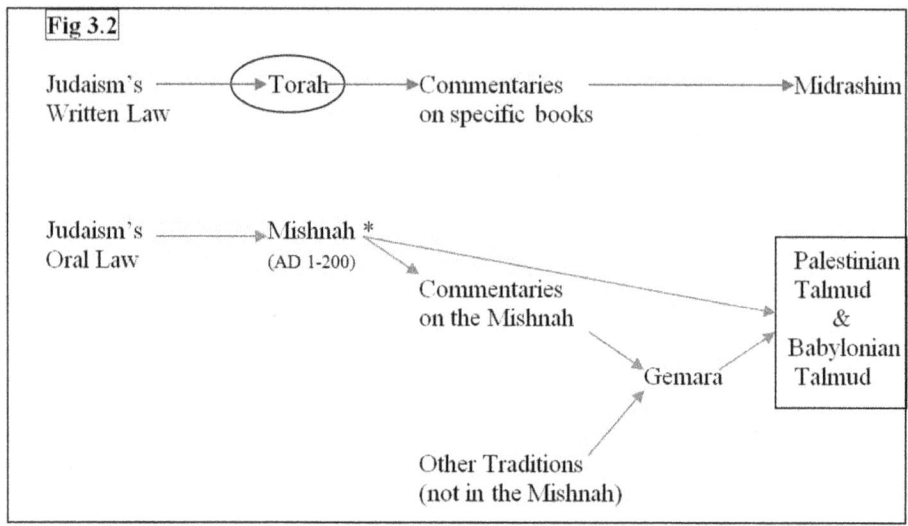

*The Mishnah is a compilation of precepts passed down as an oral tradition and collected by Judah ha-Nasi in the late second century AD, when "it became apparent that the oral decisions of the great teachers had to be collected. (These decisions were preserved by repetition; students had to repeat by memory the decisions of the masters....*mishnah* means "repetition")."[14]

Irrespective of how conclusive or not Jamnia was in formally finalising a "canon" for Judaism at the end of the 1st Century AD, it does seem reasonable to conclude that, in terms of timing at least, prior to the coming of Jesus the Messiah with his establishment of the New Covenant, no formal process of finalizing a Canon of the OT Scriptures had taken place.

[OT3] *No mad rush*: the journey of the Old Testament Canon from Jesus to Geneva/Trent

Fig 3.3, shown on the next page, is merely a repeat of Fig 3.1; keeping it in front of us will be helpful in what now follows.

Just as the journey of the Old Testament Scriptures (which we labelled OT2) was a journey that took place entirely within Judaism, the other journey of the Old Covenant Scriptures (which we are now labelling as OT3) is one that took place entirely within Christianity; albeit, as we shall now touch on, it was a journey undertaken in the first instance by Jews – those Jews who had become followers of Jesus.

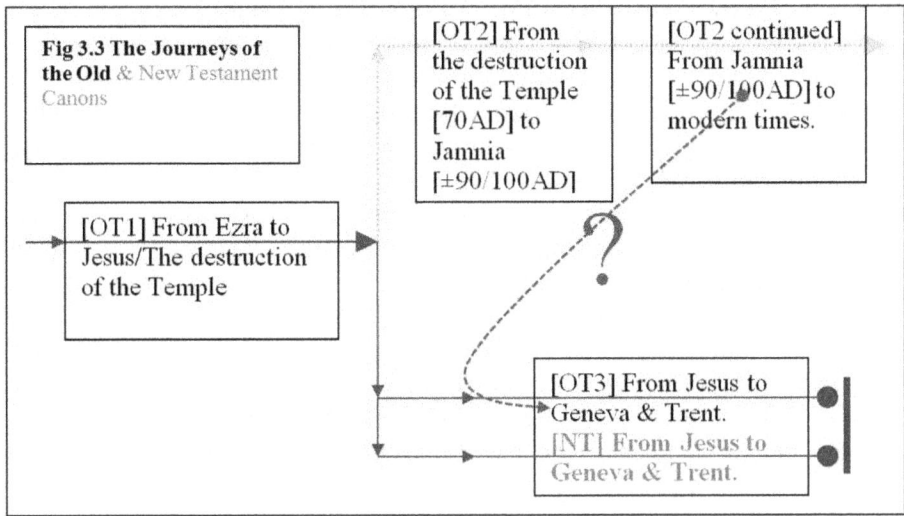

A clarification of terms: Continuity and Discontinuity

There has been a very healthy development within Christian thinking in recent decades arising from a renewed appreciation of the Hebrew character of the very earliest beginnings of the Church.[15] The New Covenant after all was introduced by a Jewish Messiah, whose inner circle throughout his entire life was Jewish, and it was at The Pasch, on the night before he died, that Jesus instituted the New Covenant in his blood,[16] in fulfilment of the prophecies in this regard by the ancient Hebrew prophets. Indeed, Jeremiah (just to take one example from many) had emphasised 600 years previously, that the new covenant he was foretelling was to be with "the house of Israel and the house of Judah" – not with some other specified nation or people.[17] And Paul, of course, being a "Hebrew of the Hebrews" himself,[18] in his letter to the Romans expounds at great length on God's covenant with Israel in the light of the actual coming of Messiah which had now taken place. So, this reminder of the **continuity** from the Old People of God to the New People of God has been a healthy correction in recent years.

This does not take from the fact that there was also a significant **discontinuity.** The Old Covenant came to an end with the establishment of the New Covenant in the blood of Messiah.[19] And that end was sudden, dramatic, and irreversible. This was not, of course, a covenant that rejected the Jews. On the contrary (as per Jeremiah's words above) it was first and foremost a new covenant with **the Jews**, a covenant into which the Gentile world was now also being invited to participate. And Paul uses the metaphor of the olive tree to emphasise that Israel is the root of this covenant (the natural branches of the olive tree) and the Gentiles are like the branches of a wild olive tree that are being grafted in amongst the natural ones.[20]

The Old Covenant came to fulfilment in the New Covenant; it had come, in other words, to **its** fullness. It had fulfilled its purposes and had no future; it had no need of a future. This issue is addressed by the author of the Letter to the Hebrews when he dealt with the transition from the Old to the New Covenant.[21] So, the Old Covenant no longer had a future, but the same was not true of the people of the Old Covenant. They did and do have a future. Those children of Abraham who recognised "the time of their visitation"[22] and who embraced their Messiah, already came to their fulfilment into the new covenant; they were subsumed into the New Creation.[23] And while that may have seemed as a mere "remnant" at the time to Paul, he - the quintessential Jew - never lost his hope (albeit heart-breaking in its longing) for "all Israel's salvation",[24] and he looked to a time in the future (our future too) when Jesus Messiah will "privately" (with us Gentiles "out of the room" as it were) again address himself to his Hebrew brothers and reveal himself anew as "their brother".[25]

If such "discontinuity-yet-with-incorporation" characterised the change from Old-to-New Covenant, and from Old-to-New People of God, how were the Old Covenant Scriptures affected by this transition?

Old Testament Scriptures viewed through Christian eyes

The answer is multifaceted. The OT Scriptures constituted the Bible that Jesus used. As we saw previously[26] he constantly referred both to the letter and to the authentic spirit of those Scriptures, and (much to the chagrin of his opponents) he repeatedly emphasised that these very Scriptures were actually speaking about him. He even went further, making outlandish statements such as "[in himself]...you have a greater than Solomon here", and "before Abraham was I am".[27] The OT Scriptures were likewise what the New Testament writers were referring to when they quoted from what they called "the Scriptures",[28] and Paul specifically endorsed the enduring value of the OT Scriptures to Christians.[29]

Accordingly, we have this intriguing paradox that, just at the moment when God intervened with a dramatic discontinuity in the journey of the people of God with his transition from Old Covenant to New Covenant, his prevailing written Word at that time (the OT Scriptures) provided a bridge of continuity from the Old Covenant to the New. Accounts such as the following capture the excitement with which the OT texts were looked at afresh – and intently – in the light of the claims of the apostolic preaching:

> And the brethren immediately sent Paul and Silas away by night to Berea. When they arrived, they went into the synagogue of the Jews. These were more noble than those in Thessalonica, in that they received the word with all readiness of mind, and searched the Scriptures daily to see if those things were so.[30]

There is thus no discontinuity in the [OT3] journey of the OT Scriptures as the transition from Old Covenant to New Covenant takes place; quite the contrary applies. They continue into the New, but with a whole new dimension added: their significance changes dramatically. The OT texts are looked at afresh. They are looked at with new eyes, and "received" anew.

Such a statement is regarded as a truism in the everyday life of people. To take a trivial example. A musical score such as the following is "received" by someone such as myself and by Marinela, my daughter in law, in very different ways. As received by me it echoes memories of torturous piano lessons at the hands of the long-suffering Miss Kilkelly. But in Marinella's case it causes her to reach for her flute and to be lifted into a different realm of creative beauty. The point is that the score - the "text" if you will - is the same but the recipients see it with different eyes.

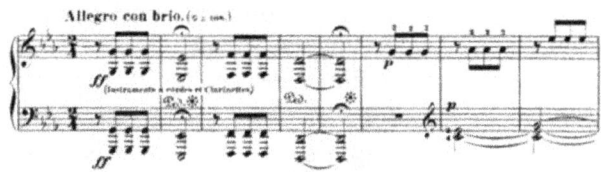

The relationship of the OT Scriptures with the People of the New Covenant would never be – could never be – the same as the relationship between those same Scriptures and the People of the Old Covenant. How could it be otherwise? The books were the same; the content was the same; the words were the same, but their place in the life of the people of the New Creation was intrinsically different from what it had been under Israel's long journey. And the people of the New Covenant (whether Jew or Gentile) now read and received these Scriptures as the Word of God as fulfilled and revealed in Jesus the Messiah.[31]

I have repeatedly pointed out throughout this *One of Us* journey that there is a pattern evident in the relationship between God and his people when it comes to him revealing himself to us: He gives; we receive. But not passively receiving. It is rather actively receiving; actively participating. So, within the New Covenant – the New Creation (this extraordinary creation called "the Body of Christ")[32] – there is a new depth of revelation being received in the OT Scriptures.

The books have not changed; but the readers have. The same inspired Word of God is unchanged but the recipients have changed. And the regenerated[33] people of the New Creation now "receive" these OT Scriptures afresh in a completely changed world, one characterised by two radically new realities: (i) the tangible – tactile - experience of having witnessed the death and subsequent resurrection of the Messiah, the very one spoken about in these same Scriptures; followed by (ii) the enlightenment of the Holy Spirit who had been poured out upon all of them shortly after the ascension of Jesus. One such eye-witness, John, the youngest of the Jewish disciples of Jesus, expressed the awesomeness of this revelation many years later in the gospel, and in the first letter, which bear his name:

> In the beginning was the Word, and the Word was with God, and the Word was God...and the Word became flesh and dwelt amongst us.[34]
>
> That which was from the beginning, which we have heard, which we have seen with our eyes, which we have looked upon, and our hands have handled, concerning the Word of life...[35]

This "Old" word had become a "New" word. Same books, same authors, same manuscripts; new revelation. A continuity, but one which involves a transformation. To illustrate: Psalm 40 was written and sung by David, and received and lived (quite correctly) by God's Old Testament people as an inspired hymn of thanksgiving and praise to YHWH:

> Sacrifice and offering
> you did not desire
> but a body you have prepared for me; [LXX][36]
> Burnt offering and sin offering
> You did not require.
> Then I said, "Behold, I come:
> In the scroll of the book
> It is written of me -
> I delight to do your will O my God,
> And your law is within my heart." [Ps 40:6-8][37]

The writer of the NT Epistle to the Hebrews still could (and presumably did) continue to sing this psalm as an inspired hymn of thanksgiving and praise to YHWH (just as we, the New Covenant people of God, continue to do so to this very day) but he also now reads it afresh in the light of the revelation of Jesus, and realises with awe, under the inspiration of the Holy Spirit, that - in addition to the original understanding - he is also in this Psalm eavesdropping on an extraordinary conversation within the Godhead: God the Father and God the Son in dialogue, in eternity; "planning" the salvation of the world through the great redemptive act:

> Therefore when he came into the world he said: "sacrifice and offering you did not desire, but a body you have prepared for me...I have come to do your will, O God." [38]

[This topic will be taken up again later in our journey, when we look more comprehensively at the dynamic of the relationship between God, His Word (not just the OT) and His Body (His People)].[39]

The Church's journey with the Old Testament seen through the prism of the New Testament

The journey that the Church now undertakes in its relationship with the OT Scriptures [**OT3** - *from Jesus to Geneva/Trent*], is accordingly a completely different journey from that which post-Temple Judaism makes [**OT2** - *from the destruction of the Temple to Jamnia and beyond*]. Each community is dealing with (almost[40]) the same physical manuscripts, but the two communities are now living markedly different revelations. Thus, for the Church, the OT Scriptures, while absolutely retaining their historical value and truth[41] as applied under the old covenant, are changed under the new covenant[42] into the new fullness as illustrated above.

It should (in my opinion) be obvious, but since it does not seem to be accepted as self-evident by all, let it also be emphasised, as Bishop Wright does, that "... our [i.e. the Church's] relationship to the New Testament is not the same as our relationship to the Old, and that we can say this without any diminution of our commitment to the Old Testament as a crucial and non-negotiable part of "holy scripture"..." [43] This is true, in my opinion, both with respect to the OT (as it was lived by Israel under the old covenant) and to the OT (as it is newly understood under the new covenant). So, although the OT Scriptures are in a sense "new" and "transformed" as read by the new covenant people of God, they can now only be appreciated within the "container" of the revelation of the NT Scriptures since these latter represent the "founding charter" of what Wright calls the fifth act (in a five-act hermeneutic of revelation: creation, the "fall", Israel, Jesus, and the Church) and the fuller understanding of the OT depends upon what has been revealed in the New; particularly **He** who is The Word, Jesus the Messiah.[44]

The Canon of the Old Testament Scriptures

In looking more closely now at the Church's journey through to the finalization of the OT Canon, we shall pay no further attention to the journey of post-Temple Judaism as it would take us outside the scope of what is being aimed for in this particular study. Accordingly, I indicate this diagrammatically in **Fig 3.1** and **Fig 4.1** by representing it in dashed lines, thus:

While the appreciation of the New Testament writings which were emerging during the formative years of the young Church obviously occupied much of its focus in those early first centuries, it did so without neglecting what, as I have emphasised, was its established Bible. But, as also previously noted, that established Bible crossed over into the Church in the same "fuzzy" Canon state with which the old covenant era had ended. The looseness of the notion of what exactly constituted Old Testament "sacred books" is reflected in citations from and references to a wide range of OT documents in the writings of the Christians. The NT writers cite the sacred books that ultimately found their way into the Hebrew Canon, especially the Law, the Prophets and Psalms. But they also echo some of the deuterocanonical books. If one studies the references in the UBS New Testament,[45] one finds allusions to Sirach, Wisdom, 1-2 Maccabees, and Tobit. Furthermore, there are allusions to what would later be considered apocryphal works, e.g., Psalms of Solomon, 1-2 Esdras, 4Maccabees, and Assumption of Moses.[46]

What is the significance of such variety? It is probably easier to say what the significance is **not**; such as – we cannot really tell from such citations and references what they tell us about the NT writers' perspective of such ancient books when they were quoting them. Were the quoted sources all regarded as a rather broad (and vague?) collection of sacred books (however they would have defined that)? Or were they perhaps assuming distinctions between them – distinctions which their NT readers would have shared with them? Who knows? On balance, current scholarship seems to imply the former – thereby endorsing this somewhat fuzzy boundary as to what constituted an OT Canon around the time of the changing of the eras.[47]

Such loose - or less clearly defined - perceptions of what constituted the "Old" sacred books are also evident in the diverse uses made by the early Church (on the one hand) of the LXX, and by the Jewish community (on the other) of the Hebrew-language sources of the OT. This is illustrated by discussions we have on record between Justin and Jews in the mid-2nd century, where Justin acknowledges the differences between the "Christian" OT and the Jewish Scriptures, just as extra-biblical writings of early Church Fathers (Clement of Rome, Polycarp, Hermas, Irenaeus, Tertullian, and others) often quote freely from a large variety of Jewish sacred books, including apocryphal works.[48] All of which is just to say that, in the first instance, there was again no "mad rush" to get "**the** list" down on parchment as far as the Old Testament was concerned.[49] The people of the New Creation began their new covenant journey as comfortable with the core of their OT canon-in-practice as we saw the people of the old covenant had been.

Gradually this began to change. The first attempts to set up a rigidly closed OT Canon for Christendom apparently reflect the Jewish debates about the Canon in 2nd century Palestine. In the late 4th century, the Western Church, as witnessed in the North African councils of Hippo (393AD) and Carthage (384AD & 419AD), accepted a fixed number of OT books including some deuterocanonicals found in the LXX mss.[50] Each of these councils approved a list of OT (and NT) books coinciding with what later would be defined by Trent. In contrast to this, writers of the Eastern Church were more aware of the shorter scriptural Canon drawn up by the Jews. Melito of Sardis (ca.

170AD) gives us our earliest Christian list of OT books – a list much like the one that eventually became the standard Hebrew list (Est is omitted). And history testifies to the diverse views that pertained on the deuterocanonical books right up to and even during the Council of Trent – Cardinal Cajetan famously favouring the exclusion of the deuterocanonicals.[51] It was under the challenge of the Reformers in the sixteenth century that the Catholic Church was finally obliged to take a specifically formal position on the OT Canon, and opted not to follow what was being advocated by the Reformers but decided to stay with what had been the *de facto* understood and liturgically utilised set of OT books for so many centuries.[52]

A question that is sometimes posed with regard to the OT Canon is whether *Jamnia* (± 100AD) should be a consideration in the Church's journey [OT3] in finalising the OT Canon of Scripture? The "?" in **Fig 3.1** illustrates this question.

Some scholars today who follow the Reformers' OT Canon of the sixteenth century, refer to the Hebrew language books of Jamnia as one of the supporting factors for their choice of Canon. Two considerations mitigate against such a line of thinking.

Firstly, the argument made by Raymond Brown, and quoted above, that one cannot really think of the Rabbinical School at Jamnia in the same terms as a decision-making Church Council under the New Covenant.

Secondly, even if this "Council" model were to apply to Jamnia, on what grounds would the Christian Church in the sixteenth (or any) century look to an Old Covenant "assembly", meeting one hundred years **after** the Old Covenant had been supplanted by, and subsumed into, the New Covenant, as an authoritative body on divine revelation instead of (actual) Councils of the body of the New Covenant? To do so would be illogical – compounded even more so if the argument is being made by people who reject the idea of Church Councils having decision-making authority in the first place.

We shall return to this latter point after we have studied the journey of the New Testament Canon in chapters 4 & 6 (as well as other considerations in chapter 7).

However, before proceeding to the topic of the NT Canon, sojourners are encouraged to study the New Advent article on the OT Canon in **Appendix A**. The date of that article (1908) does not mitigate against its validity, for the reasons which I give therein while introducing it, and it adds valuable and considerable *jot & tittle* to what I have written in this present chapter. It is a very honest article and chronicles thoroughly the journey of the OT Canon within the history of the Church both in the East and in the West, and not forgetting the journey undertaken by the Church in Africa as well during the early centuries of the Church.

* * *

1. The NT Canon will be discussed in Chapters 4 & 6.
2. This is due, in part, to the oral/written notions of Canon referred to above.
3. E.g. Book One, Chapter 17, in this collection.
4. See below for more on Jamnia.
5. Turro & Brown (Canonicity) (1968) 67:21 p 518.
6. Turro & Brown (Canonicity) (1968) 67:29 p 520-521.
7. Turro & Brown (Canonicity) (1968) 67:23 p 520. Additionally, for a comment on the Canon *at Qumran* refer to Turro & Brown (Canonicity) (1968) 67:36 p 522.
8. I am aware that *Jamnia* (which is significant in this section) was to figure prominently again at the time of the Reformation when the question of the OT Canon was revisited by the Church, and I do address that consideration below in the journey labelled OT3.
9. There are three main suggestions: (a) Ezra (±400BC), (b) the men of the so called *Great Synagogue* (working under the impetus of Ezra) - a suggestion made by the learned Jewish writer, Elias Levita, in 1538AD, and (c) Jamnia in about 90-100 AD. [Turro & Brown (Canonicity) (1968) 67:33 p 521].
10. [Own Note]: "Recently" - This is a 1968 comment.
11. [Own Note]: I have added the word "-type" lest confusion arise in the use of the term "Church" in a Jewish context. Not that the latter is wrong: one often heard of the covenant people of Israel being referred to as the "Church" of the OT. (Many of the old Puritan commentators spoke in this way).
12. [Own Note]: See Fig 3.2 for context and timing of references to the Mishnah.
13. Turro & Brown (Canonicity) (1968) 67:31-35 p521-522.
14. Brown (Apocrypha) 68:121 p559 dates the formation of the Mishnah to AD 1-200.
15. To which we owe a great deal to teachers such as the late Derek Prince and the late Dwight Pryor.
16. The character of that particular Pasch, and its relationship to The Passover in the year that Jesus was crucified, is discussed in detail in Book Seven, Chapter 6.
17. Including (inter alia) Jer 31:31-34
18. Phil 3:5. cf. Rom 11:1
19. Heb 8:13, wherein the author's comment was written from the prophet's perspective, [he is quoting Jeremiah 31:31-34] not from his own; he knew that the old covenant had already disappeared as a valid expression of the relationship between God and his people (Heb 7:12). [Bourke (Hebrews) 61:47 p396]. Cf. Rom 13:11 and more particularly Rom 10:4 upon which Matthew Henry's comment is as follows:

   > He here shows...what an unreasonable thing it was for them to be seeking justification by the works of the law, now that Christ had come, and had brought in an everlasting righteousness; considering,
   >
   > (1). The subserviency of the law to the gospel (Rom 10:4): *Christ is the end of the law for righteousness.* The design of the law was to lead people to Christ. The moral law was but for the searching of the wound, the ceremonial law for the shadowing forth of the remedy; but Christ is the end of both. See 2Co 3:7, and compare Gal 3:23, Gal 3:24. The use of the law was to direct people for righteousness to Christ. (1.) Christ is the end of the ceremonial law; he is the period of it, because he is the perfection of it. When the substance comes, the shadow is gone. The sacrifices, and offerings, and purifications appointed under the Old Testament, prefigured Christ, and pointed at him; and their inability to take away sin discovered the necessity of a sacrifice that should, by being once offered, take away sin. (2.) Christ is the end of the moral law in that he did what the law could not do (Rom 8:3), and secured the great end of it. The

end of the law was to bring men to perfect obedience, and so to obtain justification. This is now become impossible, by reason of the power of sin and the corruption of nature; but Christ is the end of the law. The law is not destroyed, nor the intention of the lawgiver frustrated, but, full satisfaction being made by the death of Christ for our breach of the law, the end is attained, and we are put in another way of justification. Christ is thus the end of the law for righteousness, that is, for justification; but it is only to *every one that believeth*. Upon our believing, that is, our humble consent to the terms of the gospel, we become interested in Christ's satisfaction, and so are justified through the redemption that is in Jesus.

(2). The excellency of the gospel above the law. This he proves by showing the different constitution of these two.

20 Rom 11:15-26
21 Hebrews chapters 8-10, and Heb 13:20
22 Luke 19:44; 23:50-51; Acts 2:36-42
23 This representation will be continued in the next chapter, in *The Canon of Scripture Process Flowchart* - **Fig 4.1** which is shown therein.
24 Rom 11:5,26-27
25 Cf. Gen 45:1f
26 Cf. Book One, Chapter 4, in this collection.
27 Mt 12:42; Jn 8:58
28 Of course I recognise that there are also those NT texts which refer to *New* Testament Scriptures but (understandably for what was a work-in-progress) these are very few in number. [cf. 2Pt3:15-16]
29 *For whatsoever was written in former times were written for our instruction, that by perseverance and encouragement of the Scriptures we might have hope.* [Rom 15:4]
30 Acts 17:10-11
31 Vatican II summarised this truth as follows: "....in them [the OT Scriptures], too, the mystery of our salvation is present in a hidden way. God, the inspirer and author of the books of both Testaments, in his wisdom has so brought it about that the New should be hidden in the Old and that the Old should be made manifest in the New[a]. For, although Christ founded the New Covenant in his blood (cf. Lk 22:20; 1Cor 11:25), still the books of the Old Testament, all of them caught up into the Gospel message[b], attain and show forth their full meaning in the New Testament (cf. Mt 5:17; Lk 24:27; Rom 16:25-26; 2Cor 3:14-16) and, in their turn, shed light on it and explain it." [Flannery, Vatican II, 1975. 58:15-16 p759-760.]

a [St. Augustine, Quaest. In Hept. 2, 73: PL 34, 623]

b [St. Irenaeus, *Adv. Haer,* III, 21, 3: PG 7, 950 (-25, 1; Harvey 2, p.115). St. Cyril of Jerusalem, *Catech.* 4, 35: PG 33, 497. Theodore of Mopsuestia, *In Soph.* 1, 4-6: Pg 66, 452D-453A].

32 Cf. Book One, Chapter 8. The theme of the Body of Christ will, (of course!), feature hugely and repeatedly in our journey: such as in Book Four, Chapter 24, Book Five in its entirety (but particularly in Chapter 12), Book Six in its entirety, and Book Seven in its entirety.
33 Regenerated: born from above, born again, born of the Spirit...cf. John 3:3-10
34 John 1:1,14
35 1John 1:1
36 [Heb]*My ears you have opened;*
37 [Lxx: Ps 39 (40): 6-8]

38 Heb 10:5...7 and the writer of the epistle adding that "By that *will* we have been sanctified through the body of Jesus Christ once for all" [Heb 10:10]

39 C.f. Book Seven, Chapter 3 [*The Welcome Table of Luke and Theophilus*]. In so doing we shall also draw upon Pope Benedict's insights on this dynamic. Cf. Benedict XVI (Jesus of Nazareth – Parts I and II).

40 I am not ignoring the difference between the use of (e.g.) the Hebrew mss. and the Greek language versions such as the LXX. But the reality was that prior to the coming of Jesus, both language versions had been in use by various Jewish communities as per their particular context and needs.

41 And it is worth noting that there is a faithful thread of truth and of values that connects the first chapters of the OT Scriptures right through to the last of the NT Scriptures, particularly when it comes to the issues such as the sovereignty of God and the importance to Him of the human race, and of each individual human person created by him in his own image and his own likeness.

42 Within the new creation inaugurated by Jesus under the new covenant, the truths of the OT revelation are "still true", and all of the OT Scriptures are relevant to the NT People of God both in their fullness (as revealed in Jesus) and as the original (but developing) revelation of YHWH the one God who is "I Am who I Am". [And let us not forget that the scope of the OT Scriptures is broader than the Abrahamic Covenant (e.g. the Covenant with Noah and the Scriptures prior to that)]. But while they still constitute "truth" and remain *relevant*, not all of their stipulations are *applicable* to the NT community because the conditions that they required have been met; they have been satisfied by Jesus and in Jesus, and accordingly vicariously by us who have "died" in Christ and have been justified and made righteous with his righteousness. (cf. Rom 5). To illustrate it simply, if bluntly, the purification stipulations and altar sacrifices of Leviticus clearly just do not *apply* to us any more. Such OT Scriptures do, as I say, still have value and meaning for us as, for example, in the way in which they have been expounded upon in the *Letter to the Hebrews* by contrasting and relating, respectively, the priesthood of Jesus to the priesthoods of the Old Testament – both the priesthood of the Old Covenant Levitical priesthood (Heb 7:11ff) and that which preceded it, the priesthood of Melchizedek (Heb 6:20ff).

43 Wright (The Last Word) (2005) p125.

44 Ibid p121, 125.

45 The United Bible Societies Greek New Testament (UBS) single text for its Third Edition now identical with the 26th Edition of the Nestle-Aland text – refer to the Bibliography.

46 Turro & Brown (Canonicity) (1968) 67:40 p 523.

47 Turro & Brown (Canonicity) (1968) 67:40 p 523.

48 Turro & Brown (Canonicity) (1968) 67:41 p 523.

49 We shall see that the same applied to the issue of a New Testament "list".

50 The longer so-called Alexandrian Canon (represented by the LXX), in contrast to the shorter Palestinian drawn up by the rabbis at Jamnia. [Turro & Brown (Canonicity) (1968) 67:21 p518]

51 Turro & Brown (Canonicity) (1968) 67:41 p523 and 67:9 p517

52 The Roman Catholic Church accepts 46 books as the canonical OT. Most Protestants accept a Canon of 39 books; the Jews of the present day have the same Canon as Protestants but a different enumeration. Thus there is a difference of seven books (plus additional parts of two other books) – the deuterocanonical or "apocryphal" books. These books are Tobit, Judith, Wisdom, Sirach (Ecclesiasticus), Baruch (including the Letter of Jeremiah), 1-2 Maccabees, and parts of Esther and Daniel. [Turro & Brown (Canonicity) (1968) 67:21 p518].

* * *

4. The journey of the New Testament Canon (Introduction)

[NT] *No mad rush*: the journey of the New Testament Canon from Jesus to Geneva/Trent (Introduction)

Rubric: Eavesdropping on cotemporaneous episcopal conversations is to be encouraged...

Accordingly, overheard...

...via *Melito* of Sardis, picking up upon the *Muratorian* fragment along the way, eavesdropping upon early discussions in the north of the African continent and probable or improbable manuscripts in Asia Minor which are tossed into the mix along with decrees by Messrs *Damascus*, *Gelasius*, and *Hormisdas*, not forgetting the letter by another such worthy - *Innocent* to *Exuperius* (never heard of him) he lived in the country of the cock, and bulls exchanged west and east, it must have been a nightmare to organise and then call it a council (no event-managers in those days and the roads my dear brother were just too terrible). Laudicea had the merits of nostalgia, Rome that of decent baths, Florence simultaneous translations, and without Martin on the one hand and Cardinal Petticoat on the other we would never have eventually arrived at Trent - you mean it took 1545 years to reach that point in the road? Well actually 1563 years because - (and I'll never complain about long meetings again) - that particular council lasted eighteen years; the devil (they say) is always in a mad rush whereas God has the patience of...well the patience of what comes with being God - he has time in his hands...

The Canon of Scripture Process Flowchart

Fig 4.1 (next page) has been referred to a number of times already, and since it is central to what follows, an unpacking of what this diagram as a whole is intended to convey will prove to be helpful at this point. The flowchart needs to be read in the following order:

Part A→Part B→Part C→Part D

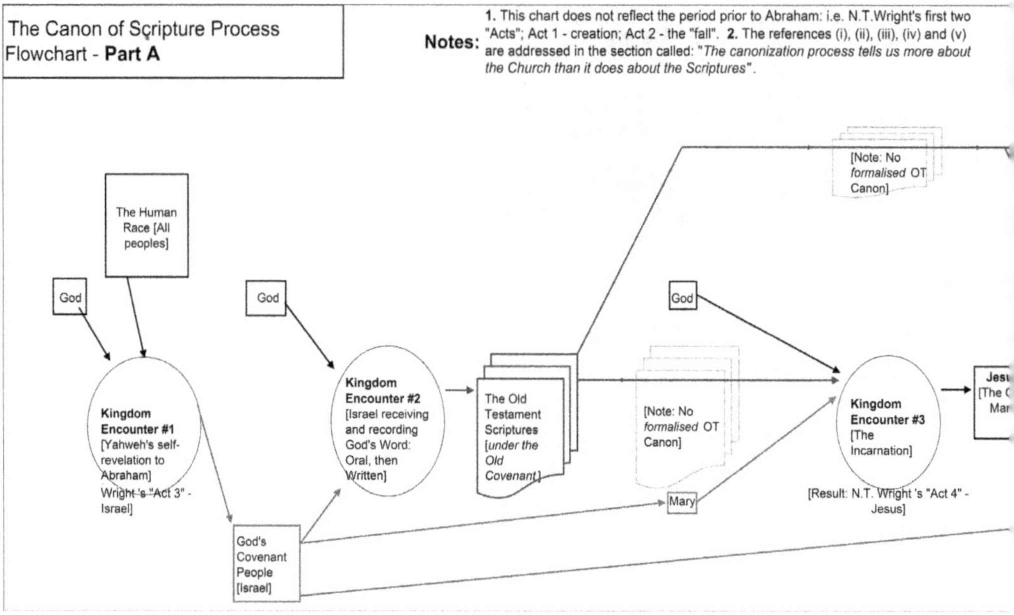

The Canon of Scripture Process Flowchart - Part A

Notes: 1. This chart does not reflect the period prior to Abraham: i.e. N.T. Wright's first two "Acts"; Act 1 - creation; Act 2 - the "fall". 2. The references (i), (ii), (iii), (iv) and (v) are addressed in the section called: "*The canonization process tells us more about the Church than it does about the Scriptures*".

- The Human Race [All peoples]
- God → **Kingdom Encounter #1** [Yahweh's self-revelation to Abraham] Wright's "Act 3" - Israel]
- God → **Kingdom Encounter #2** [Israel receiving and recording God's Word: Oral, then Written]
- The Old Testament Scriptures [*under the Old Covenant*]
- God's Covenant People [Israel]
- [Note: No *formalised* OT Canon]
- God → **Kingdom Encounter #3** [The Incarnation] — Mary
- [Result: N.T. Wright's "Act 4" - Jesus]
- Jesus [The Christ, Mar...]

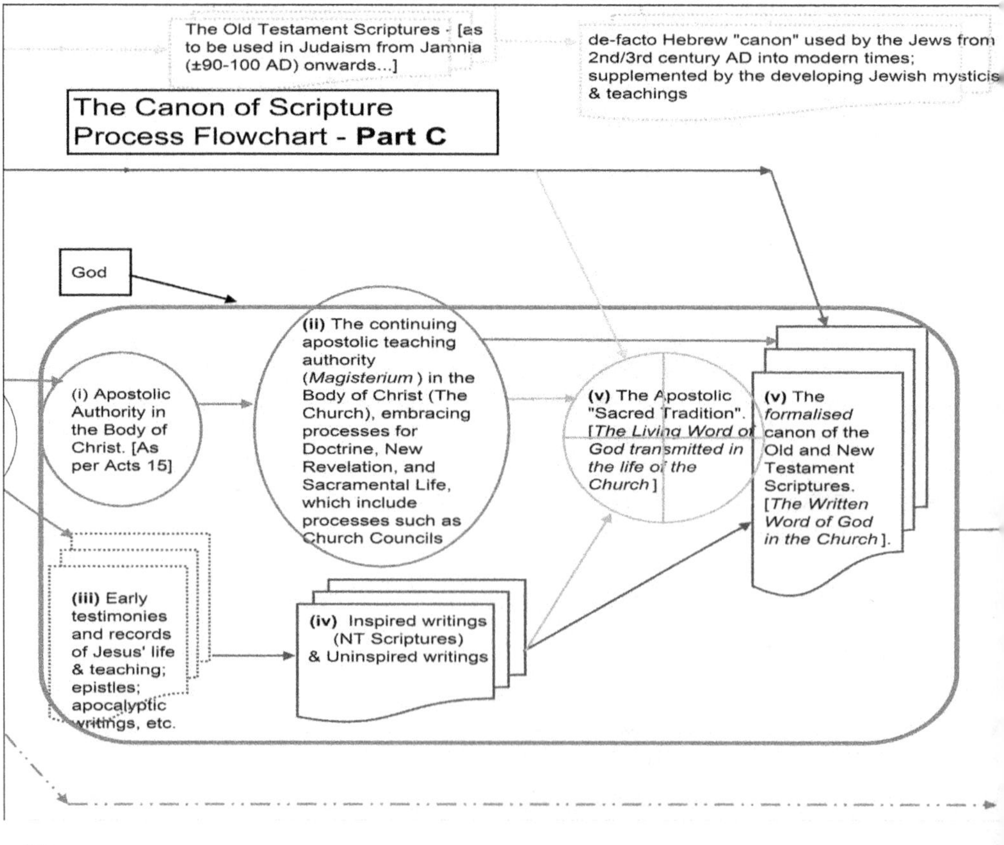

The Old Testament Scriptures - [as to be used in Judaism from Jamnia (±90-100 AD) onwards...]

de-facto Hebrew "canon" used by the Jews from 2nd/3rd century AD into modern times; supplemented by the developing Jewish mysticism & teachings

The Canon of Scripture Process Flowchart - Part C

- God
- **(i) Apostolic Authority in the Body of Christ.** [As per Acts 15]
- **(ii) The continuing apostolic teaching authority (*Magisterium*) in the Body of Christ (The Church),** embracing processes for Doctrine, New Revelation, and Sacramental Life, which include processes such as Church Councils
- **(iii) Early testimonies and records of Jesus' life & teaching; epistles; apocalyptic writings, etc.**
- **(iv) Inspired writings (NT Scriptures) & Uninspired writings**
- **(v) The Apostolic "Sacred Tradition".** [*The Living Word of God transmitted in the life of the Church*]
- **(v) The *formalised* canon of the Old and New Testament Scriptures.** [*The Written Word of God in the Church*].

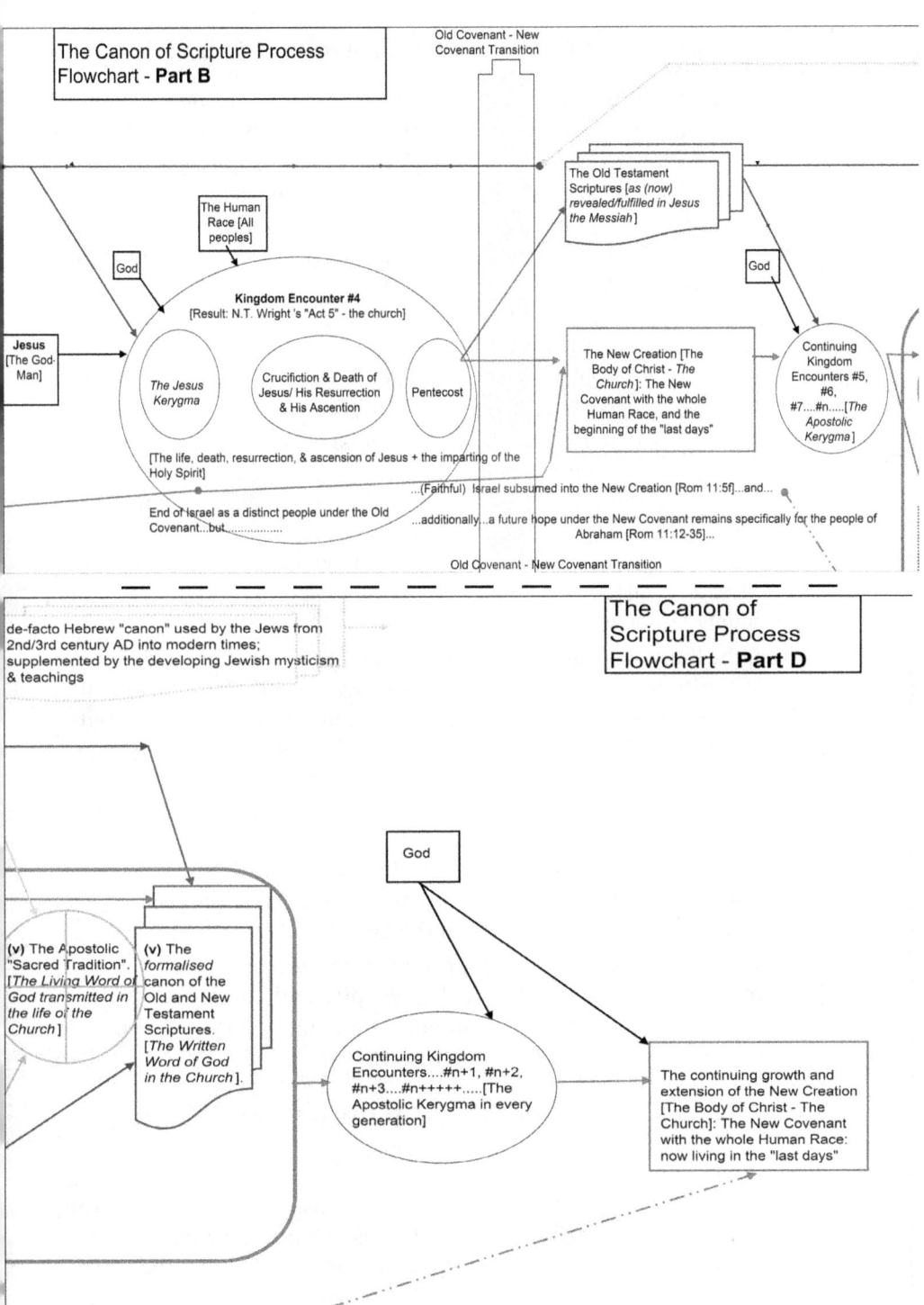

Unpacking the Canon of Scripture Flowchart (Fig 4.1)

In this diagram (**Fig 4.1**) the relationship between God and his people which led to us eventually having the Canon of Scripture is shown at a very high level as a flow of interactions.

I use the term Kingdom Encounter to describe each interaction, conscious that Kingdom is hardly a politically correct term today, but it is the most appropriate and indeed accurate one since, ultimately, what is, or should be, of concern to Christians in every age is the issue of who is on the Throne (O dear, another politically unpopular term) who is Kyrios[1] of our lives, of the Church, in the World.

A characteristic of each of these kingdom encounters is that God initiates them, and in doing so, some manifestation of his kingdom breaking through[2] into human society is experienced. The distinguished Bible scholar Bishop N.T. Wright uses a Five-Act model to describe the major interventions of God in salvation history (his model is also at a very high level) and I have mapped his "Acts" 3, 4 & 5 onto the corresponding[3] kingdom encounters (#1, #3, & #4) in this flowchart. I reference Wright primarily to show that his outcomes from these "Acts" are identical to my outcomes from the kingdom encounters in the flowchart, namely Israel, Jesus, and the Church.

Because of the limited scope of this diagram (we are herein only addressing the Canon of Scripture) I begin the flowchart with God's encounter with Abram (Abraham) as **Kingdom Encounter #1**, and do not deal at all with interactions prior to that, such as Creation and the Fall[4], and other major interactions such as the covenant with Noah. But precisely because of the specific focus of this flowchart, I do include two elements which are not in Bishop Wright's model; namely, Kingdom Encounter #2 (with the outcome of the OT Scriptures) and Continuing Kingdom Encounters (#5, #6, #7........#n) which, inter alia, in due time gave us the Canon, (and much more besides; continuing into our day, and through until the Lord Jesus returns...)

The journey through to the closing of the Canon unfolds as we track the dynamic interactions between YHWH, his People, and his Word flowing through history; these kingdom encounters appearing as dramatic images capturing each of the dominant *kyros* interactions.

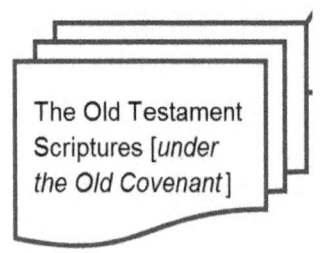

Tracking the Interactions - Kingdom Encounters #1 and #2

God sovereignly chooses, from among the entire human race, a particular man, Abram (Abraham) and with him establishes a particular covenant people, Israel (Kingdom Encounter

#1). God's subsequent interactions with Israel are manifold and include the revealing of his Word to his people in his people (Kingdom Encounter #2). In the diagram of this output the qualification *under the Old Covenant* has been chosen very deliberately since these same OT Scriptures will have two completely new designations (and associated qualifications) later in the journey.

It is noted, as well, that while these Scriptures have a de facto Canon at their core, the Canon is somewhat "fuzzy" around the edges: the definitive Canon of the OT was never to be *formally* finalised prior to the Christian era.

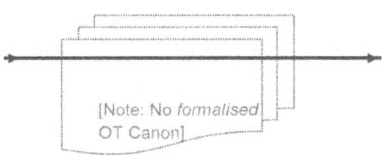

Tracking the Interactions - Kingdom Encounter #3

In Kingdom Encounter #3, the promise of the Messiah is realised in a dramatic and surprising way when the virgin of Isaiah 7:14 is revealed, and Mary utters her Fiat to God (Luke 1:38) in response to his invitation to bear the Immanuel of Isaiah 7:14/9:6.

The Incarnation takes place and Jesus is born. This Jesus Event was to change everything, even the Old Testament Scriptures. The physical documents did not change of course, neither did their contents, but what they were did change. As explained above (in OT3) from Jesus onwards they became something different. He, the Messiah, also actually embodies the Torah of the Messiah. The crisis that this presents to any Jewish ears is dramatically portrayed by the Jewish scholar Jacob Neusner in his book, "A Rabbi Talks with Jesus", a book which Pope Benedict XVI personally found very helpful in his own studies of Jesus, and from which he recounts the following extract. (Clearly "time" is cotemporaneous in all of what follows):

> In his imagination, across the millennia, Neusner has spent the day following Jesus, and then retires to discuss with the rabbi of a local village what he has heard from Jesus. The rabbi cites from the Babylonian Talmud:
>
> Rabbi Simelai expounded:
>
> *"Six hundred and thirteen commandments were given to Moses, three hundred and sixty-five negative ones, corresponding to the number of the days of the solar year, and two hundred forty-eight positive commandments, corresponding to the parts of man's body.*
>
> *David came and reduced them to eleven...*
>
> *Isaiah came and reduced them to six...*
>
> *Isaiah again came and reduced them to two...*

> *Habakkuk further came and based them on one, as it is said:*
> *"But the righteous shall live by his faith" (Hab2:4)"*

Neusner then continues his book with the following dialogue:

> *so,* the master says, *is this what the sage, Jesus, had to say?*
>
> I (Neusner): *Not exactly, but close.*
>
> He (The rabbi): *What did he leave out?*
>
> I: *Nothing.*
>
> He: *Then what did he add?*
>
> I: *Himself.*[5]

Tracking the Interactions - Kingdom Encounter #4

With this reformulation of the meaning of the OT Scriptures, we have already moved through to Kingdom Encounter #4, and the new designation (as promised above) which qualifies what the OT Scriptures have now become in the light of the Jesus (Messiah) Event is reflected in the graphic.

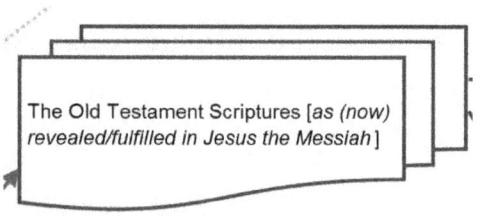

The Old Testament Scriptures [as (now) revealed/fulfilled in Jesus the Messiah]

Kingdom Encounter #4 tries to capture the impact of Jesus' life, death, resurrection, ascension and the outpouring of the Holy Spirit as one dramatic interaction, one which signalled the beginning of the "last days".[6] As stated above, the Scriptures of the Old Testament remain true – more true than ever! But the Old Covenant ends and, as foretold by Jeremiah,[7] is replaced by the promised New Covenant. This change of covenant marks the end of Israel as a distinct people under the Old Covenant,[8] but with it a new beginning for these same people under the New Covenant. As foretold by Jeremiah, the New Covenant was always going to be first of all a covenant with Israel, and not first of all with other (Gentile) nations. No surprises then, that the kernel of the new community of the New Covenant were all Jews, and (Faithful) Israel was subsumed into this New Creation. Israel is the root of the new "olive tree", as was emphasised by him who claimed to be the "most Jewish" of all of the Christians [Rom 11:1f], and the Gentiles were subsequently grafted into that tree.

With the New Covenant (a covenant with the entire human race) came the New Creation in which any dominant sense of national or tribal identity ends: in the One[9] Body of Christ there is no longer "Jew", "Gentile", "Slave", "Free", "Rich", "Poor", "Barbarian", "Greek", "Scythian", but rather a people where "Christ is all and in all".[10] Yet, additionally (and paradoxically?) a future and further hope under the New Covenant seems to remain specifically for the people of Abraham, (and the implication seems to be that this is as a distinct people - ?) [Rom 11:12ff].

The immediate outcome from Kingdom Encounter #4, in addition to the new insights into the OT Scriptures, is, as explained, the New Creation (i.e., The Church under the headship of the Resurrected Jesus):

> The New Creation [The Body of Christ - The Church]: The New Covenant with the whole Human Race, and the beginning of the "last days"

The continuing journey of the OT Scriptures within Judaism[11]

During this transition from Old Covenant to New Covenant, a parallel development takes place which is not a consequence of Kingdom Encounter #4, but occurs around the same time, namely the destruction of the Temple by the Roman empire (in AD70).[12] This tragedy for the Jewish people[13] gave rise to a new dependence by the Jews upon their Scriptures. Their subsequent journey with these Scriptures, via Jamnia to modern times is shown in the diagram as no longer being relevant to the new age of the Kingdom of God ushered in by Jesus the Messiah-King:

> The Old Testament Scriptures - [as to be used in Judaism from Jamnia (±90-100 AD) onwards...]

Note that the independence of this separate journey of the OT Scriptures by post-Temple Judaism is emphasised in **Fig 4.1** by showing that it nowhere originates from Kingdom Encounter #4, but solely from the OT Scriptures.

> de-facto Hebrew "canon" used by the Jews from 2nd/3rd century AD into modern times; supplemented by the developing Jewish mysticism & teachings

Tracking the Interactions - Kingdom Encounters #5, #6, #7...#n

The journey flowing from Kingdom Encounter #4 will bring us in due course to the revelation of the New Testament and the closing of the Canon, but it is very important to note that the New Testament Scriptures do **not** follow as an immediate and direct consequence of Kingdom Encounter #4. In saying this I am aware that it is a truism, but, unfortunately, it is my experience that many Christians have given little, if any, serious thought to the processes that went into the production of the NT Scriptures let alone the discernment process that was required for these to emerge from amongst the heterogeneous mass of early Church writings into a definitive Canon.

What one comes across instead is a kind of vague picture – a subliminal fuzzy sketch – in people's minds of the birth of Jesus, his life, the sermon on the mount, his death, resurrection, ascension, the coming of the Holy Spirit, Acts and the life of Paul, and the early Church starts living its life, the Bible in hand, bringing the gospel from Jerusalem outwards to the rest of the world.

In contrast to such a simplistic and inaccurate picture, **Fig 4.1** highlights the order in which things actually took place; showing for example that a lot of new *kingdom encounters* had to take place before the New Testament Scriptures get written and even a lot more before they are finally and formally recognised for what they are.

The first thing that happens immediately after Pentecost is that the Church begins to live its life, and to do what Jesus had said it would do after receiving the promised outpouring of the Holy Spirit: the apostles giving public testimony to the Gospel in terms of the death and resurrection of Jesus-the-Messiah. This *Apostolic Kerygma* takes over from where the *Jesus Kerygma* had left off. And this faithful proclamation of the Good News is accompanied (just as the proclamation by Jesus had been) with manifestations of the Kingdom of God: healings, miracles, repentance, changed lives in both individual and communal terms, etc: Kingdom encounters one after the other and all over the place.

> Continuing Kingdom Encounters #5, #6, #7....#n......[*The Apostolic Kerygma*]

The implications of all of this is that we are unable to complete the journey of the NT Canon without first unpacking the dynamic interactions between God, his New Covenant People, and the unfolding Word of that New Covenant. To that topic we now turn (under the title of *The Apostolic Kerygma* and Apostolic Authority) in Chapter 5, after which we shall resume the journey of the New Testament Canon in Chapter 6.

* * *

1. A term, which of course we have met before and frequently: κύριος [kurios, *koo-ree-os*]. From κῦρος kuros (*supremacy*); *supreme* in authority, that is, (as noun) *controller*; by implication *Mr.* (as a respectful title): - God, Lord, master, Sir.
2. An excellent book on this notion of manifest interventions of the Kingdom of God (the rule and reign of God) in history is Vineyard Publishing's (*Breakthrough*) by Dr. Derek Morphew.
3. "corresponding", but my numbering has to be different from his as I do not include all of Wright's "Acts" in my flowchart, and also because I have other (intermediate) "encounters", which are not in his schema.
4. Wright's Acts 1 & 2.
5. Benedict XVI (Jesus of Nazareth - Part I 2007) p104-105.
6. Heb 1:2
7. Jer 31:31ff
8. The emphasis is on the qualifier *"under the Old Covenant"*. Cf. what follows through the flowchart of Fig 4.1, and the corresponding narrative below, for Israel's implied destiny *under the New Covenant*.
9. Col 3:15
10. Col 3:11
11. Although this chapter's focus is upon the journey of the Canon of the New Testament, we have, quite rightly, needed to include the journey of the OT Canon within the New Covenant people of God. For completeness, we therefore also re-visit, albeit briefly, the continuing journey of the OT Canon within Judaism, previously alluded to in Chapter 3.
12. At least, such a connection is not self-evident. I am not here going into the theology of the prophecy by Jesus about the destruction of the Temple in Jerusalem or the timing thereof. Cf. Mt 23:37-24:2ff
13. Which was followed by their scattering throughout the whole world until the establishment of the state of Israel in 1948.

* * *

C.

Responsibility and Authority

5. The *Apostolic Kerygma* and Apostolic Authority

The Great Commission and Authority

The concluding remarks about *The journey of the OT Canon from Jesus to Geneva/Trent* [OT3] introduced – almost subliminally – the issues of responsibility and authority into the subject of the Canon because they included words like "they decided", and "they accepted", and "they opted" for this or that choice. Accordingly, in undertaking the journey of the NT Canon, it is time for us to consider who exactly did the deciding, together with the various aspects of responsibility and authority that emerged during that journey.

One of the characteristics of the ministry of Jesus which accompanied the Jesus Kerygma, was the authority of Christ. We can hardly be surprised therefore – as intimated by Jesus himself in the Great Commission - that one of the characteristics of the ministry of the Church which accompanies the Apostolic Kerygma, is the authority of the Church – the authority of the Body of Christ.

> And Jesus came and said to them, "All authority[1] in heaven and on earth has been given to me. Go therefore and make disciples of all nations, baptizing them in the name of the Father and of the Son and of the Holy Spirit, and teaching them to obey everything that I have commanded you. And remember, I am with you always, to the end of the age." [2]

Because this issue is central to the issue of the Canon of Scripture, we need to take a moment to reflect upon what is meant by the notion of "authority"; how the word is understood generally and how it is used in everyday secular practice, before we apply it to the question of the Canon.

Authority-in-practice

In everyday life, Authority can be variously spoken of as something that is **possessed**, or that is **exercised**, or that is **enforced**.

The inability to recognise the distinctions between these three aspects of authority can lead (and has lead) to a great deal of confusion in understanding how we receive and respond to God and his revelation.

It does seem self-evident, at least to me, that many entities, whether animate or inanimate, can have (i.e., possess) authority, but only animate entities can exercise and enforce authority.

To illustrate: the Constitution of the United States is a document which possesses enormous authority, but only the nine appointed-for-life distinguished justices of the Federal Supreme Court can exercise that authority in American society. They do so when they interpret the Constitution in ruling upon constitutional cases which are put before them. Even they, however, do not have the authority to enforce their own rulings. That authority resides with the various law enforcement agencies (as indicated by their very designation: *enforcement*) – the prosecuting authorities, the police, etc.

A more everyday example of legal authority, which applies in many societies today, is where an aggrieved party in a divorce case (e.g. a single mother) has been granted a maintenance order against the father of her children but he defaults on his payments. She has in her possession the authority to obtain such financial maintenance (the maintenance order issued by the court is such an authority) but that inanimate object cannot exercise that authority. Indeed, neither can she without the assistance of other legal authorities (such as law enforcement authorities). The latter, however, depend in turn upon the authority which she possesses, and they cannot exercise and execute their authority without the support of the maintenance order which the single mother has in her possession. The combination of the different authorities is required to achieve justice, and working together, they do just that.

Converse examples also apply of course, and society in general (government, business, civic society, etc.) takes grave exception if a person exercises or enforces authority which that society regards the person as not having. Just ask a bank manager who has granted a loan to a client in excess of her/his authority!

On a, tragically, grander scale we have had the Enron and Arthur Anderson debacles of recent years where people exercised authority which in fact they did not possess – authority which was not commensurate with their responsibilities. This resulted in extensive ruin for many people, and some of those who exercised such illegitimate authority are now serving prison terms.

Obviously, on the positive front, we have numerous examples in society where people are equipped with all the necessary attributes of authority to carry out their responsibilities: they possess the requisite authority, they exercise it, and they enforce it – all in one go in many instances.

These examples demonstrate: (i) that there are easily distinguished classifications of authority, [authority which is possessed, and/or which is exercised, and/or which is enforced], and (ii) that inanimate entities (documents, decisions, resolutions, agreements, contracts, etc.) can only be said to *possess* authority, while persons[3] can also *exercise* and/or *enforce* authority in addition to possessing authority.

Distinguishing between these classifications does not mean that any one class (type) of authority is, by its nature, higher than either of the other two types. To take the American Constitution example again; to say that the authority of the Constitution of the United States is different from the authority of the Supreme Court is a perfectly valid, indeed an obvious, statement. To say that its authority is less than that of the Supreme Court would be a ridiculous statement; indeed a nonsensical one since the Supreme Court is the servant of the Constitution, and only exists at all to ensure that the terms, conditions and amendments to the Constitution are upheld in American society. The Supreme Court is accordingly dependant upon the Constitution.

The converse equally applies; the Constitution depends upon the Supreme Court. Without it, the Constitution is literally powerless. The two entities are totally inter-dependant; an excellent instance of a symbiotic relationship. They are distinct entities in their own right, but individually are incapable of protecting the constitutional rights of American citizens; **each on its own cannot even fulfil its own purpose.** That is the key point; they need one another to fulfil what is in fact a single (common) purpose. [Clearly, we could include the authority-enforcement element if we wanted to complete the illustration].

Given this clarification of terminology with regards to the notions of responsibility and authority, we are now in a position to ask: what form did the journey of the New Testament Canon from Jesus to Geneva/Trent actually take and how does the issue of authority come into it?

* * *

---

1   **G1849** ἐξουσία [exousia *ex-oo-see-ah*]. From G1832 (in the sense of *ability*); *privilege*, that is, (subjectively) *force, capacity, competency, freedom*, or (objectively) *mastery*

(concretely *magistrate, superhuman, potentate, token of control*), delegated *influence:* - authority, jurisdiction, liberty, power, right, strength.

ἐξουσία, -ας, ἡ (< ἔξεστι), [in LXX: 4 Ki 20:13, Ps 113 (114):2; 135 (136):8, 9, Is 39:2, Je 28 (51):28 (הַשִּׁלְטֹן), freq. in Da for Aram. שָׁלְטָן, etc., Wi 10:14, Si 9:13, al.;] 1. prop., *liberty* or *power* to act, freedom to exercise the inward force or faculty expressed by δύναμις (q.v.): 1 Co 9:12; ἐ. ἔχειν, 2 Th 3:9; id. seq. inf., Jo 10:18, 1 Co 9:4, 5; c. gen. obj., Ro 9:21; seq. ἐπί, c. acc., Re 22:14; περί, 1 Co 7:37. 2. Later (cf. Milligan, *Th.*, 114; MM, *Exp.*, xiv), of the power of *right, authority:* Mt 21:23, Mk 11:28, Lk 20:2; of Messianic authority, Mt 9:6, Mk 2:10, al.; of apostolic authority, 2 Co 10:8; 13:10; of the authority of government: Mt 8:9; 28:18, Ju 25, Re 12:10, al.; esp. of judicial authority, Lk 20:20, Jo 19:10, 11. 3. Meton., (*a*) *jurisdiction:* Lk 23:7 (cf. 1 Mac 6:11, Is 39:2); (*b*) *a ruler* or *magistrate:* Ro 13:1–3; pl., Lk 12:11, Ro 13:1, Tit 3:1; (*c*) of supramundane powers (syn. with ἀρχή, δύναμις, θρόνος, κυριότης): 1 Co 15:24, Eph 1:21; 3:10, Col 2:10, 1 Pe 3:22, al. (Cremer, 236).

Syn.: v.s. δύναμις. [Abbott-Smith pp.161-162].

2 Mt 28:16-20. Cf. Jn 20:21-23; Mt 16:16-19.
3 I include as persons: human persons, divine persons, angelic persons, and demonic persons. To pre-empt any nit-picking let me also acknowledge that animate non-persons (such as animals) do, of course, exercise, enforce (and execute!) considerable authority – as any visitor to one our magnificent game parks in South Africa will testify.

* * *

6. The journey of the New Testament Canon (Resumed)

[NT] *No mad rush*: the journey of the New Testament Canon from Jesus to Geneva/Trent (Resumed)

As with the journey(s) of the OT Canon, that of the NT Canon also showed symptoms of *No mad rush*. And while the journeys of the OT Canon and of the NT Canon from the time of Jesus onwards concluded at the same time (**Fig 6.1 below**)[1], their beginnings were of course quite different. The former Canon, (albeit still somewhat "fuzzy" in scope at the edges as discussed above) was a major point of continuity in the transition from Old Covenant to New Covenant, whereas the latter Canon was an aspect of, and a new outcome from, the New Creation:

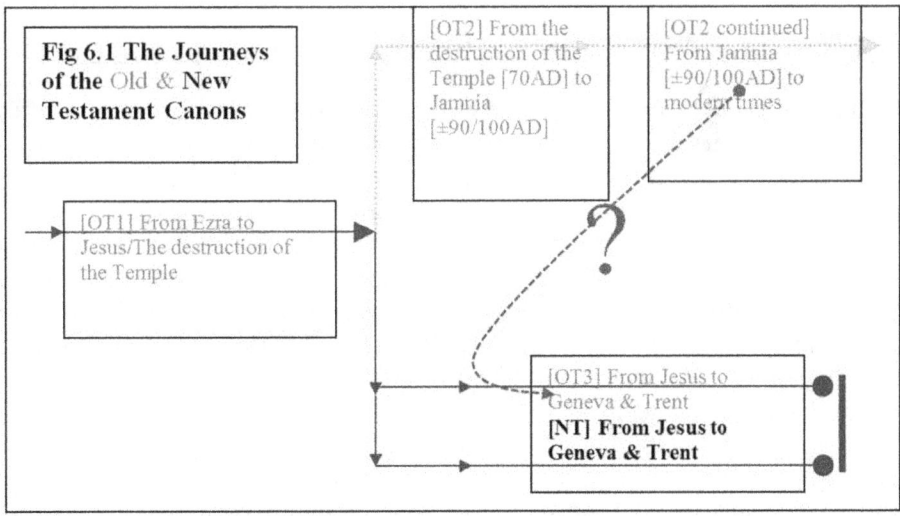

The context in which this journey of the NT Canon begins is reflected in the following extract from **Fig 4.1 on the following page**:

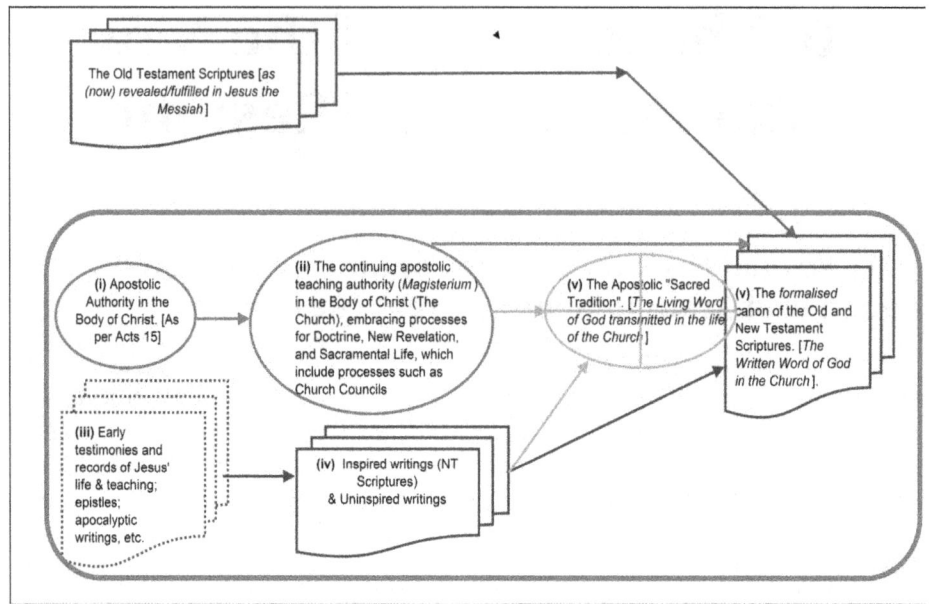

Extract from Fig 4.1

The Responsibility and Authority entrusted to the Church

The first crisis that the nascent Church faced was the issue of the Gentiles. Paul, of course, was the one chosen by Jesus to be **the** apostle to the Gentiles, but he was not the one who, as it were, got the ball rolling. That was Peter; a completely unsuspecting and reluctant Peter, who via visions, voices from heaven, and unexpected emissaries, was (eventually) persuaded to go and visit a Gentile – the Roman centurion, Cornelius. That soldier's personal "Pentecost", which shocked Peter to his boots, and which led him to then baptising Cornelius, was the trigger for the crisis. That story is so well known that there is no need to re-tell it here.[2]

But news of the event caused a stir back in Jerusalem, and the Apostles and brethren there challenged Peter on his behaviour. Luke records Peter's explanation to the assembly and how, as a result, those who had objected "became silent". But, as subsequent events were to demonstrate, it seems that what really happened was that "they let the matter pass". After all, their stated concern had been that Peter had eaten with Gentiles, and anyway, it all seemed to only involve one lone Roman soldier and his immediate staff. One isolated incident; let sleeping dogs lie; a crisis avoided...for now.[3]

Independently of all of this, Paul, supported by Barnabas and others, were experiencing significant growth in numbers and the vibrancy of Christian life in the Church at Antioch. This, in turn, had led to a major missionary initiative outwards from Antioch which had borne further fruit amongst the Gentiles encountered on Paul's (so-called) first missionary journey.[4] The reports about this caused great excitement back in Antioch.[5] But clearly, such news caused excitement of a very different kind in certain quarters back in Jerusalem, as a result of which, a group from there came down from Judea to Antioch, insisting that salvation always required submission to circumcision according to the custom of Moses. [6] This led to a major conflict; first on-site in Antioch, and then a fully-fledged crisis back in Jerusalem.[7]

Luke begins his report on the Jerusalem debate which ensued, when the leaders of the Church in Antioch and the elders in Jerusalem came together, with these words:

> [4] When they [Paul and Barnabas] came to Jerusalem, they were welcomed by the Church and the apostles and the elders, and they reported all that God had done with them. [5] But some believers who belonged to the sect of the Pharisees stood up and said, "It is necessary for them to be circumcised and ordered to keep the law of Moses." [6] The apostles and the elders met together to consider this matter. [7] After there had been much debate, Peter stood up and said...[8]

We can take it that "much debate" is something of a euphemism for actually what went on in this meeting.[9] Interestingly, other than the opening statement (quoted above) by those believers who were Pharisees (Acts 15:5) Luke does not give us any further details of what the supporters of imposing the Mosaic law on Gentile believers said in the course of "much debate". The remaining account of what became known as the Council of Jerusalem only records the arguments given by Peter, Paul and Barnabas, culminating in the positive summary of the outcome by James (the leader of the Jerusalem community) and how all of this was ultimately received positively by "the apostles and elders, and with the whole Church" in Jerusalem - resulting in a delegation being sent to Antioch. That delegation took with them verbal and written confirmation of the decision of the meeting not to impose the Mosaic law upon Gentile believers.[10]

This written letter included the famous statement:

> "...[28] For it has seemed good to the Holy Spirit and to us to impose on you no further burden than these essentials..."[11]

εδοξεν γαρ	*τω πνευματι*	*τω αγιω*	*και ημιν*
for it seemed [good]	to the spirit	- holy	and to us

The little conjunction "and" (*και*) in this declaration is of significant import; the element of collaboration is again being indicated in the process.

Intuitively we might have expected such a letter to read as follows: "For it has seemed good to the Holy Spirit to impose on you no further burden than these essentials..." But that is not what it said. The letter reads instead more like a consensus between the Holy Spirit and the assembled leaders; an indication that both parties have arrived at a common mind on this matter. An element of "partnership" is being indicated here: God's wisdom and direction, together with the leaders" responsibility in collectively owning the decision, and then exercising the authority commensurate with that responsibility in order to implement the decision. Given the "game –changing" nature of such a radically significant decision, the Apostolic Leadership also took steps to enforce their authority by sending two "chosen men of their own company to Antioch with Paul and Barnabas, namely Judas who was also named Barsabas, and Silas, leading men among the brethren".

Again, one can hardly be surprised at this. Jesus had previously indicated that consensus arrived at together by those assembled on earth would be ratified in heaven.[12]

For the purposes of our immediate issue (the journey of the NT Canon) the authority established via the [Acts 15] Council of Jerusalem marks two important milestones in the canonization journey.

First Milestone

The first milestone is the event itself. An assembly constituted by the Apostles and elders accepted the responsibility for addressing a critical issue – (call it "doctrine", call it "policy", call it "pastoral theology") – and, with the self-understanding that with the responsibility it possessed the commensurate authority, they exercised that authority; placed the decision on record and acted upon it. In the letter we can actually identify elements of all three characteristics which we have associated with the notion of authority in general, wherein authority can be possessed, exercised, and enforced.

This comes across in Luke's introduction to what the KJV's sub-heading calls "The Jerusalem Decree", together with the actual contents of the letter. This is such a key moment in the emerging nature of the Church that it is worth quoting the verses referred to in full:

> [22] Then the apostles and the elders, with the consent of the whole Church, decided to choose men from among their members and to send them to Antioch with Paul and Barnabas. They sent Judas called Barsabbas, and Silas, leaders among the brothers, [23] with the following letter: "The brothers, both the apostles and the elders, to the believers of Gentile origin in Antioch and Syria and Cilicia, greetings. [24] Since we have heard that certain persons who have gone out from us, though with no instructions from us, have said things to disturb you and have unsettled your minds, [25] we have decided unanimously to choose representatives and send them to you, along with our beloved Barnabas and Paul, [26] who have risked their lives for the sake of our Lord Jesus Christ. [27] We have therefore

sent Judas and Silas, who themselves will tell you the same things by word of mouth. ²⁸ For it has seemed good to the Holy Spirit and to us to impose on you no further burden than these essentials: ²⁹ that you abstain from what has been sacrificed to idols and from blood and from what is strangled and from fornication. If you keep yourselves from these, you will do well. Farewell."¹³

We can recognize the three generic elements of authority in this passage as follows:

Possessing authority

This is indicated by Luke's introduction. In Acts 15:22, he refers to the body which is engaged in the decision-making as "the apostles [τοις αποστολοις] and elders [τοις πρεσβυτεροις], together with the whole Church [ολη τη εκκλησια]". The implied authority is then embedded within the letter itself, where, in Acts 15:23, the leaders identify themselves with these same designations: "The brothers, both the apostles [οι αποστολοι] and the elders [οι πρεσβυτεροι],¹⁴ to the believers of Gentile origin in Antioch and Syria and Cilicia, greetings...". The authority associated with such appellations as *apostle* and, more particularly, with *elder/presbyter*, was well-defined in pre-Christian society (in both Gentile and Jewish communities) and later in our journey, a full exposition is undertaken of those roles in society, and how they then were taken over and deployed in the early Church.¹⁵ For our present purposes, we can just assert that such designations carried an authority, the nature of which would have been recognised and understood by the recipients of the letter – be they Jew or Gentile.

The claim to having authority to issue such a decree is reinforced later in the letter by the reference made by the apostles and elders to the fact that the authority of God – the Holy Spirit – underwrites their ruling, (Act 15:28).

Exercising authority

Excuse the truism, but in the interests of completeness, it is worth just drawing attention to the fact that the apostles and elders went through the formal process of actually writing the decree, and, in addition, handpicking "chosen men from among their members..."; leaders who are named (Acts 15:22); whose names (Judas and Silas) are specified in the letter (Acts 15:27).

Furthermore, as the letter states, these men are charged with the responsibility of verifying the written decree orally: "...who themselves will tell you the same things by word of mouth" (Acts 15:27) while at the same time validating the status of Paul and Barnabas, (Acts 15:25-26) knowing that they are the representatives of the Antioch Church in this whole matter. The apostles and elders would not have been hesitant about such endorsement, including with regards to Barnabas, since he had been one of the early converts within the original Jerusalem community, a Levite from Cyprus,[16] whom the Jerusalem Church had originally sent to Antioch to help build up that new Church. His arrival there had even pre-dated that of Paul, whom he had been instrumental in bringing to Antioch.[17]

Enforcing authority

This is implied by two aspects of the process described. Firstly, (fairly obviously) by the strong endorsement given to Paul and Barnabas, now supported in person by the further presence in Antioch of the two leaders sent from Jerusalem with the letter, (Judas and Silas).

Secondly (and more subtly) by including within the letter, the strongly worded rebuke which the Jerusalem leadership had given to their own members who, without authority, had seriously unsettled the Antioch community in the first place with their insistence upon conformity to the Mosaic law. It is actually in that passage that the subject of authority occurs in the letter:

> Since we have heard that certain persons who have gone out from us, though with no *instructions* from us, have said things to disturb you and have unsettled your minds... [Acts 15:24 NRSV]

The word translated by the NRSV as *instructions* in verse 24, can equally be translated as *authorization*. Indeed, that is how the NIV so translates it:

> We have heard that some went out from us without our *authorization* and disturbed you, troubling your minds by what they said. [Acts 15:24 NIV84]

The Greek verb used here for *authorization* is $\delta\iota\alpha\sigma\tau\acute{\epsilon}\lambda\lambda o\mu\alpha\iota$ [diastellomai],[18] and is variously translated elsewhere in the NT as *commanding*,[19] or to express the verb with which Jesus *charged* his disciples not to reveal certain things that they had seen, including the transfiguration.[20]

This signal event – The Council of Jerusalem - also laid down the process to be followed with respect to conflicts in the years and centuries which lay ahead for the Church; and there would be many as we now know.

Before proceeding to the generic implementation of the process thus established, let us add one observation about this outcome. It is interesting, is it not, that neither side in this dispute could appeal to Jesus (i.e. to his words/expressed views) for clear guidelines on the matter?[21] Indeed, there is no suggestion in Luke's description of this "council/debate" that either party even attempted to quote him in this regard. If the gospels had been written by this time (AD 49), then one could perhaps hypothetically imagine protagonists from the opposing sides taking – selectively taking – some of Jesus' sayings about missions on either "only to the house of Israel" (one view) or "go to the whole world etc." (the alternate emphasis) to support their case. But these gospel records would only be finalised in written form from the 60s onwards; indeed even oral traditions as to the sayings of Jesus were not even referred to in this dispute. No, God designed it this way: The Holy Spirit is the one to whom the Church turns in order to guide it in negotiating such completely new waters, deploying, of course, the revelation of God's word available to it... and then expects us to take responsibility for giving effect to the outcomes.

Furthermore, we have the advantage of knowing (from the written Gospels) that Jesus had himself undergirded this process when he said to the apostles at the Last Supper that, after he had left them (Jn 16:5) the Holy Spirit would come and be their guide into all truth, and that in doing so he would be reliably representing Jesus himself and (for good measure!) the Father as well. (Jn 16:13-15).

Second Milestone

The second milestone in the canonization journey is, accordingly, the process which has thereby been established. In the form in which it was to develop, it is represented in the extract of points (i) and (ii) from Fig 4.1 (Part C) as follows:

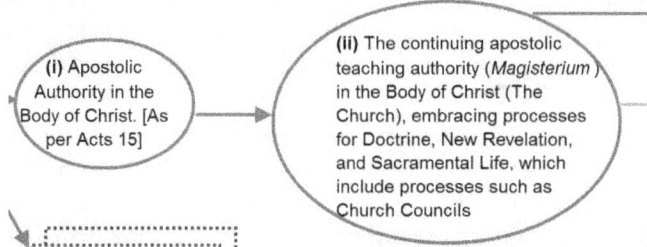

In parallel with this life of the Church leading up to the Council of Jerusalem, the testimonies of the Jesus Event are being proclaimed (the Apostolic Kerygma) and they are being relayed orally from person to person, from community to community. Written versions start appearing together with other writings, such as the epistles of Paul and other Apostles, and (in due course) apocalyptic writings. These, in turn, develop into what would become, in due course, the NT Scriptures – points (iii) and (iv) from Fig 4.1 (Part C) refer.

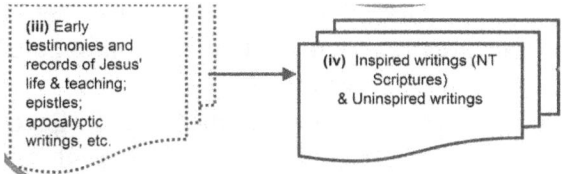

Note that in **Fig 4.1** (and including these four extracts) there is *no* arrow of dependency of these outcomes **(iii)/(iv)** upon that of Church authority **(i)/ii)**. This very important factor is discussed in detail below in the context of the statement: "In canonizing, the Church **discovers** inspiration; it does not create it." We shall note, in due course, that the Canon of Scripture is an outcome from a number of factors, one of which is the authority of the Church. The point being emphasised at this point in the canonization journey is that, in contrast to the journey of the Canon, the journey of the **content** of the inspired texts of Scripture themselves is not dependent upon, nor an outcome from, any aspect of Church authority.

From The Jerusalem Council to Geneva/Trent

In writing history (in general) one of the endemic risks is that the perspective of the writer can influence the narrative in a way that may result in inaccuracies – (as exposed, that is, by other or subsequent investigations!). The same applies to the writing of (let us call it) sacred history.

What is then exposed is perhaps the writer's presumption that this is what happened because the writer thinks that is what must have happened given the circumstances of the day, or even what should have happened given the writer's world/theological view. I suspect that this is often done subconsciously. There is not an intention to deceive being inferred here. I have given one example previously; the unwarranted designation of Jamnia as a Council (along the lines of a Church Council that we have become familiar with).

Could the same be said about the way in which the assembly of Acts 15 has also been designated here as a Council (along the lines of a Church Council that we have become familiar with)? In this regard, it is interesting to note that when the Jerome Biblical Commentary refers to the Jerusalem Council of Acts 15, it puts it in quotes thus: The Apostolic "Council",[22] without explaining why it does so. The New Advent article on the NT Canon [**Appendix B** refers] is quite happy to deploy the term as we are doing here, while at the same time giving a detailed description of the various classes of councils and synods in the history of the Church.[23]

I mention all this because, in now looking forward from the Jerusalem Council (or "Council") as we continue our journey of the New Testament Canon from Jesus to Geneva/Trent, it is my intention to try my best to identify what God actually did in working with the Church as it grappled with the issues of finalising the Canon, and not what we think he should have done, or what we assume that he must have done.

In the first instance, we can say that when the issue of what constituted the Canon became a contentious issue, God entrusted the resolution of that issue to a council (and councils) of the Church. After robust debates on the issues involved - debates not unlike those which accompanied the resolution of the highly contentious Gentile/Torah issue referred to above at the Jerusalem Council - the outcomes from such council(s) were owned by the Church as the conclusion of God's will on the matter; much in the same spirit as that of Acts 15:28, but I think I am right in saying that while the Holy Spirit would have been invoked in such councils, the specific wording of "It has been decided by the Holy Spirit and by us" has not been deployed in council pronouncements since that of Acts 15.

There were, of course, as already mentioned, robust debates along the way; the unsigned NT Letter to the Hebrews was periodically challenged as canonical,[24] - depending upon who in the West and in the East you were talking to. Likewise, the Second letter of Peter.

In the second instance, the maxim - "conflict being the catalyst which leads to clarity" - which we have met before on our journey,[25] kicked in periodically when people of one kind or another stirred the pot of religious controversy, particularly when they took exception to one or other aspect of Christianity – oft times a personally challenging aspect – and wanted to eliminate or change books of Scripture to accommodate their views, e.g. Marcion who (circa 144 AD) pushed for a Canon composed of a cocktail of Gnosticism and Christianity and also wanted the entire OT discarded as well as Acts and Revelation.

The Muratorian Fragment

We have evidence that, from the time that Marcion was stirring things up, the idea of actually drawing up a list of books that were being accepted across the Churches as trusted inspired (NT) Scripture was finding some favour. One such "list" which has become quite famous is the one known as the Muratorian Fragment.

The manuscript version which we have of this list is actually dated much later than the Marcion era: it is an 8th Century[26] Latin manuscript which was discovered by [Cardinal] Ludovico Antonio Muratori in the Ambrosian Library in Milan, and published by him in 1740.

The reason why this ms. gained notoriety was because it was recognised that this Latin version was a translation of a much older ms. in Greek (no longer extant) and that the text of the Muratorian Fragment includes the remark: "But Hermes composed *The Shepherd* very recently in our times, in the city of Rome, while his brother, Pius, the bishop, occupied the [episcopal] seat of the city of Rome". Given that Pius was pope [d.155AD][27] during the reign of Antoninus Pius as emperor,[28] the implication was that the original Greek-language version of the list must therefore have been drawn up in the second century around AD 170. This date has however been challenged in recent years by other scholars who date it to the fourth century. Either way, the Muratorian Fragment remains a remarkable document as it gives us a window into the mind of Christian leaders and scholars in the first four centuries of the Church when other lists (such as the Festal Letter of Athanasius of 367 AD) formed the basis for approval of versions of the Canon at Church Councils held at the close of the fourth century, Hippo (in 393 AD) and Carthage (in 397 AD).

I am personally attracted to the Muratorian Fragment for a couple of reasons. Firstly, the scribe who produced the Greek-to-Latin translation is regarded as having a very low proficiency in Latin. So, immediately I recognise a kindred spirit; his success in formal Latin examinations would have matched mine. The insults heaped upon him by scholars are brutal, with words such as "torturous Latin" with "barbarous spelling" being used by critics; the kindest designate his work as "vulgar Latin". This notwithstanding, his ms. is regarded as a treasure today; so three cheers for "The Bog-Latin Club!"

Sojourners can see his original much-maligned Latin version (along with a so-called restored version) in **Appendix C**. Two presentations of the ms. text are included in that Appendix. The first contains the translation into English by the famous scholar Bruce Metzger, and the second, in the columnar form, shows the original Latin and an amended version.

All of the NT books are included in the Muratorian Fragment with the following exceptions: The Gospel of Matthew is not mentioned (the assumption being that this reference was lost when the ms. got damaged – viz., its designation as a fragment); only two of John's epistles are mentioned (he does not identify which two); and the Letter of James and the Letter to the Hebrews are both absent. The apocalypse of John (i.e. Revelation) is included, but so also is an apocalypse of Peter which, of course, did not end up in the Canon, but the letters to the Laodiceans and Alexandrians are specifically excluded as forgeries.

The Council of Trent

The most serious conflict over the biblical Canon was of course reached in the sixteenth century when the Reformers questioned the scope of the OT Canon. The result was the Council of Trent (1545-63) which formally canonised the list of OT books which the [Catholic] Church had effectively regarded as inspired from around the early fifth century.[29]

As some of the NT books were also being reassessed for canonicity by some of the Reformers (e.g. The Letter of James) Trent also formally finalised the Canon of the New Testament in terms of the 27 books that we have today.

So the full Canon of Old Testament (46)[30] and New Testament (27) books was really only formally recorded in a Church council in the sixteenth century; an extraordinary thing really in terms of timing (if one views it from a 21st century world view and the importance we place on written constitutions, charters and contracts).

An invalid juxtaposition: The authority of the Church or the authority of Scripture?

The concern often expressed about the Catholic position on the process of the formation of the Canon, is that it seems to imply that the Church is asserting the supremacy of the Church over the Bible.[31] Is this the case?

So often these matters are posed in the manner of a binary choice. Jesus had questions thrown at him repeatedly in such a "binary choice" manner, and time and time again he demonstrated that the unspoken assumption – or presumption – underlying the question was invalid, and he responded by approaching the issue from an entirely different perspective; from a different plain.

This is the case here. It is necessary to approach the issue from a different angle, viewing it through a different "window". In our next chapter, which is entitled: *"Discovering" the Scriptures*, we will look at this question through such a "window" starting with a quotation from the Jerome Biblical Commentary.

* * *

---

1 Fig 6.1 is identical to Fig 3.1 with the exception that the NT Canon is now highlighted.
2 Acts 10:1-48.
3 Act 11:1-18.
4 Acts 13:1-14:26.
5 Acts 14:27-28.
6 Acts 15:1.
7 Acts 15:2-5.
8 Acts 15:4-6.
9 Acts 15:7 records that there was *much dispute/many discussions* depending upon the translation; Peterson probably captures the mood well: as *the arguments went on and on, back and forth, getting more and more heated.*
10 Acts 15:7-29.
11 Acts 15:28.
12 Cf. Mt 18:18-20.

13 Acts 15:22-29.
14 Presbyters are synonymous with Elders. Book Four in this collection refers.
15 Cf. Book Four, Chapters 4-11, in this collection.
16 Acts 4:36-37.
17 Acts 11:19-26. Cf. Acts 9:26-27.
18 **G1291** διαστέλλομαι [diastellomai *dee-as-tel"-lom-ahee*]. Middle voice from G1223 and G4724; to *set* (oneself) *apart* (figuratively *distinguish*), that is, (by implication) to *enjoin:* - charge, that which was (give) commanded (-ment).
19 E.g., Heb 12:20.
20 Mt 16:20; Mk 5:43; 7:36; 8:15; 9:9.
21 Cwiekowski (1988) p94.
22 Dillon & Fitzmyer (Acts) (1968) 45:72 p194; Fitzmyer (A Life of Paul) (1968) 46:28-31; Fitzmyer (Galatians) (1968) 49:7 p237.
23 Cf. the further reference to this New Advent article (Appendix B), below.
24 It is interesting, in the light of its early contentious history, that in the eyes of some modern day scholars, the Epistle to the Hebrews has been referred to as "perhaps the most self-authenticating contribution to the Holy Scriptures". F.F. Bruce quotes this statement without either endorsing or querying it, but I mention it as a further example of the mind-set - (fully understandable but, to me, missing the point about the *process* of authenticating) - which goes in a straight line and in just a single step from presenting the "case"/the evidence to "voila" it's in the Canon! i.e. in the Bible". I am audacious enough to say that (as a BIG fan of the Epistle to the Hebrews) I can well appreciate the many reasons why it should be in the Canon, but those reasons are not the immediate reason why this Epistle is in the canon. The actual reason is that the Church, under the guidance of the Holy Spirit, decided that it belonged in the canon.
25 Including Book Two, Chapter 10, of this collection.
26 Or possibly 7th century.
27 Johnson (Papacy) p.210.
28 Period of rule: AD 138-161.
29 Again, the New Advent articles in Appendices A & B refer.
30 The "46" is the Catholic Church number, including, as it does, the Deutero-Canonicals
31 E.g. Wright (Last Word) (2005) p62-63.

***

7. "Discovering" the Scriptures

The Jerome Biblical Commentary's introduction to this concept

> Viewed objectively, the Canon of Scripture stands as a body of literature endowed with an inner cohesion. Undoubtedly, this cohesion came about because these books were being used by a community guided by the Holy Spirit. They nourished the prayer life of the group, called forth reflection, and provided a rule of life. Books not conforming to this internal cohesion fall, by that very fact, outside the pale of the Canon. The faculty for judging such conformity or nonconformity resides in the Church. Acknowledgment from any other quarter would be what Zwingli feared, namely, a human seal of approval set upon the work of God. In part it was this consideration that prompted Augustine's well-known observation, "I would not believe the Gospel did not the authority of the Catholic Church move me to this" (Contra epistolam Manichaei 5.6.; PL 42.176).
>
> Inspiration, then, demands canonization, but canonization is not to be understood as working a change in the inspired book. Nothing is added, but a light is thrown upon the book in order to make manifest something that is already there. In canonizing, the Church discovers inspiration; it does not create it. The Fathers apparently sensed the intimate connection between Bible and Church, for at times they spoke of the books of Scripture interchangeably as "canonical books" and "Church-books."[1]

The words, "In canonizing, the Church *discovers* inspiration; it does not create it," which Turro and Brown apply here to the Canon in general, finds an echo in the comments of other biblical scholars. Most seem to agree that the Scriptures were "discovered" and are not a "creation" of the Church. And yet, I find, that the way in which this expression is interpreted by different scholars/theologians, reflects significantly different understandings of the role of the Church in such "discovery". Accordingly, let us unpack this word a little bit, (just as we unpacked the common meaning of the word *authority*), before we apply it to the *discovery* of the Canon.

What constitutes "Discovery" in general

Let us first look at an example of how the word "*discovery*" is used generally. This example, while it deals with the discovery of certain ancient manuscripts, does not relate directly to the issue of the Canon or of inspiration, but just to the use of the word "discovery" - one that would apply in any archaeological situation.

"Discovery." An illustration of the terminology: Who discovered the Dead Sea Scrolls?[2]

Approximately 24 km southeast of Jerusalem, Wadi En-Nar, a desolate, dry watercourse runs eastward down to the Dead Sea. A broken line of cliffs stretches behind the shoreline plain. On this plain, in the hot days and contrasting cold nights of autumn, the Ta'amireh Bedouin tend their flocks of sheep and goats.

In the year 1947, while tending the flocks, a young Bedouin shepherd threw a stone into a small opening in the crumbling face of a cliff. He was startled by the noise it caused, apparently by shattering an earthenware jar.

He fled in fear, but two days later he returned and climbed some 100 metres to enter through a larger, higher opening. As his eyes became accustomed to the darkness, he saw ten tall jars lining the walls of the cave, and a mass of broken pottery amid fallen rocks littered the floor. Most of the jars were empty, but one contained some scrolls, two of which were cloth-covered. He took the manuscripts back to the Bedouin camp and left them there for about a month, hanging in a bag on a tent pole. Finally, some Bedouin took the scrolls to Bethlehem to see how much they would fetch. The Bedouin were unceremoniously turned away from one monastery, being told that the scrolls were of no value whatever. Another dealer said that the manuscripts had no archaeological merit, and he suspected that they had been stolen from a Jewish synagogue.

Eventually, in 1948, their worth was rightfully established when seven of the scrolls were sold by the Bedouin to a cobbler and antiquities dealer called Kando. He in turn sold three of the scrolls to Eleazar L. Sukenik of Hebrew University, and four to Metropolitan Mar Athanasius Yeshue Samuel of the Syrian Orthodox monastery of St. Mark. Mar Athanasius in turn brought his four to the American School of Oriental Research, where they came to the attention of American and European scholars.

It was not until 1949 that the site of the find was identified as the cave now known as Qumran Cave 1, and in that year, G.L. Harding and R.de Vaux excavated that particular cave. It was that identification which led to more explorations and excavations of the area of Khirbet Qumran. Further search of Cave 1 revealed archaeological finds of pottery, cloth and wood, as well as a number of additional manuscript fragments. It was these discoveries that proved decisively that the scrolls were indeed ancient and authentic.

So, who discovered the Dead Sea Scrolls?

The immediate answer is that the Bedouin discovered them. And that has to be a correct and accurate answer. But is it a complete answer? Since they did not know the nature of the artefacts that they had discovered, their scale of discovery could best be described as not fully meeting the conditions of being (using language much beloved in mathematics and rugby) "necessary and sufficient."[3] As far as they were concerned, they had discovered these jars, some of which had manuscripts inside them, which, for whatever reason, were of value to archaeologists and scholars. In findings of other Dead Sea scrolls by the Bedouin, since they were being paid for each individual fragment, they cut remaining manuscripts into small fragments before selling them off. They would presumably never have done this if they had realised what they had discovered. Of course, once this cutting-up process became known, it caused great consternation amongst the scholarly recipients who were further down the discovery channel of these artefacts.

The scholars' scale of discovery could equally be described as not meeting the conditions of being "necessary and sufficient." Their discovery was certainly necessary, but hardly sufficient; without the role of the Bedouin in the first place, the scholars would have had nothing to examine and, accordingly, nothing further to "discover".

The complete answer to the question therefore lies in recognising the different stages and the different contributions that went into the discovery of the Dead Sea scrolls, including, in the final stage, the illumination brought to the process by scholars in distinguishing between those scrolls which were of a biblical nature, those of equal value in other domains of study, and yet others which had relatively little (or no) value to archaeology or to history at all.

This multi-layered process of discovery is, unsurprisingly, actually reflected in the (multi-layered) dictionary definition of the word "discover": 1. to be the first to find or find out about. 2. to learn about or encounter for the first time; realize. 3. to find after study or search. 4. to reveal or make known.

Discovery of the Inspired Scriptures: What this really means

It is with this sort of framework in mind that the previous comments by Turro and Brown can be appreciated:

> "Inspiration, then, demands canonization, but canonization is not to be understood as working a change in the inspired book. Nothing is added, but a light is thrown upon the book in order to make manifest something that is already there. In canonizing, the Church **discovers** inspiration; it does not create it."

And this process of discovery includes (by definition) distinguishing between books which are inspired (and therefore belong in the Canon) and those which are not inspired (and accordingly do not belong). The books did not come pre-labelled as either inspired or not. The Church did not come across an unambiguous collection of books in a jar, all neatly wrapped and classified and distinguished as either canonical or not canonical. As emphasised previously, God did not make it easy for us by "leaving a list". The Church had to sift, over time, through a number of writings all of which laid claim in various ways to being expressions of revelation from God. In other words: in the *discovery* process, the Church, under the guidance of the Holy Spirit, had to *discover* which of these documents were inspired (and which were not).

All of this reflects, of course, the position of the Catholic Church. What is the perspective of other Christians – and specifically Evangelical Christians?

Evangelical scholarship and the Canon of Scripture

Evangelical scholarship on the Bible – on the Word of God – is probably the singularly most distinctive characteristic of Evangelical Christianity. There are, of course, many other outstanding characteristics, such as: the emphasis on personal conversion to Jesus Christ, discipleship and following Jesus in relieving human suffering by means of ministry akin to his, evangelisation and missions, individual personal prayer and inspiring communal worship, the responsibility to engage in intercessionary prayer, recognising the universality of the Body of Christ, etc. etc. But ultimately, whatever characteristic is considered, it is all founded on the written Word of God and utilises that Word. In saying all of this, I speak as an "insider". My Christian spirituality embraces the Evangelical and Catholic-Sacramental in a uniform, integrated, and mystical life in Christ.[4]

Given then, this centrality of the Word, it comes as something of a surprise to the student of the Canon of Scripture to realise that Evangelical scholarship on the topic of the Canon is so sparse. There are great works on the Canon –

Professor F. F. Bruce's volume, referenced below, is a case in point. But what is absent is scholarship on the decision-making processes that gave rise to the formation and closing of the Canon – in other words, scholarship on the issue of responsibility/authority.

Accordingly, my present goal in approaching this topic is to try and find an answer to the following question, posed as a paradox.

The Canonical Paradox:

> The Catholic position with respect to the Canon of Scripture is that the Church was entrusted with the responsibility of discovering, under the guidance of the Holy Spirit, from among all of the writings which emerged from the Old Covenant people of God and from the people of the New Covenant, which writings were divinely inspired and which were not. Having done so, the Church possessing the responsibility, exercised the commensurate authority to define the former as constituting the Canon of Scripture.
>
> The Evangelical position is that the constitution of the Canon is not subject to any ecclesiastical authority and indeed that no human agency has either the responsibility or the authority to define what constitutes the Canon.
>
> The paradox that I wish to pose to my Evangelical sojourners is the following: Given that the Reformers did not have, and did not desire or claim to have, the responsibility or the authority to determine what constituted the Canon of Scripture, why (in deciding to exclude the Deutero-Canonical books from the Old Testament Canon) did they in fact exercise such authority?

The unspoken assumption (somewhat tongue in cheek) behind this paradox is that the printer/book binder did not accept responsibility/authority for such a decision, and took it upon himself to leave the books out!

Furthermore, it needs to be emphasised that this paradox is not resolved by resorting to criteria of canonicity, liturgical practices, or other reasons or arguments for or against the Deutero-Canonical books. In other words, in order to try and resolve the paradox it is not going to be sufficient to repeat the case for and/or the case against such inclusion/exclusion. All that will do is re-present a case – a point of view – as to why a particular book should have been included or excluded; it does not identify the authority which sanctioned the actual outcome.

To again take an example from the American Constitution: Legal arguments were presented on both sides of the notorious Roe vs. Wade landmark case in 1975; some in favour of abortion and some against. The reason that the law was changed was not because one case was stronger or weaker than the other – that will always remain a matter of subjective opinion. What brought about the change in the law was that the Supreme Court of the United States decided and directed that it had to be changed. Why the Court did that can be discussed at length. The point is that those nine justices had the constitutional responsibility and authority to make that decision and the associated authority to exercise it. The enforcement authorities then implemented it.

Undoubtedly, criteria of canonicity and other factors did play a major part in influencing the Church during its journey of discernment-discovery on what books were inspired and which were not, culminating in the decisions that were taken in regard to the Canon. The point being made is that, whatever the reasons, such decisions **were** taken, and they were taken (on the one hand) by people who claimed to have the authority to do so, and (on the other hand) by others who (paradoxically) did not claim to have such authority.

I draw upon five Evangelical sources in looking at this paradox. The first, Dr. Wayne Grudem, does include the issue of authority in his study of the Canon. The second, Professor F. F. Bruce, focuses his comments primarily on criteria of canonicity. For my third source I refer to a work, not on the Canon per se but on the subject of Authority, by Dr. Martin Lloyd-Jones. In the fourth source, Anglican Bishop N. T. Wright addresses very specifically the ecclesiastical authority issue. And finally, Dr. M. J. Sawyer recognises the paradox which I have posed and presents it as such to his Evangelical brethren.

Most of my quotations from these scholars are quite brief.

Dr. Wayne Grudem

Grudem's comments appear as his Appendix B (The Canon of Scripture) in his 1988 book *The GIFT of Prophecy – in the New Testament and Today*.

In discussing the question of divine inspiration with respect to certain New Testament writings which were not authored by one of the Apostles, Grudem uses the word *recognizing* with reference to the process that the early Church followed in addressing such writings:

> ...in these [non-apostle-authored] cases, the early Church had the task of *recognizing* [his italics] which writings had the characteristic of being God's own words (through human authors).[5]

Grudem does not couple the notion of responsibility/authority with such *recognizing*, but his application of the word *recognising* is strikingly similar to the way in the word *discovering* has been used above by Turro & Brown. It is a pity that the actual Catholic position (i.e., that of *discovering* inspiration) is not more widely recognised or understood, because (like many people, including, I suspect, many Catholics) Grudem assumes that the Catholic

Church sees itself as having bestowed divine authority upon certain writings. He accordingly, juxtaposes the posture adopted on authority by different Christian groups in this manner:

> ...it must be remembered in connection with any historical investigation that the work of the early Church was not to *bestow divine authority* [his italics] or even ecclesiastical authority upon some merely human writings, but rather to *recognize* [his italics] the divinely authored characteristic of writings that already had such a quality. This is because the ultimate criterion of canonicity is diving authorship, not human or ecclesiastical approval.[6]

The End Note added by Grudem to this comment reads:

> It is as at this point that evangelical Protestants differ both with Roman Catholics (who would say the official Church endorsement is a means of giving divine authority to a writing) and with some non-evangelical Protestants (who would not agree with the idea of a category of writings that have joint human and divine authorship and would therefore question the idea of a canon based on such a criterion).[7]

This note reflects – quite understandably – a misunderstanding on Grudem's part as compared to what the Catholic Church's position (as per Turro & Brown) actually is.

With humble honesty, Grudem also asks the following "what if" hypothetical question that some other Evangelical scholars pose:[8]

> "...what should we do if another of Paul's epistles were discovered... Would we add it to Scripture?"

Grudem is obviously thinking here of the so called "other" or "missing" letters supposed to have been written by Paul to the Corinthians, and while ultimately acknowledging (for very good reasons which he spells out) that this is so unlikely that the question is almost so hypothetical as to be ridiculous, the thought processes revealed in his (equally hypothetical and speculative) answer are very revealing:

> "...The answer would probably be that if a great majority of believers were convinced that this was indeed an authentic Pauline epistle, written in the course of Paul's fulfilment of his apostolic office, then the nature of Paul's apostolic authority would require that this epistle would also be in God's own words, and that therefore it should be added to Scripture...."[9]

The intrinsic assumption in such a fine scholar as Wayne Grudem is that the very idea that a God-given mandate resides in the Church for just such an instance, is not a possibility. Instead re resorts to a speculative "majority" (which, apart from anything else, would be impossible to "poll"). His posture is, of course, perfectly understandable precisely because it begs the question of what is meant by "the Church" and the decision-making authority of "the Church".

That notwithstanding, I do find in such scholars – and Grudem is no exception – an acknowledgement (which I am convinced is subliminal) that decision-making processes had to have taken place with regards to issues such as the Canon. This comes through in terminology such as the following...

> "...In the case of several New Testament books which were slow to gain approval by the whole Church (books such as 2 Peter and 3 John), much of the hesitancy can be attributed to...etc."[10]

...where the word *approval* is used.

Professor F. F. Bruce

For the classic work by Evangelical scholarship on the issue of the Canon, sojourners are referred to the late F.F. Bruce, known worldwide as "the dean of evangelical scholarship", and to his book, The Canon of Scripture (1988).[11]

Whatever one's Church background, Bruce's book is essential reading for this topic. His confident, but humble, authority comes through in every page, and his style is eminently readable – a true delight actually. Nonetheless, he still leaves us without an Evangelical solution to the decision-making process issue, notwithstanding the fact that (as with Grudem above) he (subliminally) also uses words such as "recognised" in the discernment sense, and "acknowledged" in a decision-making sense; the latter in an instance such as the following:

> In a Christian context, we might define the word [canon] as "the list of the writings acknowledged by the Church as documents of divine revelation."[12]

Yes, acknowledged by people – by persons who then acted upon the conclusions which they had come to acknowledge.

Dr. D. Martin Lloyd-Jones

The "Dr." title is actually that of a medical doctor, and Martin Lloyd-Jones was recognised as a brilliant medical man who had intentionally swopped the stethoscope for the pulpit.

Dear Sojourner, if one has a pre-disposition for great preaching in the Puritan tradition, whether expository or thematic, as this narrator has, then the good Doctor will be to your liking, and many of his sermons between 1957 and 1980 in Westminster Chapel and elsewhere were recorded for posterity.

If he ever touched upon the topic of the Canon of Scripture in preaching or in writing I am not aware of it. However, what I do have in my possession is his book on the topic of Authority. It is not a large book – it has only three chapters: The Authority of Jesus Christ, The Authority of the Scriptures, and The Authority of the Holy Spirit.

In this book Lloyd-Jones presents me with two dilemmas. The first is that he deals with his three subjects of authority (Jesus, the Scriptures, and the Holy Spirit) as if all three are the same type of authority, and certainly in terms of the distinctions that I have made above in Chapter 5, that is patently not the case, which can be explained as follows.

Jesus and the Holy Spirit are, of course, persons, and (if it were our topic) I could demonstrate that these two persons possess authority, have exercised/enforced authority, and still continue to do so. In other words both Jesus and the Holy Spirit manifest all of the three characteristics of authority. It is true that sometimes they involve people in the exercise/enforcing of their authority; other times they do not. That is God's prerogative.

The same is not true of the authority of Scripture. The Scripture possesses enormous authority, but that authority cannot be exercised without the involvement of some person or persons. [Such a person can indeed be the person of the Holy Spirit himself, a preacher, another person, indeed a person reading Scripture him/herself, or groups of persons acting in consort.] It is in this respect that it is a different type of authority from the other two. Let me emphasise that referring to the Scripture in this way does not designate it as an authority that is to be regarded as of a lower class or lower authoritative type than the authority of Jesus or the Holy Spirit.[13] After all, the Scripture, as I have been at pains to emphasise, is the Eternal Logos enfleshed ("incarnate") in human language. Yet, the nature of its authority is different, and as our American Constitution example demonstrated, such distinctions are commonplace in everyday life. This notwithstanding, Dr. Lloyd-Jones not only overlooks the fact that, in some manner or other, persons have to come into the picture for the authority of Scripture to be exercised, he specifically rejects it.[14]

My second dilemma with Dr. Lloyd-Jones is that in a book on Authority he does not have a chapter on the Authority of the Church. He does touch very briefly on aspects of Church authority but only in passing and not in any way related to the Canon of Scripture.

However, just as noted with Grudem and Bruce, the element of authority is also present in Lloyd-Jones' book in a subliminal manner. Thus, when he presents a case for the apostolic authority behind the NT Scriptures, he uses expressions such as the "early Christians all recognised it" [the apostolic authority]; there were certain decisions that were "universally accepted"; the "early Church also accepted it"; "the test of canonicity" (presumably some persons must have been selecting and applying such "tests"?), etc.[15]

Clearly, at some stage (the "early Church" stage) there were people who were exercising authority. As I say, it may have been so subconsciously in his mind, the persons doing the "accepting" are somewhat "fuzzy" in definition ("early Church", "universal", etc.) but persons they are. He does not dwell on the process, and certainly does not deal at all with the long periods of (multi-generational) time involved between the Early Church and the Reformation, and the associated debates about what was "in" and what was "out", which in one sense is understandable since, as pointed out, he does not have a chapter on the Authority of the Church.[16]

Bishop (now Professor) N. T. Wright

In his excellent book, *God's Last Word*, which he wrote while he was still the Anglican Bishop of Durham, the distinguished biblical scholar N.T. Wright deals with some of the current secular attempts to undermine the authenticity of early Church development and the reliability of the New Testament and indeed of the Old Testament Scriptures.[17]

In the course of his defence of such Church development he addresses the process of canon-formation and its relationship with the authority of the Church. The passage in question reads as follows:

> *...People sometimes suggest, indeed, that the process of canonization is the sign that the Church itself was the final authority. This proposal is sometimes made by Catholic traditionalists asserting the supremacy of the Church over the Bible, and sometimes by postmodern sceptics asserting that the Canon itself, and hence the books included in it, were all part of a power-play for control within the Church and social respectability in the world. This makes a rather obvious logical mistake analogous to that of a soldier who, receiving orders through the mail, concludes that the letter carrier is his commanding officer. Those who transmit, collect and distribute the message are not in the same league as those who write it in the first place.*
>
> *Such proposals have, in fact, little to recommend them historically, despite enthusiastic advocacy in some quarters. They represent, among other things, a serious de-Judaizing of the Christian tradition. The canonization of scripture, both Jewish and Christian, was no doubt complicated by all kinds of less-than-perfect human motivations, as indeed in the writing of scripture in the first place. But canonization was never simply a matter of a choice of particular books on a "who's in, who's out" basis. It was a matter of setting out the larger story, the narrative framework, which makes sense of and brings order to God's world and God's people.[18]*

It may seem presumptuously audacious for an old computer hack to beg to differ from the views of such a renowned and eminent scholar in the field of biblical studies. But herewith, for what they are worth, a few comments on some of the points made by Bishop Wright. In each instance, I quote Bishop Wright's words, and then I comment upon them.

First Point: *People sometimes suggest, indeed, that the process of canonization is the sign that the Church itself was the final authority. This proposal is sometimes made by Catholic traditionalists asserting the supremacy of the Church over the Bible...,*

Comment: Classically, the Catholic Church does not adopt positions which contradict the Bible or claim that its position is superior to that of the Bible. It is not in competition with the Bible. Furthermore, the authority of what the Bible says and teaches is not the immediate issue being addressed here; it is, rather, which books make up that Bible, and the Catholic Church did indeed claim to have the responsibility (and the commensurate) authority to make *that* particular call - to define what constituted the Canon. However, once that has been done, the Church still states unambiguously (as quoted previously) that it remains the servant of the Bible and subject to its authority. So, I would want to add some clarification (the words in **bold type** below) to Bishop Wright's words if we wish to be clear about what exactly the Catholic Church is claiming authority for: *...that the process of canonization is the sign that the Church itself was the final authority* **on defining the Canon.**

Second Point: Bishop Wright's illustration: *This makes a rather obvious logical mistake analogous to that of a soldier who, receiving orders through the mail, concludes that the letter carrier is his commanding officer.*

Comment: Again, I would want to challenge Bishop Wright's illustration, in which the letter-carrier (the courier) is pictured as a passive conduit with no responsibility other than delivering a package. I emphasised previously with regard to the writing of Scripture (e.g., Luke writing his gospel) that Luke was no passive scribe, sitting, quill in hand, waiting to "hear" the next noun or verb which the Holy Spirit was to "dictate" to him before he could continue putting "quill to parchment". On the contrary, Luke was the trusted active partner of the Divine Author of Scripture in the production of his gospel.

Such an *active vs. passive* distinction, applies also to the discovery of the Canon. The canonization process is thus more akin to a loyal courier, who is in a position of personal trust with his commanding officer. Upon arriving at his destination, the courier opens his mail bag, and sees that there are more letters in his bag than when he began his journey. Clearly, some erroneous letters have found their way into his bag. Problem: which are the original authentic orders?

On the assumption that he is unable to refer back to his commanding officer, the courier, being in a position of personal trust, is free to open all of the letters, and begins the difficult task of distinguishing the authentic ones from the others. It is not a straightforward exercise. All the letters bear some resemblance to one another: they are written on the same sort of paper, share a similar format, and address the same sort of issues.

Despite these challenges, he knows that he has to accept the responsibility of discovering - (and this is best done in consultation with other trusted couriers, and indeed with the soldier who is going to have to act on the orders) - which set of orders best reflect the will of the commanding officer, and are consistent with what they already know of him from their relationship with him and his approach to previous issues similar to those now being addressed via these orders. On the basis of such a process, he settles upon the orders which he concludes are the authentic ones, and these are the ones which the receiving soldier receives as his orders.

Accordingly, the receiving soldier is under no illusion that the letter-carrier is his commanding officer. But what he does know is that this person is his commanding officer's personal courier, one to whom he has entrusted previous orders.

The letter-carrier's role in this illustration is thus not a passive one. It is active, and carries with it great responsibility. The letter-carrier has, of course, not added anything to the orders - neither in content nor in value - neither has he changed the orders. The courier's discernment process does however include **discovering** which of the (supposed) orders reflect the commanding officer's voice and have an inner cohesion with orders commissioned by the commander on previous occasions. It is on such a basis that the courier takes responsibility for determining which set of orders he places into the awaiting soldier's hands.

> **Third Point:** *But canonization was never simply a matter of a choice of particular books on a "who's in, who's out" basis. It was a matter of setting out the larger story, the narrative framework, which makes sense of and brings order to God's world and God's people.*

Comment: I like Bishop Wright's emphasis on the *larger story* and the *narrative framework*. I also appreciate that canonization was never simply **only** a question of which books were "in" and which were "out", but surely the larger story does not exclude completely that very fundamental issue?[19] Bishop Wright seems to want to by-pass that aspect completely and ignore it. It is a truism to state that canonization most certainly did include such choices. Otherwise, what was the 16th century disagreement over the OT Canon all about? A disagreement that we still live with today.

Dr. M. James Sawyer

As mentioned at the beginning of this section, Evangelical scholarship on this topic is sparse. There just seems to be very little attention given the subject of **how** the Canon came to be established. After searching high and low for more material, I was fortunate to come across an excellent piece of research on the Canon of the New Testament by one Dr. M. James Sawyer (Ph.D.

from Dallas Theological Seminary); research which had been undertaken by him while he was Western Seminary's Associate Professor of Theology and Church History at its San Jose campus.

Dr. Sawyer introduces his paper, *Evangelicals and The Canon of the New Testament*, with these opening words:[20]

Canon Determination for Evangelicals

Over the past two decades American Evangelical scholarship has ably risen to the defence of the doctrine of the inerrancy of the Bible as a touchstone upholding the historic position of the Church of Jesus Christ with reference to its authority. While volumes have been penned discussing the nature of biblical inspiration and the consequent authority of the scripture, it seems curious that in all the bibliological discussions one crucial issue is scarcely mentioned; that issue is the issue of Canon. Apart from R. Laird Harris' *Inspiration and Canonicity of the Bible*, David Dunbar's chapter, "The Biblical Canon" in *Hermeneutics, Authority and Canon*, Geisler and Nix's discussion in their *General Introduction to the Bible* and the recent series of articles in *Christianity Today*,[21] American Evangelicals who affirm the inerrancy of Scripture have had little to say concerning the shape of the Canon. [22] The sixty-six books which compose the Protestant Scriptures are assumed to be the complete written revelation of God to man without further comment or debate.

It has been charged that conservative evangelicalism's reticence to discuss the issue of Canon is due to the fact that it "finds itself imprisoned within a 19th century biblicism *which believes that to question the Canon is to undermine the authority of Scripture.*"[23] Outside the evangelical fold, the question of Canon has been debated for decades with the discussion centering on the nature of Canon itself. Emil Bruner has noted:

The question of Canon has never, in principle, been answered, but is being continually reopened. Just as the Church of the second, third and fourth centuries had the right to decide what was "apostolic" and what was not, on their own responsibilities as believers, so in the same way every Church in every period in the history of the Church possesses the same right and the same duty.[24]

While Bruner may overstate the case, the question he raises is the question of the certainty of historical knowledge. This question has profound implications for the faith.

I would propose that the evangelical approach to Canon determination has historically been the weakest link in its bibliology. This weakness has persisted for several reasons. (1) Canon has not been a pressing issue of debate on the larger theological horizon.

(2) It has been *assumed* that the Canon of the New Testament was closed definitively in the fourth century. (3) Apostolicity has been assumed as the controlling issue because of the early mention of this feature by the Fathers. (4) The New Testament Canon has been accepted uncritically because of the theological assumption that through divine providence the early Church was led (infallibly) to its canonical decisions.

In this paper I want to (1) address the question of Canon, (2) look critically at the traditional inerrantist apologetic for the Canon, (3) trace briefly the development of the New Testament Canon up through the Reformation, and (4) propose an alternative determination process.

* * *

Sawyer's complete article is dated as June 3rd 2004,[25] and a copy is enclosed as **Appendix D**. Sojourners are strongly encouraged to read it in full.

What particularly attracted me to Sawyer's paper was the humility and honesty with which the topic of the Canon was approached, and Sawyer was one of the few Evangelical academics that I came across who had decided (and he says so explicitly) to grapple with the "how" issue that I have continuously stressed is at the heart of this topic; the process issue - the decision-making-process issue.

His paper's scope includes valuable insights into the historical dynamics at the time of the Reformation, as well as the way in which criteria for canonization proposed at the time of the Reformation (including the significance, even the meaning of apostolic authorship, the "witness of the Spirit", etc.,) as well as other criteria which are put forward today and then retro-applied to historical situations in the journey of the Canon, have been used to try and arrive at a solution which would align with Evangelical theology.

In his paper,[26] Sawyer introduces Bruce Metzger's[27] perspective on the importance of "the list" of books, as footnotes [*a and *b] to his own insights, as follows:

> Discussions of Canon tend to develop in one of two directions depending upon the definition of Canon adopted by the theologian. Warfield and Geisler and Nix adopt a *material* definition and stress the objective existence of a God-given standard, which exists by virtue of its divine inspiration. In this sense, Canon emphasizes the inherent authority of the writing. The second type of discussion, taking its clue[28] from the original usage of the term "canon," stresses the *formal* development of the Canon in the sense of a completed list, an authoritative collection, a closed collection, if you will, to which nothing can be added.*[a] These discussions view the formal recognition process and usually see the Church in some sense as giving its official approval to the collection.*[b]

*(a) Bruce Metzger notes that the term Canon had both a material and a formal sense:

> ...ecclesiastical writers during the first three centuries used the word *kanon* to refer to what was for Christianity an inner law and binding norm of belief ("rule of faith" and/or "rule of truth"). From the fourth century onward the word also came to be used in connection with the sacred writings of the Old and New Testaments . . . . according to Zahn and Souter, the formal meaning of Canon as "a list" was primary, for otherwise it would be difficult to explain the use of the verb *kanonizein* ("to include in a canon") when it is applied to particular books and to the books collectively. *The Canon of the New Testament* (Oxford: Clarendon Press, 1987), 293.

*(b) The question of whether the Canon is a "collection of authoritative books" or an "authoritative collection of books" hinges on what definition of Canon one adopts. If one argues that the individual writings are canonical because of their divine inspiration, then he would logically see the Canon as a collection of authoritative books. If on the other hand, one views the Canon in the sense of a completed list to which nothing can be added, he would tend to see the Canon as an authoritative collection. However, I believe that at this point to be consistent one would have to admit that the authority of the *collection* is imposed by ecclesiastical authority. [29]

Sawyer concludes his paper by (again) giving a frank and honest assessment of the outcomes from such analysis as well as a survey of possible "solutions" to the dilemma which are available today – introducing the dynamic of personal faith into the debate in a way that I had not come across previously in this context. I put the word "solutions" in quotes because his paper ends with having to hold such "solutions" in tension – to the point where he suspects that the process (from an Evangelical perspective) might just have to remain as something of a dilemma with which individual Christians will have to continue to grapple in the years ahead.

* * *

Evangelicals and The Canon of the New Testament - Epilogue

At the time (May 2014) of going to press with this volume, [Book Three, *Spoiling the Hands*], I have by chance come across a recently published book (December 2013) which by its title and description looks as if it may well provide a serious and (at 438 pages) substantial contribution to this subject. I have not had time to acquire or study it. It is entitled "The Formation and Significance of the Christian Biblical Canon: A Study in Text, Ritual and Interpretation", by Dr. Thomas Bokedal, currently on the staff of the School of Divinity, History, and Philosophy at Kings College, University of Aberdeen. The publication description of his book reads as follows:

> This book offers a fresh cross-disciplinary approach to the current discussion on the Christian canon formation process. By carefully integrating historical, hermeneutical and theological aspects to account for the emergence of the canon, it seeks to offer a more comprehensive picture of the canon development than has previously been achieved. The formation and continuous usage of the Christian biblical canon is here viewed as an act of literary preservation and actualization of the Church's apostolic normative tradition - "the Scriptures and the Lord" - addressing, first of all, the Church, but also the wider society. In order to grasp the complex phenomenon of the biblical canon, the study is divided into four parts, focusing respectively on linguistic and effective-historical, textual and material, performative, and ideational aspects of the canon. Attention is given to the scribal nomina sacra convention, the codex format, oral and written Gospel, early Christian liturgical praxis and the Rule of Faith. Bokedal argues that the canon was formed in a process, with its own particular intention, history, and direction. Throughout the study, history and theology, past and present are considered alongside each other. By using a Gadamerian hermeneutics of tradition, the reader's attention is directed to historical dimensions of the canon and its interpretative possibilities for our time. The notion of effective history (Wirkungsgeschichte), as well as the interaction between text, community and reader are crucial to the argument. The canonical text as text, its interpretation and ritual contextualization are highlighted as unifying elements for the communities being addressed.

* * *

Discovering the Scriptures: The Catholic Framework

According to the framework that I am following it is my position that in order to complete the journey of the Canon, the Church had to sift through a number of writings which laid claim to being expressions of revelation from God, and under the guidance of the Holy Spirit, had to *discover* which of these documents were inspired (and which were not).

This *discovery* process was represented in **Fig 4.1 Part C** in the step from stage (iv) to stage (v). As pointed out previously, stage (iv) did **not** depend upon Church decision-making. In contrast stage (v) did. In other words, deciding upon which of the various writings of the early Church were inspired by the Holy Spirit and which were not **did** involve human decision-making in the discovery/discernment process. Speaking in terms of "self-selection" (by inanimate artefacts which may well possess authority but have no means of enacting such), and/or of "the inner witness of the spirit"(whose spirit?), is not going to explain away this decision-making issue.

The graphical representation of that process is so central to this issue that it is repeated again here, wherein it is to be noted that the exact same process applied equally to the Canon of the Old Testament as much as it did to the New Testament.

Of course, none of this happened in a single day! The process was undertaken by the Church over many years.

* * *

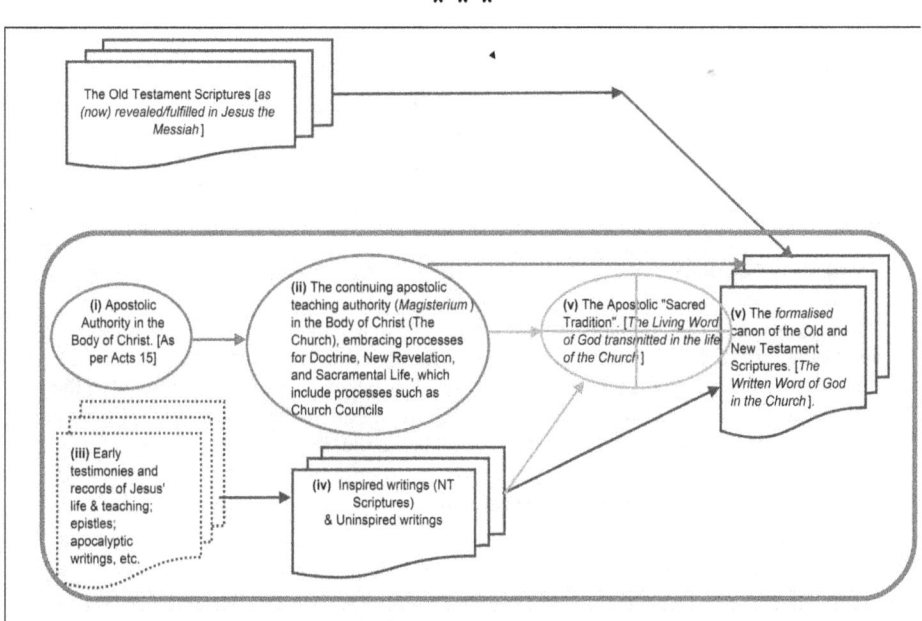

Extract from Fig 4.1

* * *

---

1   Turro & Brown (Canonicity) (1968) 67:7 p516
2   Cf., *The Great Collaboration*, (Book Two in the *One of Us* collection) for examples of manuscript artefacts discovered at Qumran.
3   To illustrate: **Mathematics:** In a simple arithmetic progression (such as 1, 4, 7, 10....... n+3), it is *necessary* for the successive numbers in the sequence to be larger than the previous number. However, this in itself is an *insufficient* condition since, in the example shown, the number "9" satisfies the necessary condition specified but fails a further condition (n+3). **Rugby:** For a try to be scored in rugby it is *necessary* for a player to cross the opponent's line with the ball in hand. But that in itself is not *sufficient*; a number of other conditions have to be satisfied as well (including grounding the ball with a

downward pressure and doing so without crossing either the dead-ball line or the touch-in-goal line).

4   I trust that the Evangelical element is explicitly self-evident from a reading of Books One and Two in this collection, and that of the Catholic from a reading of Books Five, Six, and Seven on the Eucharist. [Book Four has elements reflecting both, while this present volume predominantly reflects the Catholic perspective on the Canon of Scripture].

5   Grudem (1988, 1992) p.287.

6   Grudem (1988, 1992) p.294.

7   Grudem (1988, 1992), p.294 and End Note #138, p.330.

8   Cf. Sawyer's paper in Appendix D.

9   Grudem (1988, 1992), p.295.

10 Grudem (1988, 1992), p.294.

11 Sawyer also quotes a number of times from Bruce's book.

12 Bruce (Canon) p.17

13 The Scripture itself says (of itself) that "the word of God is living and powerful..." (Heb 4:12), which statement does not conflict with what is being said here. Clearly, the original creating word that spoke creation into existence (what Matthew Henry refers to as the *essential* word in his comments on this verse) and which I have always equated with the pre-incarnation God-the-Son being the Word that was "spoken" as the act of creation [Gen 1:3(a); John 1:1; Col 1:15-17; Heb 1:3], is intrinsically "alive" and life-giving, and the written word of the Scriptures is likewise [cf. Dt 32:47] *as we interact with it*. Matthew Henry describes the life-giving, life-changing power of such a Word: "That [the word] is *quick;* it is very lively and active, in all its efforts, in seizing the conscience of the sinner, in cutting him to the heart, and in comforting him and binding up the wounds of the soul. Those know not the word of God who call it a dead letter; it is quick, compared to the light, and nothing quicker than the light; it is not only quick, but quickening; it is a vital light; it is a living word, *zōn*. Saints die, and sinners die; but the word of God lives. *All flesh is grass, and all the glory thereof as the flower of grass. The grass withereth, and the flower thereof falleth away, but the word of the Lord endureth for ever* [Is 40:8]."

14 Lloyd-Jones (Authority) p59.

15 Lloyd-Jones (Authority) p59

16 Lloyd-Jones" remarks quoted here are all from his chapter on the Authority of Scripture.

17 Wright (Last Word) (2005) Chapter 5.

18 E.g. Wright (Last Word) (2005) p62-63.

19 The primacy assigned to the matter of a "list" of books by distinguished scholars in Biblical Studies such as Theodor Zahn and Alexander Souter likewise cannot just be ignored. C.f., the reference to Zahn and Souter in Sawyer's paper below.

20 **The Notes reflected here are all Sawyer's own.** [I have taken the liberty of converting his Foot Notes to End Notes for the sake of e-book formatting].

21 The February 5, 1988 issue of *Christianity Today* included five brief articles covering different issues and perspectives on the subject of canon; Ronald Youngblood, "The Process; How We Got Our Bible," Richard B. Gaffin, Jr., "The New Testament: How Do We Know for Sure?"; Klyne Snodgrass; "Providence Is Not Enough"; David G. Dunbar, "Why The Canon Still Rumbles"; Kenneth S. Kantzer, "Confidence in the Face of Confusion."

22 Throughout this paper the term "conservative Evangelical" will be employed in

the restricted sense of one who affirms the inerrancy of Scripture. More latitudinal Evangelicals have recently published significant works on the NT canon. Bruce Metzger's *The Canon of The New Testament* (Oxford: Clarendon, 1987) is the most significant of these.

23 Richard Lyon Morgan, "Let's be Honest About the Canon", *The Christian Century* 84 (May 31, 1967), 717.84 (May 31, 1967), 717 (italics added). This confounding of the questions of inspiration and canonicity occurs on both the conservative and liberal side of the theological spectrum. One need only remember that some of those who do not profess evangelical convictions attempt to prove that Luther did not hold to inerrancy since he questioned books on the fringes of the canon.

24 Ibid.

25 Sawyer, 2004: https://Bible.org/article/evangelicals-and-canon-new-testament

26 Appendix D.

27 It is to be noted that F. F. Bruce in his book also references Bruce Metzger's contribution to the topic of the Canon.

28. In his original paper, Dr. Sawyer uses the word "clue", but perhaps he had intended to use cue. Cf., https://Bible.org/article/evangelicals-and-canon-new-testament

29 As quoted by Sawyer in Appendix D.

* * *

8. The Canonization journey tells us more about the Church than it does about the Scriptures

From the previous chapter, some observations are apposite:

First Observation: Sacred Tradition

This formal promulgation of the Canon is an example of Divine Revelation that the Catholic Church refers to as Sacred Tradition. More shall be said on this topic below, but the formal designation by the Church of what constitutes the Canon illustrates a broader position held by the Catholic Church wherein it holds that God reveals himself to his people both through the means of Sacred Scripture and by on-going revelation to the Church. One may agree or disagree in general with this position, but at least in the particular instance of the Canon it is hard to find a way around it, since as I have repeatedly pointed out, nowhere in Scripture (either OT or NT) is the scope of the Canon of Scriptures specified: God did not leave a list. Yet, we do have a list. How we got that list has been the subject of what has been said above.

If one is a Catholic, one is accepting the historical judgement of the Church meeting in Council. If one is not, then one is accepting the historical judgement of other individuals/groups of the Reformation – [unless one wants to allow for variations in the content of the Canon on a personal and individual "inner witness" basis, or a personal preference or conscience basis. The latter approach is not one I have come across except in isolated cases.[1]] Either way, the reality is that we, the Church, have accepted a critical truth, namely the scope of the Sacred Scriptures, without the definitive endorsement of Scripture itself.

Second Observation: The drivers of Sacred Tradition

The Catholic Church does not make this sort of judgement-call (that of Sacred Tradition) lightly or casually, but neither does it do so reluctantly. It says, in effect: "This is what we do; it is in our nature to do so; it is normative for the Church that Jesus said he would continue to be with "until the end" ".

It is also important to note that situations of conflict are not the only ones in which Sacred Tradition comes into play. In fact, within Sacred Tradition, one can identify three broad drivers.

The first driver, as we have seen, is *Contention*. When contention leads to serious conflict, it requires clarification and ultimately resolution. The second is when God himself takes the initiative in revealing some new dimension of the Truth to the Church. The third driver is the continuing formation by God of his Church - of the life of his own Body - of whom, let us never forget, He is the Head. One illustration of each of these may aid in appreciating the concept, without necessarily presenting a supporting case for each example.

An example of a contentious issue: We have already discussed the contention around the scope of the Canon, but herewith a second example: the doctrine of The Trinity. Clearly, the vast majority of those who claim to be "Christian" believe this doctrine (albeit that the word Trinity is nowhere to be found in the Scriptures) but not all. Some contemporary groups, such as the Oneness Pentecostals (I have personally known folk in such a group here in South Africa), the Mormons, and the Jehovah's Witnesses,[2] dogmatically reject this doctrine.

In the fourth century, the Arian heresy, which denied that Christ was of one substance with the Father (but rather a creature raised by the Father to the dignity of Son of God), caused turmoil on a massive scale within the Church. Clearly this was a denial of the divinity of Jesus, and undermined the heart of the Christian message: the Incarnation, Atonement, and Resurrection. The Council of Nicaea (AD 325) was assembled specifically to address this issue, and it is from this council, and others which followed it, that we have the language used in the professing creeds of the Church to reinforce core doctrines such as the Trinity. This was an instance of where a Council reinforced a truth previously implied by Sacred Scripture, and the dogmatic statements on the truth of the Trinity then become a part of Sacred Tradition.

An example of a new dimension of the truth: The *perpetual* virginity of Mary, the mother of Jesus, is an example of Sacred Tradition where God revealed a dimension of the truth to the Church which was not specifically stated in the Scriptures. All Christians hold to the doctrine of the Virgin Birth, but the Catholic Church (as well as the Orthodox, and some Anglicans) further believe that Mary retained her virginity for the whole of her life and never gave birth to any children other than Jesus. The vast majority of Evangelicals, on the other hand, would say that she had other children and would point to biblical references to the brothers of Jesus in support of that. The Catholic Church takes such references as meaning family relatives in a broader sense.[3]

An example of God's continuing formation of the Church: The most well developed example of this third "driver" of Sacred Tradition is the Catholic Liturgy of the Eucharist (The Sacrifice of the Mass).

"For the liturgy is made up of unchangeable elements divinely instituted, and of elements subject to change. These latter not only may be changed but ought to be changed with the passage of time, if they have suffered from the intrusion of anything out of harmony with the inner nature of the liturgy or have become less suitable."

This sentence is a quotation from the most recent example of God's continuing formation of his Church in the Second Vatican Council. The words are taken from the *Constitution on the Sacred Liturgy* issued by the council on 4th December 1963. The 282 pages of this particular document make it the longest of all of the Constitutions, Decrees, and Declarations issued by the Council (there were sixteen such publications in total, running to over 1000 pages).[4]

Third Observation: Big "T" or little "t"?

Moving from these examples, and accordingly from the specific to the general, a key aspect of Sacred Tradition needs to be borne in mind; namely, its scope. Sacred Tradition, understood as a dimension of Divine Revelation (we could refer to is as big "T") is not to be confused with Church traditions (small "t") many of which are of a local nature although some can be universal, which have developed as pastoral practices and are time conditioned and/or context conditioned.

The latter practices range across topics as diverse as the nature and colour of liturgical vestments, the commemoration of the feast days of saints, and the use of Latin or the Vernacular in the Church's liturgy. The scope, or perhaps one should say the domain of Sacred Tradition (big "T") is reserved for those major issues which are either of a dogmatic (*faith and morals*) nature or those unchangeable elements of a sacramental and/or liturgical nature in the living organism which constitutes the Body of Christ, (i.e. as quoted above, the elements of which are unchangeable being divinely instituted, as distinct from those elements subject to change).[5]

Fourth Observation:

The fourth observation that I want to make as a result of our examination of *the journey of the New Testament Canon from Jesus to Geneva/Trent*, is one of timing, and the implications thereof:

> Undertaking this journey has told us more about the Church than it has about the Scriptures.

It is a truism to state that the Canon tells us much about Scripture: it defines the very scope of what constitutes Scripture. The body of Scriptures prior to Trent (OT and NT) was a *de facto* Canon. After fifteen hundred years into the life of the Church the authority of this Canon had been assumed; no longer seriously questioned. Then came the Reformation, and with it the canon of Scripture was challenged, including at some stages, elements of both the Old and New Testaments.

This Canon was not changed as a result of Trent; it was formally confirmed. So, from a Catholic perspective and practice as far as the scope, usage, and significance of the Scriptures were concerned, Trent changed nothing.

What Trent did do, however, in the **process** of closing the Canon, was in effect to make a very loud statement about the responsibility and authority of the Church. By dogmatically closing the Canon once and for ever the Church was demonstrating its claim to be **the** authoritative body with the responsibility of protecting the canon of arguably the Church's most important asset, the Holy Scriptures.

If this formal action had been taken in the second century or even (say) the third or fourth, it would probably (and here I can only speculate) have been accepted then by the whole Church, and also be accepted now by the Church worldwide – whether Catholic, Protestant or Orthodox, since a council in such an early century could still be regarded as being sufficiently close to the Apostolic age to still have, as it were, "retained the minds of the Apostles" on such matters, and on that basis be regarded as reliable and authoritative – Apostolic Authority. That this did not happen was (as discussed previously) a consequence of the issue of the Canon per se not being a sufficiently contentious issue to warrant such a move.

The Church in the early centuries had worked through the issues over particular books (such as Hebrews and 2Peter) without, as it were, coming to blows. When the Council of Trent made its declarations on the Canon of Scripture it was, in effect, laying claim to such Apostolic Authority, as its basis for exercising such authority. Given the lapse of fifteen centuries since the death of the apostles, not to mention the unholy character of many of the leaders of the Church at the time leading up to the Reformation and to Trent, this claim may seem to many people to lack credibility. I however, maverick that I am, see the deliberate hand of God in the late timing of all of this. I believe that he wanted us – and wants us – to see that Apostolic Authority did continue, and still does continue, to reside in the Church long after the age of the Apostles.

From a purely human point of view this, as I say, is difficult to swallow when one looks at the motley crew that gathered at Trent for the Council, and the somewhat chaotic image of a process which started, stopped, resumed, stopped again, reconvened again (and again...) with varying numbers of bishops participating; as few as twenty nine bishops and five heads of Orders when it got going on 15th December 1545, increasing to sixty-six in June, down to fifty a few months later, and back up to seventy by January 1546...sounds more like a rolling maul in rugby than a formal assembly of distinguished prelates! But by that January of 1546, the idea of a Council was catching on... The final attendance scorecard of the Council (over a discontinuous eighteen years – a period encompassing five popes) was Sessions 1-10 (Dec 1545-June 1547), 29-69 bishops; Sessions 11-17 (May 1551-May 1552), 44-51 bishops; and Sessions 18-25 (1562-63), 105-228 bishops.[6]

Pope Paul III was the pontiff who initiated the process leading to the Council. An archetype of the age, Alessandro Farnese had been named a cardinal-deacon (while not yet even a priest) at the age of twenty-four by Pope Alexander VI, and was known as "Cardinal Petticoat" because his sister Giulia was the pope's mistress.

Farnese himself was not known to be a holy man, and had a mistress who bore him four children even while he held several important Church positions. But after he was ordained to the priesthood in 1519 and appointed bishop of Parma, he underwent a remarkable conversion (*about time*, I hear you say!) ending his relationship with his mistress and joining the reform party.

As Pope Paul III he confirmed or reconfirmed several new religious orders, including the Capuchins, the Ursulines, and the Society of Jesus (Jesuits), brought several influential Catholic reformers to Rome whom he appointed cardinals, and it was their report of 1537 which became the foundation for the work of the Council of Trent. He continued, however, to embody within himself a strange combination of reforming instincts with Renaissance display, including giving the "red hat" to two of his grandchildren. But he nonetheless had a sense of what was wrong with the Catholic Church and what to do about it.[7]

Can God work with such a setup? Can he work with such people and through such people? History's answer is "yes". The Bible's answer is "yes".

In Old Testament terms, and as I first pointed out when we looked at God's dealings with Abraham,[8] God, sovereign and ever-amazingly humble, continues to recognise the full dignity inherent in the human creation – warts and all, the Fall and all. A study of God's dealings with David, the Psalm-writing king who was also an adulterer, manipulator, liar, betrayer, and murderer, brings us to the same conclusion.

And this is not only an Old Testament phenomenon. In New Testament terms, Paul had the prophetic insight to warn the leaders of the Church of his day that from among their own number men would rise up attempting to pervert the Church from within.[9]

God is tactile; when he interacts with us it is not by remote control; he touches us. He gets his hands dirty in the process...but he knows what he is doing, and remains irrevocably committed to his covenant. It does not stop him from judging the Church, and on that score, it is not as if we had never been warned: "For the time has come for judgement to begin with the household of God..."[10] And the much needed reform of the Church was indeed accompanied with judgement – including the wars and terrible suffering of the Sixteenth Century that we brought upon ourselves. But our God, incarnate at heart, sticks with us through it all and works in us, through us, and in spite of us.

Fifth Observation: Reformation or Replacement?

When we look at the failings of the men who occupied much of the leadership of the Church at this time, I am reminded of the words of Jesus when he spoke to his disciples and to the multitudes of his day:

> The scribes and the Pharisees occupy the chair of Moses. You must therefore do what they tell you and listen to what they say; but do not do according to what they do; for they do not practice what they preach.[11]

It must have been immensely difficult for reformers such as Luther, Calvin, Zwingli and others to try and apply this maxim in their context. An opportunity lost perhaps? Only God knows. But I do suspect that it was an opportunity lost. And I say this for the following reason: The goal of the Reformers was reformation; what actually came about was replacement.

In spite of the many benefits which ensued from the Reformation, the outcome from a structural and responsibility/accountability perspective has not been orderly; one of the reasons being that a huge vacuum was created in the domain previously occupied by a well-defined authority. Under the new post-Reformation emerging order, the aspiration was to have the authority of Scripture as the sole authority. Scripture possessed authority, (as it still possesses authority). No question about that. It was true in the Roman Catholic Church (irrespective of whoever sat upon Peter's chair), and it remained true for the Reformers. But, as explained above,[12] to possess authority does not intrinsically mean that such authority can be exercised, let alone enforced. Only persons can exercise the authority of Scripture and only persons can enforce the authority of Scripture.

This unrecognised vacuum was not filled at the time, and has remained essentially unfilled (and possibly in some measure unrecognised) to this very day...which brings us to our next observation.

Sixth Observation: Inter-dependence or Independence?

The choice is between trusting that God has continued to bring revelation to the Church,[13] or that all divine revelation stopped with the written revelation of the NT Canon.

The effects of such a choice are extensive, covering a broad range of issues. One example relates to the very models of "Church" itself.

The Catholic approach, as evidenced above, is that God has laid the foundation for the model of the Church in Scripture but that he did not provide all of the detail therein, depending instead upon leading the Church as a body of interdependent people, by means of his Holy Spirit, from the Apostolic age forward, until it arrived at the model that finally emerged in history.

The contrary posture holds that God has provided within the pages of Scripture all that one needs in order to live the Christian life and how we (in the twenty-first century) are to structure that life individually and collectively in terms of biblically-ordained leadership roles and responsibilities, without any reference as to how this has already been worked through in history.

The latter posture sounds very attractive; it just has not proved to be viable in practice. The multiplicity of diverse models that have ensued from it – a process continuing exponentially in our day – is indicative of its intrinsic weakness. The different interpretations, independently formulated, which have been built upon the (common) foundational Scriptural base have resulted in very different Church models, including Church accountability structures. The existence of so many incompatible models is itself evident that, subliminally or otherwise, individuals/independent groups have had to "fill in the gaps" themselves on the processes of implementation that God actually did **not** include in the written Scriptures by the year 100AD.

This lack of detail (I would contend) was not an "oversight" on God's part. It was deliberate. Much of what I have said above has been given over to making the case that God never intended that the fullness of his revelation would be closed in **written** form by the year 100AD.

One really has to ask: where did the idea come from that it had been his intention to do so? It bears repeating: God's full revelation is his Son – Jesus the Messiah, God the Son. The night before he died, Jesus himself stated quite clearly to the Twelve that he still had many things to say to them but, since they were not in a position to be able to receive it at that point in time, it would be the responsibility of the Spirit of truth to guide them into all truth.[14] In saying this, Jesus emphasised that what the Spirit would bring would be an authentic revelation of both the Father and of Jesus.[15]

Divine revelation comes to us through the written Scriptures **and** in God's continuing unfolding of the mystery of Christ in and to the Body of Christ. If this is true, then it is futile to expect to find every "t" crossed and every "i" dotted by the year 100AD. The **content** is there in the Scriptures; the principles are there, even the designations of the office-bearers in the Church, etc., but the very fact that these have been implemented in a wide variety of diverse ways (particularly in the last five hundred years) clearly demonstrates that the **processes** of implementation were not "self-selecting" on the basis of Scripture alone. Instead, what actually happened in history was that the processes of implementation were revealed by the Holy Spirit to the Church over time. And one of the main "lessons" learned during the Church's journey of the formative years of the first century was that God was only willing to work with us on a collaborative basis of mutual inter-dependence.

God - *The Dependent God*[16] - does not "do" independence. Instead he majors on inter-dependence and collaboration. This is true within the Godhead, and it is true in his relationships with us. Can we really be so surprised then to discover that he expects us in our relationships with one another to live as one Body in an interdependent and collaborative manner? Yes, it is difficult. Yes, it is very messy. Yes, we get our hands dirty in the process. And yes, it is very painful. Such is love.[17]

I have great sympathy for the reformers – not least because of my own personal journey. I expect that replacement ensued (rather than reformation per se) because, from their perspective, hope of reforming the existing ecclesiastical office-bearers and the existing types of Church structures had faded beyond recovery. Where else to turn? Where else but to where one always has to return – to the written words of Scripture. But doing this – *and this alone* – was not going to resolve all of the difficulties faced by the reformers, and within a very short period of time, one finds (for example) Luther and Zwingli adopting radically different doctrinal positions with respect to the fundamental issue of the Eucharist – in spite of them both appealing to the authority of Scripture. With platforms (such as collaborative Church councils) no longer available, the tendency towards independence and to fragmentation accordingly developed more and more with each contentious doctrinal issue which emerged...

Seventh Observation: Apostolic Authority is a function of Apostolic Succession[18]

The Catholic Church assembled at Trent debated the contents of the Canon and then also promulgated the Canon, but it did so on the same basis of responsibility and authority as it had claimed throughout its history, namely that the apostles left bishops as their successors, and (to quote the words of the early Church Father, *Irenaeus*) that the apostles gave their successors "their own position of teaching authority".

For further comment on the notion of Apostolic Authority continuing into the life of the Church, sojourners are referred to **Appendix F** wherein the document of Vatican II entitled "Dogmatic Constitution on Divine Revelation" is particularly helpful on a number of grounds. Firstly, the four short articles (Articles 7-10) in Chapter II, *The Transmission of Divine Revelation*, lay out very clearly the Catholic Church's up-to-date (1965) position on the God-given process that enables Divine Revelation to be transmitted from age to age. Secondly, the content of the Dogmatic Constitution itself is an illustration of that process in action – specifically by referring back to Scripture, previous Church Councils, Papal Encyclicals, and early Church Fathers. In other words, within itself, this appendix is an "instance" of the very process it is describing. Thirdly, it summarizes succinctly the relationship between "Christ the Lord, in whom the entire Revelation of the most high God is summed up (cf. 2Cor 1:20; 3:16-4:6)", Sacred Scripture, Sacred Tradition, and the teaching authority (*Magisterium*) of the Church.

* * *

The long and the short of it...

In Chapter 2 of this book, in order to give concrete expression to the subject of the Canon of Scripture, the issue was expressed in very simple terms as follows:

> Why is the very personal letter of Paul to Philemon "in" the Canon, and the "gospel" of the apostle Thomas "out"?

The short answer to that question is simply that the Church, under the inspiration of the Holy Spirit, discovered (recognised, discerned) that one was divinely inspired and that the other was not. Accordingly, the Church took the decision to include the one in the Canon and to exclude the other.

The long answer is what this volume on *Soiling the Hands* has been all about.

* * *

Periscope

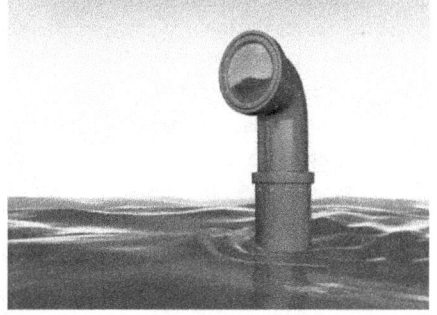

We have now completed the first three books in the seven-volume journey which was labelled, *The journey with One-of-Us*, and have taken the journey of the Scriptures and the Canon of Scripture as far as we can at this stage. Where to from here?

As explained in the section immediately preceding the Bibliography (The Collection: One of us – an overview), the journey from this point onwards consists of Books Four-Seven in that collection.

Book Four chronicles the journey of the Apostolic (AD 33-67) and Sub-Apostolic Church (AD 67-100) under the title of "The Jigsaw Puzzle Church", and explores that journey in the decades immediately following the death and resurrection of Jesus. In doing so, it attempts to address two of the key issues which characterised the first seventy years of the Church. Firstly, how did the Church survive during its first forty years with virtually no written New Testament Scriptures? And secondly, how did the Church survive in the decades from 67 AD onwards in the absence of the original Apostolic leadership, most of whom had been killed by around 67AD?

This will then be followed by a trilogy on the Eucharist, covering its theology (Book Five), its resilience over time (Book Six), and the relationship between the Eucharist and Scripture (Book Seven).

* * *

---

1. Cf. The "Conclusion" section of the article by Sawyer in Appendix D.
2. Jehovah Witnesses are not Christians, but latterly have been claiming to be such.
3. E.g., regarding James, the "brother" of the Lord, who became head of the Jerusalem Community. As perhaps the half-brother of Jesus, he might have been a son of Joseph from a previous marriage.
4. Cf. Flannery (Vatican II) for the documents in written form or from the Web [http://www.vatican.com/]: the major declarations/documents are: (i) The Constitution on the Sacred Liturgy. (ii) Decree on the Means of Social Communication. (iii) Dogmatic Constitution on the Church. (iv) Decree on the Catholic Eastern Churches. (v) Decree on Ecumenism. (vi) Decree on the Pastoral Office of Bishops in the Church. (vii) Decree on the Up-To-Date Renewal of Religious Life. (viii) Decree on the Training of Priests. (ix) Declaration on Christian Education. (x) Declaration on the Relation of the Church to Non-Christian Religions. (xi) Dogmatic Constitution on Divine Revelation. (xii) Decree on the Apostolate of Lay People. (xiii) Declaration on Religious Liberty. (xiv) Decree on the Church's Missionary Activity. (xv) Decree on the Ministry and Life of Priests. (xvi) Pastoral Constitution on the Church in the Modern World.
5. Cf. the excellent assessment of these principles in the Jerome Biblical Commentary when it addresses the topic of the Church interpretation of Scripture: Brown (Hermeneutics) (1968) 71:82-90 p619-621.
6. Vidmar (2005) pp236-7
7. Johnson (Papacy) (1997) p135; Vidmar (2005) p233-235.
8. Cf. Book One, Chapter 14.
9. Act 20:30.
10. 1Pt 4:17(a)
11. Mt 23:1-3. The term used within the Catholic Church to describe God's faithfulness to the authority of the offices that He has established in the Church is that of the *Character* of the office. An individual priest may have serious sin in his life, a particular bishop may be seriously flawed in his own personal character, a pope may have a mistress, and yet the God-established *Office*, with the functions performed therein, remain intact in accordance with the Covenant established by God. The priest in question can still preside at the Eucharist and it is a valid Eucharist. The bishop in question can still ordain priests and the ordinations are valid. The pope in question can still appoint and ordain bishops and

the appointments stand. This sort of thing is a source of scandal and, of course, has very serious consequences for the corrupt holders of these offices, but God nonetheless allows this to happen in accordance with his sovereign will and purposes. This is not to suggest that he is indifferent to such goings on. As mentioned above, history shows us that such times are usually accompanied by parallel actions of judgement and reform movements by God.

12 Chapter 5.
13 Cf. John 16:12-15.
14 John 16:12-13.
15 John 16:13-15.
16 Cf. Book One in this collection.
17 The "how to do and be Church" journey of the first century is developed in quite some detail in Book Four of this collection: Book Four: The Jigsaw Puzzle Church [The journey of the Apostolic (AD 33-67) and Sub-Apostolic Church (AD 67-100)]
18 An article on Apostolic Succession from the perspective of a scholar from the Eastern Orthodox Church is included below as **Appendix E**.

* * *

Appendices

A - F

Appendix A - Canon of the Old Testament

[New Advent article (Catholic) (1908)][1]

> Narrator's Note with respect to the dating, terminology, and ecumenical posture of the two articles from New Advent: Appendix A & Appendix B.
>
> These articles[2] are from New Advent's copy of articles in the Catholic Encyclopaedia of 1908. Because they are articles about the Canon of Scripture, and not about the content of individual books of the Old and New Testaments, (and therefore not dependent upon the considerable advances made in textual criticism and exegesis during the past century), they retain, in essence, their value as a (still) valid expression of the Catholic Church's understanding of the Canon of Scripture.
>
> Being more than a hundred years old, the terminology deployed reflects the age and the era in which they were written. Thus, when e.g., the articles speak of The Vatican Council they are referring to the First Vatican Council of 1870 (!) and not to Vatican II. For the same reason the ecumenical posture is virtually non-existent by our standards; accordingly, sojourners are asked to extend a generous measure of grace when the articles use terms such as "[those] outside the Church" (meaning "outside the Catholic Church") when quoting the views of Eastern Orthodox and Protestant Churches.

Overview

The word Canon as applied to the Scriptures has long had a special and consecrated meaning. In its fullest comprehension it signifies the authoritative list or closed number of the writings composed under Divine inspiration, and destined for the well-being of the Church, using the latter word in the wide sense of the theocratic society which began with God's revelation of Himself to the people of Israel, and which finds its ripe development and completion in the Catholic organism.

The whole Biblical Canon therefore consists of the canons of the Old and New Testaments. The Greek *kanon* means primarily a reed, or measuring-rod: by a natural figure it was employed by ancient writers both profane and religious to denote a rule or standard. We find the substantive first applied to the Sacred Scriptures in the fourth century, by St. Athanasius; for its derivatives, the Council of Laodicea of the same period speaks of the *kanonika biblia* and Athanasius of the *biblia kanonizomena*. The latter phrase proves that the passive sense of Canon — that of a regulated and defined collection — was already in use, and this has remained the prevailing connotation of the word in ecclesiastical literature.

The terms *protocanonical* and *deuterocanonical*, of frequent usage among Catholic theologians and exegetes, require a word of caution. They are not felicitous, and it would be wrong to infer from them that the Church successively possessed two distinct Biblical Canons. Only in a partial and restricted way may we speak of a first and second Canon. Protocanonical (*protos*, "first") is a conventional word denoting those sacred writings which have been always received by Christendom without dispute. The protocanonical books of the Old Testament correspond with those of the Bible of the Hebrews, and the Old Testament as received by Protestants. The deuterocanonical (*deuteros*, "second") are those whose Scriptural character was contested in some quarters, but which long ago gained a secure footing in the Bible of the Catholic Church, though those of the Old Testament are classed by Protestants as the "Apocrypha". These consist of seven books: Tobias, Judith, Baruch, Ecclesiasticus, Wisdom, First and Second Maccabees; also certain additions to Esther and Daniel.

It should be noted that *protocanonical* and *deuterocanonical* are modern terms, not having been used before the sixteenth century. As they are of cumbersome length, the latter (being frequently used in this article) will be often found in the abbreviated form *deutero*.

The scope of an article on the sacred Canon may now be seen to be properly limited regarding the process of
» what may be ascertained regarding the process of the collection of the sacred writings into bodies or groups which from their very inception were the objects of a greater or less degree of veneration;
» the circumstances and manner in which these collections were definitely *canonized*, or adjudged to have a uniquely Divine and authoritative quality;
» the vicissitudes which certain compositions underwent in the opinions of individuals and localities before their Scriptural character was universally established.

It is thus seen that canonicity is a correlative of inspiration, being the extrinsic dignity belonging to writings which have been officially declared as of sacred origin and authority. It is antecedently very probable that according as a book was written early or late it entered into a sacred collection and attained a canonical standing. Hence the views of traditionalist and critic (not implying that the traditionalist may not also be critical) on the Canon parallel, and are largely influenced by, their respective hypotheses on the origin of its component members.

The Canon among the Palestinian Jews (protocanonical books)

It has already been intimated that there is a smaller, or incomplete, and larger, or complete, Old Testament. Both of these were handed down by the Jews; the former by the Palestinian, the latter by the Alexandrian, Hellenist, Jews.

The Jewish Bible of today is composed of three divisions, whose titles combined form the current Hebrew name for the complete Scriptures of Judaism: *Hat-Torah, Nebiim, wa-Kéthubim*, i.e. The Law, the Prophets, and the Writings. This triplication is ancient; it is supposed as long-established in the Mishnah, the Jewish code of unwritten sacred laws reduced to writing, c. A.D. 200. A grouping closely akin to it occurs in the New Testament in Christ's own words, Luke 24:44: "All things must needs be fulfilled, which are written in the law of Moses, and in the prophets, and in the psalms concerning me". Going back to the prologue of Ecclesiasticus, prefixed to it about 132 B.C., we find mentioned "the Law, and the Prophets, and others that have followed them".

The Torah, or Law, consists of the five Mosaic books, Genesis, Exodus, Leviticus, Numbers, Deuteronomy. The Prophets were subdivided by the Jews into the Former Prophets [i.e. the prophetico-historical books: Josue, Judges, 1 and 2 Samuel (I and II Kings), and 1 and 2 Kings (III and IV Kings)] and the Latter Prophets (Isaias, Jeremias, Ezechiel, and the twelve minor Prophets, counted by the Hebrews as one book). The Writings, more generally known by a title borrowed from the Greek Fathers, Hagiographa (holy writings), embrace all the remaining books of the Hebrew Bible. Named in the order in which they stand in the current Hebrew text, these are: Psalms, Proverbs, Job, Canticle of Canticles, Ruth, Lamentations, Ecclesiastes, Esther, Daniel, Esdras, Nehemias, or II Esdras, Paralipomenon.

Traditional view of the Canon of the Palestinian Jews

Proto-Canon

In opposition to scholars of more recent views, conservatives do not admit that the Prophets and the Hagiographa represent two successive stages in the formation of the Palestinian Canon. According to this older school, the principle which dictated the separation between the Prophets and the

Hagiographa was not of a chronological kind, but one found in the very nature of the respective sacred compositions. That literature was grouped under the Ké-thubim, or Hagiographa, which neither was the direct product of the prophetical order, namely, that comprised in the Latter Prophets, nor contained the history of Israel as interpreted by the same prophetic teachers--narratives classed as the Former Prophets.

The Book of Daniel was relegated to the Hagiographa as a work of the prophetic *gift* indeed, but not of the permanent prophetic *office*. These same conservative students of the Canon--now scarcely represented outside the Church--maintain, for the reception of the documents composing these groups into the sacred literature of the Israelites, dates which are in general much earlier than those admitted by critics. They place the practical, if not formal, completion of the Palestinian Canon in the era of Esdras (Ezra) and Nehemias, about the middle of the fifth century B.C., while true to their adhesion to a Mosaic authorship of the Pentateuch, they insist that the canonization of the five books followed soon after their composition.

Since the traditionalists infer the Mosaic authorship of the Pentateuch from other sources, they can rely for proof of an early collection of these books chiefly on Deuteronomy 31:9-13, 24-26, where there is question of a books of the law, delivered by Moses to the priests with the command to keep it in the ark and read it to the people on the feast of Tabernacles. But the effort to identify this book with the entire Pentateuch is not convincing to the opponents of Mosaic authorship.

The Remainder of the Palestinian-Jewish Canon

Without being positive on the subject, the advocates of the older views regard it as highly probable that several additions were made to the sacred repertory between the canonization of the Mosaic Torah above described and the Exile (598 B.C.). They cite especially Isaiah 34:16; 2 Chronicles 29:30; Proverbs 25:1; Daniel 9:2.

For the period following the Babylonian Exile the conservative argument takes a more confident tone. This was an era of construction, a turning-point in the history of Israel. The completion of the Jewish Canon, by the addition of the Prophets and Hagiographa as bodies to the Law, is attributed by conservatives to Esdras, the priest-scribe and religious leader of the period, abetted by Nehemias, the civil governor; or at least to a school of scribes founded by the former. (Cf. Nehemiah 8-10; 2 Maccabees 2:13, in the Greek original.)

Far more arresting in favour of an Esdrine formulation of the Hebrew Bible is a the much discussed passage from Josephus, "Contra Apionem", I, viii, in which the Jewish historian, writing about A.D. 100, registers his conviction and that of his coreligionists--a conviction presumably based on tradition-

-that the Scriptures of the Palestinian Hebrews formed a closed and sacred collection from the days of the Persian king, Artaxerxes Longiamanus (465-425 B.C.), a contemporary of Esdras. Josephus is the earliest writer who numbers the books of the Jewish Bible. In its present arrangement this contains 40; Josephus arrived at 22 artificially, in order to match the number of letters in the Hebrew alphabet, by means of collocations and combinations borrowed in part from the Septuagint. The conservative exegetes find a confirmatory argument in a statement of the apocryphal Fourth Book of Esdras (xiv, 18-47), under whose legendary envelope they see an historical truth, and a further one in a reference in the Baba Bathra tract of the Babylonian Talmud to hagiographic activity on the part of "the men of the Great Synagogue", and Esdras and Nehemias.

But the Catholic Scripturists who admit an Esdrine Canon are far from allowing that Esdras and his colleagues intended to so close up the sacred library as to bar any possible future accessions. The Spirit of God might and did breathe into later writings, and the presence of the deuterocanonical books in the Church's Canon at once forestalls and answers those Protestant theologians of a preceding generation who claimed that Esdras was a Divine agent for an inviolable fixing and sealing of the Old Testament. To this extent at least, Catholic writers on the subject dissent from the drift of the Josephus testimony. And while there is what may be called a consensus of Catholic exegetes of the conservative type on an Esdrine or quasi-Esdrine formulation of the Canon so far as the existing material permitted it, this agreement is not absolute; Kaulen and Danko, favouring a later completion, are the notable exceptions among the above-mentioned scholars.

Critical views of the formation of the Palestinian Canon

Its three constituent bodies, the Law, Prophets, and Hagiographa, represent a growth and correspond to three periods more or less extended. The reason for the isolation of the Hagiographa from the Prophets was therefore mainly chronological. The only division marked off clearly by intrinsic features is the legal element of the Old Testament, viz., the Pentateuch.

The Torah, or Law

Until the reign of King Josias, and the epoch-making discovery of "the book of the law" in the Temple (621 B.C.), say the critical exegetes, there was in Israel no written code of laws or other work, universally acknowledged as of supreme and Divine authority. This "book of the law" was practically identical with Deuteronomy, and its recognition or canonization consisted in the solemn pact entered into by Josias and the people of Juda, described in 2 Kings 23. That a written sacred Torah was previously unknown among the Israelites, is demonstrated by the negative evidence of the earlier prophets, by the absence of any such factor from the religious reform undertaken by Ezechias (Hezekiah), while it was the mainspring of that carried out by Josias, and lastly by the plain surprise and consternation of the latter ruler at the finding of such a work. This argument, in fact, is the pivot of the current system of Pentateuchal criticism, and will be developed more at length in the article on the Pentateuch, as also the thesis attacking the Mosaic authorship and promulgation of the latter as a whole. The actual publication of the entire Mosaic code, according to the dominant hypothesis, did not occur until the days of Esdras, and is narrated in chapters viii-x of the second book bearing that name. In this connection must be mentioned the argument from the Samaritan Pentateuch to establish that the Esdrine Canon took in nothing beyond the Hexateuch, i.e. the Pentateuch *plus* Josue. (See PENTATEUCH; SAMARITANS.)[3]

The Nebiim, or Prophets

There is no direct light upon the time or manner in which the second stratum of the Hebrew Canon was finished. The creation of the above-mentioned Samaritan Canon (c. 432 B.C.) may furnish a *terminus a quo*; perhaps a better one is the date of the expiration of prophecy about the close of the fifth century before Christ. For the other *terminus* the lowest possible date is that of the prologue to Ecclesiasticus (c. 132 B.C.), which speaks of "the Law, and the Prophets, and the others that have followed them". But compare Ecclesiasticus itself, chapters 46-49, for an earlier one.

The Kéthubim, or Hagiographa Completes of the Jewish Canon

Critical opinion as to date ranged from c. 165 B.C. to the middle of the second century of our era (Wildeboer). The Catholic scholars Jahn, Movers, Nickes, Danko, Haneberg, Aicher, without sharing all the views of the advanced exegetes, regard the Hebrew Hagiographa as not definitely settled till after Christ. It is an incontestable fact that the sacredness of certain parts of the Palestinian Bible (Esther, Ecclesiastes, Canticle of Canticles) was disputed by some rabbis as late as the second century of the Christian Era (Mishna, Yadaim, III, 5; Babylonian Talmud, Megilla, fol. 7). However differing as to dates, the critics are assured that the distinction between the Hagiographa and the Prophetic Canon was one essentially chronological. It was because the Prophets already formed a sealed collection that Ruth, Lamentations, and Daniel, though naturally belonging to it, could not gain entrance, but had to take their place with the last-formed division, the Kéthubim.

The protocanonical books and the New Testament

The absence of any citations from Esther, Ecclesiastes, and Canticles may be reasonably explained by their unsuitability for New Testament purposes, and is further discounted by the non-citation of the two books of Esdras. Abdias, Nahum, and Sophonias, while not directly honoured, are included in the quotations from the other minor Prophets by virtue of the traditional unity of that collection. On the other hand, such frequent terms as "the Scripture", the "scriptures", "the holy Scriptures", applied in the New Testament to the other sacred writings, would lead us to believe that the latter already formed a definite fixed collection; but, on the other, the reference in St. Luke to "the Law and the Prophets and the Psalms", while demonstrating the fixity of the Torah and the Prophets as sacred groups, does not warrant us in ascribing the same fixity to the third division, the Palestinian-Jewish Hagiographa. If, as seems certain, the exact content of the broader catalogue of the Old Testament Scriptures (that comprising the deutero books) cannot be established from the New Testament, a fortiori there is no reason to expect that it should reflect the precise extension of the narrower and Judaistic Canon.

We are sure, of course, that all the Hagiographa were eventually, before the death of the last Apostle, divinely committed to the Church as Holy Scripture, but we know this as a truth of faith, and by theological deduction, not from documentary evidence in the New Testament. The latter fact has a bearing against the Protestant claim that Jesus approved and transmitted *en bloc* an already defined Bible of the Palestinian Synagogue.

Authors and standards of canonicity among the Jews

Though the Old Testament reveals no formal notion of inspiration, the later Jews at least must have possessed the idea (cf. 2 Timothy 3:16; 2 Peter 1:21). There is an instance of a Talmudic doctor distinguishing between a composition "given by the wisdom of the Holy Spirit" and one supposed to be the product of merely human wisdom. But as to our distinct concept of canonicity, it is a modern idea, and even the Talmud gives no evidence of it. To characterize a book which held no acknowledged place in the divine library, the rabbis spoke of it as "defiling the hands", a curious technical expression due probably to the desire to prevent any profane touching of the sacred roll.[4] But though the formal *idea* of canonicity was wanting among the Jews the *fact* existed. Regarding the sources of canonicity among the Hebrew ancients, we are left to surmise an analogy.

There are both psychological and historical reasons against the supposition that the Old Testament Canon grew spontaneously by a kind of instinctive public recognition of inspired books. True, it is quite reasonable to assume that the prophetic office in Israel carried its own credentials, which in a large measure extended to its written compositions. But there were many pseudo-prophets in the nation, and so some authority was necessary to draw the line between the true and the false prophetical writings. And an ultimate tribunal was also needed to set its seal upon the miscellaneous and in some cases mystifying literature embraced in the Hagiographa. Jewish tradition, as illustrated by the already cited Josephus, Baba Bathra, and pseudo-Esdras data, points to authority as the final arbiter of what was Scriptural and what not.

The so-called Council of Jamnia (c. A.D. 90) has reasonably been taken as having terminated the disputes between rival rabbinic schools concerning the canonicity of Canticles. So while the intuitive sense and increasingly reverent consciousness of the faithful element of Israel could, and presumably did, give a general impulse and direction to authority, we must conclude that it was the word of official authority which actually fixed the limits of the Hebrew Canon, and here, broadly speaking, the advanced and conservative exegetes meet on common ground. However the case may have been for the Prophets, the preponderance of evidence favours a late period as that in which the Hagiographa were closed, a period when the general body of Scribes dominated Judaism, sitting "in the chair of Moses", and alone having the authority and prestige for such action. The term *general body* of Scribes has been used advisedly; contemporary scholars gravely suspect, when they do not entirely reject, the "Great Synagogue" of rabbinic tradition, and the matter lay outside the jurisdiction of the Sanhedrim.

As a touchstone by which uncanonical and canonical works were discriminated, an important influence was that of the Pentateuchal Law. This was always the Canon *par excellence* of the Israelites. To the Jews of the Middle Ages the Torah was the inner sanctuary, or Holy of Holies, while the Prophets were the Holy Place, and the *Kéthubim* only the outer court of the Biblical temple, and this medieval conception finds ample basis in the pre-eminence allowed to the Law by the rabbis of the Talmudic age. Indeed, from Esdras downwards the Law, as the oldest portion of the Canon, and the formal expression of God's commands, received the highest reverence.

The Cabbalists of the second century after Christ, and later schools, regarded the other section of the Old Testament as merely the expansion and interpretation of the Pentateuch. We may be sure, then, that the chief test of canonicity, at least for the Hagiographa, was conformity with the Canon *par excellence*, the Pentateuch. It is evident, in addition, that no book was admitted which had not been composed in Hebrew, and did not possess the antiquity and prestige of a classic age, or name at least. These criteria are negative and exclusive rather than directive. The impulse of religious feeling or liturgical usage must have been the prevailing positive factors in the decision. But the negative tests were in part arbitrary, and an intuitive sense cannot give the assurance of Divine certification. Only later was the infallible voice to come, and then it was to declare that the Canon of the Synagogue, though unadulterated indeed, was incomplete.

The Canon among the Alexandrian Jews (deuterocanonical books)

The most striking difference between the Catholic and Protestant Bibles is the presence in the former of a number of writings which are wanting in the latter and also in the Hebrew Bible, which became the Old Testament of Protestantism. These number seven books: Tobias (Tobit), Judith, Wisdom, Ecclesiasticus, Baruch, I and II Machabees, and three documents added to protocanonical books, viz., the supplement to Esther, from x, 4, to the end, the Canticle of the Three Youths (Song of the Three Children) in Daniel, iii, and the stories of Susanna and the Elders and Bel and the Dragon, forming the closing chapters of the Catholic version of that book. Of these works, Tobias and Judith were written originally in Aramaic, perhaps in Hebrew; Baruch and I Machabees in Hebrew, while Wisdom and II Machabees were certainly composed in Greek. The probabilities favour Hebrew as the original language of the addition to Esther, and Greek for the enlargements of Daniel.

The ancient Greek Old Testament known as the Septuagint was the vehicle which conveyed these additional Scriptures into the Catholic Church. The Septuagint version was the Bible of the Greek-speaking, or Hellenist, Jews, whose intellectual and literary centre was Alexandria (see SEPTUAGINT). The oldest extant copies date from the fourth and fifth centuries of our era,[5] and were therefore made by Christian hands; nevertheless scholars generally admit that these faithfully represent the Old Testament as it was current among the Hellenist or Alexandrian Jews in the age immediately preceding Christ. These venerable manuscripts of the Septuagint vary somewhat in their content outside the Palestinian Canon, showing that in Alexandrian-Jewish circles the number of admissible extra books was not sharply determined either by tradition or by authority. However, aside from the absence of Machabees from the Codex Vaticanus (the very oldest copy of the Greek Old Testament), all the entire manuscripts contain all the deutero writings; where the manuscript Septuagints differ from one another, with the exception noted, it is in a certain excess above the deuterocanonical books. It is a significant fact that in all these Alexandrian Bibles the traditional Hebrew order is broken up by the interspersion of the additional literature among the other books, outside the law, thus asserting for the extra writings a substantial equality of rank and privilege.

It is pertinent to ask the motives which impelled the Hellenist Jews to thus, virtually at least, canonize this considerable section of literature, some of it very recent, and depart so radically from the Palestinian tradition. Some would have it that not the Alexandrian, but the Palestinian, Jews departed from the Biblical tradition. The Catholic writers Nickes, Movers, Danko, and more recently Kaulen and Mullen, have advocated the view that originally the Palestinian Canon must have included all the deuterocanonicals, and so stood down to the time of the Apostles (Kaulen, c. 100 B.C.), when, moved by the fact that the Septuagint had become the Old Testament of the Church, it was put under ban by the Jerusalem Scribes, who were actuated moreover (thus especially Kaulen) by hostility to the Hellenistic largeness of spirit and Greek composition of our deuterocanonical books. These exegetes place much reliance on St. Justin Martyr's statement that the Jews had mutilated Holy Writ, a statement that rests on no positive evidence. They adduce the fact that certain deutero books were quoted with veneration, and even in a few cases as Scriptures, by Palestinian or Babylonian doctors; but the private utterances of a few rabbis cannot outweigh the consistent Hebrew tradition of the Canon, attested by Josephus--although he himself was inclined to Hellenism--and even by the Alexandrian-Jewish author of IV Esdras. We are therefore forced to admit that the leaders of Alexandrian Judaism showed a notable independence of Jerusalem tradition and authority in permitting the sacred boundaries of the Canon, which certainly had been fixed for the Prophets, to be broken by the insertion of an enlarged Daniel and the Epistle of Baruch. On the assumption that the limits of the Palestinian Hagiographa remained undefined until a relatively late date, there was less bold innovation in the addition of the other books, but the wiping out of the lines of the triple division reveals that the Hellenists were ready to extend the Hebrew Canon, if not establish a new official one of their own.

On their human side these innovations are to be accounted for by the free spirit of the Hellenist Jews. Under the influence of Greek thought they had conceived a broader view of Divine inspiration than that of their Palestinian brethren, and refused to restrict the literary manifestations of the Holy Ghost to a certain terminus of time and the Hebrew form of language. The Book of Wisdom, emphatically Hellenist in character, presents to us Divine wisdom as flowing on from generation to generation and making holy souls and prophets (7:27, in the Greek). Philo, a typical Alexandrian-Jewish thinker, has even an exaggerated notion of the diffusion of inspiration (Quis rerum divinarum hæres, 52; ed. Lips., iii, 57; De migratione Abrahæ, 11,299; ed. Lips. ii, 334). But even Philo, while indicating acquaintance with the deutero literature, nowhere cites it in his voluminous writings. True, he does not employ several books of the Hebrew Canon; but there is a natural presumption that if he had regarded the additional works as being quite on the same plane as the others, he would not have failed to quote so stimulating and congenial a production as the Book of Wisdom. Moreover, as has been pointed out by several authorities, the independent spirit of the Hellenists could not have gone so far as to setup a different *official* Canon from that of Jerusalem, without having left historical traces of such a rupture. So, from the available data we may justly infer that, while the deuterocanonicals were admitted as sacred by the

Alexandrian Jews, they possessed a lower degree of sanctity and authority than the longer accepted books, i.e., the Palestinian Hagiographa and the Prophets, themselves inferior to the Law.

The Canon of the Old Testament in the Catholic Church

The most explicit definition of the Catholic Canon is that given by the Council of Trent, Session IV, 1546. For the Old Testament its catalogue reads as follows:

The five books of Moses (Genesis, Exodus, Leviticus, Numbers, Deuteronomy), Josue, Judges, Ruth, the four books of Kings, two of Paralipomenon, the first and second of Esdras (which latter is called Nehemias), Tobias, Judith, Esther, Job, the Davidic Psalter (in number one hundred and fifty Psalms), Proverbs, Ecclesiastes, the Canticle of Canticles, Wisdom, Ecclesiasticus, Isaias, Jeremias, with Baruch, Ezechiel, Daniel, the twelve minor Prophets (Osee, Joel, Amos, Abdias, Jonas, Micheas, Nahum, Habacuc, Sophonias, Aggeus, Zacharias, Malachias), two books of Machabees, the first and second.

The order of books copies that of the Council of Florence, 1442, and in its general plan is that of the Septuagint. The divergence of titles from those found in the Protestant versions is due to the fact that the official Latin Vulgate retained the forms of the Septuagint.

The Old Testament Canon (including the deuteros) in the New Testament

The Tridentine decrees from which the above list is extracted was the first infallible and effectually promulgated pronouncement on the Canon, addressed to the Church Universal. Being dogmatic in its purport, it implies that the Apostles bequeathed the same Canon to the Church, as a part of the *depositum fidei*. But this was not done by way of any formal decision; we should search the pages of the New Testament in vain for any trace of such action. The larger Canon of the Old Testament passed through the Apostles' hands to the Church tacitly, by way of their usage and whole attitude toward its components; an attitude which, for most of the sacred writings of the Old Testament, reveals itself in the New, and for the rest, must have exhibited itself in oral utterances, or at least in tacit approval of the special reverence of the faithful. Reasoning backward from the status in which we find the deutero books in the earliest ages of post-Apostolic Christianity,[6] we rightly affirm that such a status points of Apostolic sanction, which in turn must have rested on revelation either by Christ or the Holy Spirit. For the deuterocanonicals at least, we needs must have recourse to this legitimate prescriptive argument, owing to the complexity and inadequacy of the New Testament data.

All the books of the Hebrew Old Testament are cited in the New except those which have been aptly called the *Antilegomena* of the Old Testament, viz., Esther, Ecclesiastes, and Canticles; moreover Esdras and Nehemias are not employed. The admitted absence of any explicit citation of the deutero writings does not therefore prove that they were regarded as inferior to the above-mentioned works in the eyes of New Testament personages and authors. The deutero literature was in general unsuited to their purposes, and some consideration should be given to the fact that even at its Alexandrian home it was not quoted by Jewish writers, as we saw in the case of Philo. The negative argument drawn from the non-citation of the deuterocanonicals in the New Testament is especially minimized by the indirect use made of them by the same Testament. This takes the form of allusions and reminiscences, and shows unquestionably that the Apostles and Evangelists were acquainted with the Alexandrian increment, regarded its books as at least respectable sources, and wrote more or less under its influence. A comparison of Hebrews, xi and II Machabees, vi and vii reveals unmistakable references in the former to the heroism of the martyrs glorified in the latter. There are close affinities of thought, and in some cases also of language, between 1 Peter 1:6-7, and Wisdom 3:5-6; Hebrews 1:3, and Wisdom 7:26-27; 1 Corinthians 10:9-10, and Judith 8:24-25; 1 Corinthians 6:13, and Ecclesiasticus 36:20.

Yet the force of the direct and indirect employment of Old Testament writings by the New is slightly impaired by the disconcerting truth that at least one of the New Testament authors, St. Jude, quotes explicitly from the "Book of Henoch", long universally recognized as apocryphal, see verse 14, while in verse 9 he borrows from another apocryphal narrative, the "Assumption of Moses". The New Testament quotations from the Old are in general characterized by a freedom and elasticity regarding manner and source which further tend to diminish their weight as proofs of canonicity. But so far as concerns the great majority of the Palestinian Hagiographa- -a fortiori, the Pentateuch and Prophets--whatever want of conclusiveness there may be in the New Testament, evidence of their canonical standing is abundantly supplemented from Jewish sources alone, in the series of witnesses beginning with the Mishnah and running back through Josephus and Philo to the translation of the above books for the Hellenist Greeks. But for the deuterocanonical literature, only the last testimony speaks as a Jewish confirmation. However, there are signs that the Greek version was not deemed by its readers as a closed Bible of definite sacredness in all its parts, but that its somewhat variable contents shaded off in the eyes of the Hellenists from the eminently sacred Law down to works of questionable divinity, such as III Machabees.

This factor should be considered in weighing a certain argument. A large number of Catholic authorities see a canonization of the deuteros in a supposed wholesale adoption and approval, by the Apostles, of the Greek, and therefore larger, Old Testament. The argument is not without a certain force; the New Testament undoubtedly shows a preference for the Septuagint; out of the 350 texts from the Old Testament, 300 favour the language of the Greek version rather than that of the Hebrew. But there are considerations which bid us hesitate to admit an Apostolic adoption of the Septuagint *en bloc*. As remarked above, there are cogent reasons for believing that it was not a fixed quantity at the time. The existing oldest representative manuscripts are not entirely identical in the books they contain. Moreover, it should be remembered that at the beginning of our era, and for some time later, complete sets of any such voluminous collection as the Septuagint in manuscript would be extremely rare; the version must have been current in separate books or groups of books, a condition favourable to a certain variability of compass. So neither a fluctuating Septuagint nor an inexplicit New Testament conveys to us the exact extension of the pre-Christian Bible transmitted by the Apostles to the Primitive Church. It is more tenable to conclude to a selective process under the guidance of the Holy Ghost, and a process completed so late in Apostolic times that the New Testament fails to reflect its mature result regarding either the number or note of sanctity of the extra-Palestinian books admitted. To historically learn the Apostolic Canon of the Old Testament we must interrogate less sacred but later documents, expressing more explicitly the belief of the first ages of Christianity.

The Canon of the Old Testament in the Church of the first three centuries

The sub-Apostolic writings of Clement, Polycarp, the author of the Epistle of Barnabas, of the pseudo-Clementine homilies, and the "shepherd" of Hermas, contain implicit quotations from or allusions to all the deuterocanonicals except Baruch (which anciently was often united with Jeremias) and I Machabees and the additions to David. No unfavourable argument can be drawn from the loose, implicit character of these citations, since these Apostolic Fathers quote the protocanonical Scriptures in precisely the same manner.

Coming down to the next age, that of the apologists, we find Baruch cited by Athenagoras as a prophet. St. Justin Martyr is the first to note that the Church has a set of Old Testament Scriptures different from the Jews', and also the earliest to intimate the principle proclaimed by later writers, namely, the self-sufficiency of the Church in establishing the Canon; its independence of the Synagogue in this respect. The full realization of this truth came slowly, at least in the Orient, where there are indications that in certain quarters the spell of Palestinian-Jewish tradition was not fully cast off for some time. St. Melito, Bishop of Sardis (c. 170), first drew up a list of the canonical books of the Old Testament. While maintaining the familiar arrangement of the Septuagint, he says that he verified his catalogue by inquiry among Jews; Jewry by that time had everywhere discarded the Alexandrian books, and Melito's Canon consists exclusively of the protocanonicals *minus* Esther. It should be noticed, however, that the document to which this catalogue was prefixed is capable of being understood as having an anti-Jewish polemical purpose, in which case Melito's restricted Canon is explicable on another ground. St. Irenæus, always a witness of the first rank, on account of his broad acquaintance with ecclesiastical tradition, vouches that Baruch was deemed on the same footing as Jeremias, and that the narratives of Susanna and Bel and the Dragon were ascribed to Daniel. The Alexandrian tradition is represented by the weighty authority of Origen. Influenced, doubtless, by the Alexandrian-Jewish usage of acknowledging in practice the extra writings as sacred while theoretically holding to the narrower Canon of Palestine, his catalogue of the Old Testament Scriptures contains only the protocanonical books, though it follows the order of the Septuagint. Nevertheless Origen employs all the deuterocanonicals as Divine Scriptures, and in his letter of Julius Africanus defends the sacredness of Tobias, Judith, and the fragments of Daniel, at the same time implicitly asserting the autonomy of the Church in fixing the Canon (see references in Cornely). In his Hexaplar edition of the Old Testament[7] all the deuteros find a place. The sixth-century Biblical manuscript known as the "Codex Claromontanus" contains a catalogue to which both Harnack and Zahn assign an Alexandrian origin, about contemporary with Origen. At any rate it dates from the period under examination and comprises all the deuterocanonical books, with IV Machabees besides. St. Hippolytus (d. 236) may fairly be considered as representing the primitive Roman tradition. He comments on the Susanna chapter, often quotes Wisdom as the work of Solomon, and employs as Sacred Scripture Baruch and the Machabees. For the West African Church the larger Canon has two strong witnesses in Tertullian and St. Cyprian. All the deuteros except Tobias, Judith, and the addition to Esther, are biblically used in the works of these Fathers. (With regard to the employment of apocryphal writings in this age see under APOCRYPHA.)

The Canon of the Old Testament during the fourth, and first half of the fifth, century

In this period the position of the deuterocanonical literature is no longer as secure as in the primitive age. The doubts which arose should be attributed largely to a reaction against the apocryphal or pseudo-Biblical writings with which the East especially had been flooded by heretical and other writers. Negatively, the situation became possible through the absence of any Apostolic or ecclesiastical definition of the Canon. The definite and inalterable determination of the sacred sources, like that of all Catholic doctrines, was in the Divine economy left to gradually work itself out under the stimulus of questions and opposition. Alexandria, with its elastic Scriptures, had from the beginning been a congenial field for apocryphal literature, and St. Athanasius, the vigilant pastor of that flock, to protect it against the pernicious influence, drew up a catalogue of books with the values to be attached to each. First, the strict Canon and authoritative source of truth is the Jewish Old Testament, Esther excepted. Besides, there are certain books which the Fathers had appointed to be read to catechumens for edification and instruction; these are the Wisdom of Solomon, the Wisdom of Sirach (Ecclesiasticus), Esther, Judith, Tobias, the Didache, or Doctrine of the Apostles, the Shepherd of Hermas. All others are apocrypha and the inventions of heretics (Festal Epistle for 367). Following the precedent of Origen and the Alexandrian tradition, the saintly doctor recognized no other formal Canon of the Old Testament than the Hebrew one; but also, faithful to the same tradition, he practically admitted the deutero books to a Scriptural dignity, as is evident from his general usage. At Jerusalem there was a renascence, perhaps a survival, of Jewish ideas, the tendency there being distinctly unfavourable to the deuteros. St. Cyril of that see, while vindicating for the Church the right to fix the Canon, places them among the apocrypha and forbids all books to be read privately which are not read in the Churches. In Antioch and Syria the attitude was more favourable. St. Epiphanius shows hesitation about the rank of the deuteros; he esteemed them, but they had not the same place as the Hebrew books in his regard. The historian Eusebius attests the widespread doubts in his time; he classes them as *antilegomena*, or disputed writings, and, like Athanasius, places them in a class intermediate between the books received by all and the apocrypha. The 59th (or 60th) Canon of the provincial Council of Laodicea (the authenticity of which however is contested) gives a catalogue of the Scriptures entirely in accord with the ideas of St. Cyril of Jerusalem. On the other hand, the Oriental versions and Greek manuscripts of the period are more liberal; the extant ones have all the deuterocanonicals and, in some cases, certain apocrypha.

The influence of Origen's and Athanasius's restricted Canon naturally spread to the West. St. Hilary of Poitiers and Rufinus followed their footsteps, excluding the deuteros from canonical rank in theory, but admitting them in practice. The latter styles them "ecclesiastical" books, but in authority unequal to the other Scriptures. St. Jerome cast his weighty suffrage on the side unfavourable to the disputed books. In appreciating his attitude we must remember that Jerome lived long in Palestine, in an environment where everything outside the Jewish Canon was suspect, and that, moreover, he had an excessive veneration for the Hebrew text, the *Hebraica veritas* as he called it. In his famous "Prologus Galeatus", or Preface to his translation of Samuel and Kings, he declares that everything not Hebrew should be classed with the apocrypha, and explicitly says that Wisdom, Ecclesiasticus, Tobias, and

Judith are not on the Canon. These books, he adds, are read in the Churches for the edification of the people, and not for the confirmation of revealed doctrine. An analysis of Jerome's expressions on the deuterocanonicals, in various letters and prefaces, yields the following results: first, he strongly doubted their inspiration; secondly, the fact that he occasionally quotes them, and translated some of them as a concession to ecclesiastical tradition, is an involuntary testimony on his part to the high standing these writings enjoyed in the Church at large, and to the strength of the practical tradition which prescribed their readings in public worship.

Obviously, the inferior rank to which the deuteros were relegated by authorities like Origen, Athanasius, and Jerome, was due to too rigid a conception of canonicity, one demanding that a book, to be entitled to this supreme dignity, must be received by all, must have the sanction of Jewish antiquity, and must moreover be adapted not only to edification, but also to the "confirmation of the doctrine of the Church", to borrow Jerome's phrase.

But while eminent scholars and theorists were thus depreciating the additional writings, the official attitude of the Latin Church, always favourable to them, kept the majestic tenor of its way. Two documents of capital importance in the history of the Canon constitute the first formal utterance of papal authority on the subject. The first is the so-called "Decretal of Gelasius", *de recipiendis et non recipiendis libris*, the essential part of which is now generally attributed to a synod convoked by Pope Damasus in the year 382. The other is the Canon of Innocent I, sent in 405 to a Gallican bishop in answer to an inquiry. Both contain all the deuterocanonicals, without any distinction, and are identical with the catalogue of Trent.

The African Church, always a staunch supporter of the contested books, found itself in entire accord with Rome on this question. Its ancient version, the *Vetus Latina* (less correctly the *Itala*), had admitted all the Old Testament Scriptures. St. Augustine seems to theoretically recognize degrees of inspiration; in practice he employs protos and deuteros without any discrimination whatsoever. Moreover in his "De Doctrinâ Christianâ" he enumerates the components of the complete Old Testament. The Synod of Hippo (393) and the three of Carthage (393, 397, and 419), in which, doubtless, Augustine was the leading spirit, found it necessary to deal explicitly with the question of the Canon, and drew up identical lists from which no sacred books are excluded. These councils base their Canon on tradition and liturgical usage. For the Spanish Church valuable testimony is found in the work of the heretic Priscillian, "Liber de Fide et Apocryphis"; it supposes a sharp line existing between canonical and uncanonical works, and that the Canon takes in all the deuteros.

The Canon of the Old Testament from the middle of the fifth to the close of the seventh century

This period exhibits a curious exchange of opinions between the West and the East, while ecclesiastical usage remained unchanged, at least in the Latin Church. During this intermediate age the use of St. Jerome's new version of the Old Testament (the Vulgate) became widespread in the Occident. With its text went Jerome's prefaces disparaging the deuterocanonicals, and under the influence of his authority the West began to distrust these and to show the first symptoms of a current hostile to their canonicity. On the other hand, the Oriental Church imported a Western authority which had canonized the disputed books, viz., the decree of Carthage, and from this time there is an increasing tendency among the Greeks to place the deuteros on the same level with the others--a tendency, however, due more to forgetfulness of the old distinction than to deference to the Council of Carthage.

The Canon of the Old Testament during the Middle Ages

The Greek Church

The result of this tendency among the Greeks was that about the beginning of the twelfth century they possessed a Canon identical with that of the Latins, except that it took in the apocryphal III Machabees. That all the deuteros were liturgically recognized in the Greek Church at the era of the schism in the ninth century, is indicated by the "syntagma Canonum" of Photius.

The Latin Church

In the Latin Church, all through the Middle Ages we find evidence of hesitation about the character of the deuterocanonicals. There is a current friendly to them, another one distinctly unfavourable to their authority and sacredness, while wavering between the two are a number of writers whose veneration for these books is tempered by some perplexity as to their exact standing, and among those we note St. Thomas Aquinas. Few are found to unequivocally acknowledge their canonicity. The prevailing attitude of Western medieval authors is substantially that of the Greek Fathers. The chief cause of this phenomenon in the West is to be sought in the influence, direct and indirect, of St. Jerome's depreciating Prologus. The compilatory "Glossa Ordinaria" was widely read and highly esteemed as a treasury of sacred learning during the Middle Ages; it embodied the prefaces in which the Doctor of Bethlehem had written in terms derogatory to the deuteros, and thus perpetuated and diffused his unfriendly opinion. And yet these doubts must be regarded as more or less academic. The countless manuscript copies of the Vulgate produced by these ages, with a slight, probably accidental, exception, uniformly embrace the complete Old Testament; Ecclesiastical usage and Roman tradition held firmly to the canonical equality of all parts of the Old Testament. There is no lack of evidence that during this long period the deuteros were read in the Churches of Western Christendom. As to Roman authority, the catalogue of Innocent I appears in the collection of ecclesiastical canons sent by Pope Adrian I to Charlemagne, and adopted in 802 as the law of the Church in the Frankish Empire; Nicholas I, writing in 865 to the bishops of France, appeals to the same decree of Innocent as the ground on which all the sacred books are to be received.

The Canon of the Old Testament and the general councils

The Council of Florence (1442)

In 1442, during the life, and with the approval, of this Council, Eugenius IV issued several Bulls, or decrees, with a view to restore the Oriental schismatic bodies to communion with Rome, and according to the common teaching of theologians these documents are infallible statements of doctrine. The "Decretum pro Jacobitis" contains a complete list of the books received by the Church as inspired, but omits, perhaps advisedly, the terms Canon and *canonical*. The Council of Florence therefore taught the inspiration of all the Scriptures, but did not formally pass on their canonicity.

The Council of Trent's definition of the Canon (1546)

It was the exigencies of controversy that first led Luther to draw a sharp line between the books of the Hebrew Canon and the Alexandrian writings. In his disputation with Eck at Leipzig, in 1519, when his opponent urged the well-known text from II Machabees in proof of the doctrine of purgatory, Luther replied that the passage had no binding authority since the books was outside the Canon. In the first edition of Luther's Bible, 1534, the deuteros were relegated, as apocrypha, to a separate place between the two Testaments. To meet this radical departure of the Protestants, and as well define clearly the inspired sources from which the Catholic Faith draws its defence, the Council of Trent among its first acts solemnly declared as "sacred and canonical" all the books of the Old and New Testaments "with all their parts as they have been used to be read in the Churches, and as found in the ancient vulgate edition". During the deliberations of the Council there never was any real question as to the reception of all the traditional Scripture. Neither--and this is remarkable--in the proceedings is there manifest any serious doubt of the canonicity of the disputed writings. In the mind of the Tridentine Fathers they had been virtually canonized, by the same decree of Florence, and the same Fathers felt especially bound by the action of the preceding ecumenical synod. The Council of Trent did not enter into an examination of the fluctuations in the history of the Canon. Neither did it trouble itself about questions of authorship or character of contents. True to the practical genius of the Latin Church, it based its decision on immemorial tradition as manifested in the decrees of previous councils and popes, and liturgical reading, relying on traditional teaching and usage to determine a question of tradition. The Tridentine catalogue has been given above.

The Vatican Council (1870)

The great constructive Synod of Trent had put the sacredness and canonicity of the whole traditional Bible forever beyond the permissibility of doubt on the part of Catholics. By implication it had defined that Bible's plenary inspiration also. The Vatican Council took occasion of a recent error on inspiration to remove any lingering shadow of uncertainty on this head; it formally ratified the action of Trent and explicitly defined the Divine inspiration of all the books with their parts.

The Canon of the Old Testament outside the [Roman Catholic][8] Church

Among the Eastern Orthodox

The Greek Orthodox Church preserved its ancient Canon in practice as well as theory until recent times, when, under the dominant influence of its Russian offshoot, it is shifting its attitude towards the deuterocanonical Scriptures. The rejection of these books by the Russian theologians and authorities is a lapse which began early in the eighteenth century. The Monophysites, Nestorians, Jacobites, Armenians, and Copts, while concerning themselves little with the Canon, admit the complete catalogue and several apocrypha besides.

Among Protestants

The Protestant Churches have continued to exclude the deutero writings from their canons, classifying them as "Apocrypha". Presbyterians and Calvinists in general, especially since the Westminster Synod of 1648, have been the most uncompromising enemies of any recognition, and owing to their influence the British and Foreign Bible Society decided in 1826 to refuse to distribute Bibles containing the Apocrypha. Since that time the publication of the deuterocanonicals as an appendix to Protestant Bibles has almost entirely ceased in English-speaking countries. The books still supply lessons for the liturgy of the Church of England, but the number has been lessened by the hostile agitation. There is an Apocrypha appendix to the British Revised Version, in a separate volume. The deuteros are still appended to the German Bibles printed under the auspices of the orthodox Lutherans.[9]

* * *

About this page:

APA citation. Reid, G. (1908). Canon of the Old Testament. In The Catholic Encyclopedia. New York: Robert Appleton Company. Retrieved April 26, 2010 from New Advent: http://www.newadvent.org/cathen/03267a.htm

MLA citation. Reid, George. "Canon of the Old Testament." The Catholic Encyclopedia. Vol. 3. New York: Robert Appleton Company, 1908. 26 Apr. 2010 <http://www.newadvent.org/cathen/03267a.htm>.

Transcription. This article was transcribed for New Advent by Ernie Stefanik.

Ecclesiastical approbation. *Nihil Obstat.* November 1, 1908. Remy Lafort, S.T.D., Censor. *Imprimatur.* +John Cardinal Farley, Archbishop of New York.

Contact information. The editor of New Advent is Kevin Knight. My email address is webmaster@newadvent.org.

* * *

---

1   See the Bibliography under New Advent, including WWW.NewAdvent.org

2   [Own Note] For Appendix B, I have added numbers to the sub-paragraph headings within the article.

3   [Own Note]. These, and similar entries in Appendices A & B, are cross references to articles elsewhere within New Advent.

4   [Own Note]. This reading of "Defiling (Soiling) the hands" reads somewhat differently from that of the Jerome Biblical Commentary's understanding as quoted in the opening paragraph of this book (*A paradoxical designation* - introducing Section A).

5   [Own Note]. Obviously, this 1908 Article predated the radical Qumran and other mss. discoveries of the Twentieth Century. Cf. The 21 Old Testament and New Testament manuscript examples in Book Two, *The Great Collaboration*, in this collection.

6   [Own Note] The period 100 AD onwards was called the sub-Apostolic age by the Catholic Encyclopaedia of 1908, but is what Raymond E. Brown et al referred to as the post-Apostolic age. Brown reserved the designation sub-Apostolic to the earlier period of AD 67–100. Cf. Section B of Book Four (*The Jigsaw Puzzle Church*) in this collection.

7   [Own Note] Cf. Chapter 10 (Artefact # 7), and Appendix C, of Book Two, *The Great Collaboration*, in this collection.

8   [Own Note]. My introductory remarks to Appendices A & B refer.

9   [Own Note]. The editors of New Advent add the following to the end of this Article

* * *

Appendix B - Canon of the New Testament

[New Advent article (Catholic) (1908)][1]

> Narrator's Note with respect to the dating, terminology, and ecumenical posture of the two articles from New Advent: Appendix A & Appendix B.
>
> These articles[2] are from New Advent's copy of articles in the Catholic Encyclopaedia of 1908. Because they are articles about the Canon of Scripture, and not about the content of individual books of the Old and New Testaments, (and therefore not dependent upon the considerable advances made in textual criticism and exegesis during the past century), they retain, in essence, their value as a (still) valid expression of the Catholic Church's understanding of the Canon of Scripture.
>
> Being more than a hundred years old, the terminology deployed reflects the age and the era in which they were written. Thus, when e.g., the articles speak of The Vatican Council they are referring to the First Vatican Council of 1870 (!) and not to Vatican II. For the same reason the ecumenical posture is virtually non-existent by our standards; accordingly, sojourners are asked to extend a generous measure of grace when the articles use terms such as "[those] outside the Church" (meaning "outside the Catholic Church") when quoting the views of Eastern Orthodox and Protestant Churches.

Canon of the New Testament [The classical Roman Catholic position][3]

The Catholic New Testament, as defined by the Council of Trent, does not differ, as regards the books contained, from that of all Christian bodies at present. Like the Old Testament, the New has its *deuterocanonical* books and portions of books, their canonicity having formerly been a subject of some controversy in the Church. These are for the entire books: the Epistle to the Hebrews, that of James, the Second of St. Peter, the Second and Third of John, Jude, and Apocalypse; giving seven in all as the number of the New Testament contested books.

The formerly disputed passages are three: the closing section of St. Mark's Gospel, xvi, 9-20 about the apparitions of Christ after the Resurrection; the verses in Luke about the bloody sweat of Jesus, xxii, 43, 44; the *Pericope Adulteræ*, or narrative of the woman taken in adultery, St. John, vii, 53 to viii, 11. Since the Council of Trent it is not permitted for a Catholic to question the inspiration of these passages.

A. THE FORMATION OF THE NEW TESTAMENT Canon (A.D. 100-220)

The idea of a complete and clear-cut Canon of the New Testament existing from the beginning, that is, from Apostolic times, has no foundation in history. The Canon of the New Testament, like that of the Old, is the result of a development, of a process at once stimulated by disputes with doubters, both within and without the Church, and retarded by certain obscurities and natural hesitations, and which did not reach its final term until the dogmatic definition of the Tridentine Council.

1. The witness of the New Testament to itself: The first collections

Those writings which possessed the unmistakable stamp and guarantee of Apostolic origin must from the very first have been specially prized and venerated, and their copies eagerly sought by local Churches and individual Christians of means, in preference to the narratives and *Logia*, or Sayings of Christ, coming from less authorized sources. Already in the New Testament itself there is some evidence of a certain diffusion of canonical books: II Peter, iii, 15, 16, supposes its readers to be acquainted with some of St. Paul's Epistles; St. John's Gospel implicitly presupposes the existence of the Synoptics (Matthew, Mark, and Luke). There are no indications in the New Testament of a systematic plan for the distribution of the Apostolic compositions, any more than there is of a definite new Canon bequeathed by the Apostles to the Church, or of a strong self-witness to Divine inspiration. Nearly all the New Testament writings were evoked by particular occasions, or addressed to particular destinations. But we may well presume that each of the leading Churches--Antioch, Thessalonica, Alexandria, Corinth, Rome-- sought by exchanging with other Christian communities to add to its special treasure, and have publicly read in its religious assemblies all Apostolic writings which came under its knowledge. It was doubtless in this way that the collections grew, and reached completeness within certain limits, but a considerable number of years must have elapsed (and that counting from the composition of the latest book) before all the widely separated Churches of early Christendom possessed the new sacred literature in full. And this want of an organized distribution, secondarily to the absence of an early fixation of the Canon, left room for variations and doubts which lasted far into the centuries. But evidence will presently be given that from days touching on those of the last Apostles there were two well defined bodies of sacred writings of the New Testament, which constituted the firm, irreducible, universal minimum, and the nucleus of its complete Canon: these were the Four Gospels, as the Church now has them, and thirteen Epistles of St. Paul[4]-- the *Evangelium* and the *Apostolicum*.

2. The principle of canonicity

Before entering into the historical proof for this primitive emergence of a compact, nucleative Canon, it is pertinent to briefly examine this problem: During the formative period what principle operated in the selection of the New Testament writings and their recognition as Divine?--Theologians are divided on this point. This view that Apostolicity was the test of the inspiration during the building up of the New Testament Canon, is favoured by the many instances where the early Fathers base the authority of a book on its Apostolic origin, and by the truth that the definitive placing of the contested books on the New Testament catalogue coincided with their general acceptance as of Apostolic authorship. Moreover, the advocates of this hypothesis point out that the Apostles' office corresponded with that of the Prophets of the Old Law, inferring that as inspiration was attached to the *munus propheticum* so the Apostles were aided by Divine inspiration whenever in the exercise of their calling they either spoke or wrote. Positive arguments are deduced from the New Testament to establish that a permanent prophetical *charisma* (see CHARISMATA)[5] was enjoyed by the Apostles through a special indwelling of the Holy Ghost, beginning with Pentecost: Matth., x, 19, 20; Acts, xv, 28; I Cor., ii, 13; II Cor., xiii, 3; I Thess., ii, 13, are cited. The opponents of this theory allege against it that the Gospels of Mark and of Luke and Acts were not the work of Apostles (however, tradition connects the Second Gospel with St. Peter's preaching and St. Luke's with St. Paul's); that books current under an Apostle's name in the Early Church, such as the Epistle of Barnabas and the Apocalypse of St. Peter, were nevertheless excluded from canonical rank, while on the other hand Origen and St. Dionysius of Alexandria in the case of Apocalypse, and St. Jerome in the case of II and III John, although questioning the Apostolic authorship of these works, unhesitatingly received them as Sacred Scriptures. An objection of a speculative kind is derived from the very nature of inspiration *ad scribendum*, which seems to demand a specific impulse from the Holy Ghost in each case, and preclude the theory that it could be possessed as a permanent gift, or charisma. The weight of Catholic theological opinion is deservedly against mere Apostolicity as a sufficient criterion of inspiration. The adverse view has been taken by Franzelin (De

Divinâ Traditione et Scripturâ, 1882), Schmid (De Inspirationis Bibliorum Vi et Ratione, 1885), Crets (De Divinâ Bibliorum Inspiratione, 1886), Leitner (Die prophetische Inspiration, 1895--a monograph), Pesch (De Inspiratione Sacræ, 1906). These authors (some of whom treat the matter more speculatively than historically) admit that Apostolicity is a positive and partial touchstone of inspiration, but emphatically deny that it was exclusive, in the sense that all non-Apostolic works were by that very fact barred from the sacred Canon of the New Testament They hold to doctrinal tradition as the true criterion.

Catholic champions of Apostolicity as a criterion are: Ubaldi (Introductio in Sacram Scripturam, II, 1876); Schanz (in Theologische Quartalschrift, 1885, pp. 666 sqq., and A Christian Apology, II, tr. 1891); Székely (Hermeneutica Biblica, 1902). Recently Professor Batiffol, while rejecting the claims of these latter advocates, has enunciated a theory regarding the principle that presided over the formation of the New Testament Canon which challenges attention and perhaps marks a new stage in the controversy. According to Monsignor Batiffol, the *Gospel* (i.e. the words and commandments of Jesus Christ) bore with it its own sacredness and authority from the very beginning. This Gospel was announced to the world at large, by the Apostles and Apostolic disciples of Christ, and this message, whether spoken or written, whether taking the form of an evangelic narrative or epistle, was holy and supreme by the fact of containing the Word of Our Lord. Accordingly, for the primitive Church, *evangelical character* was the test of Scriptural sacredness. But to guarantee this character it was necessary that a book should be known as composed by the official witnesses and organs of the Evangel; hence the need to certify the Apostolic authorship, or at least sanction, of a work purporting to contain the Gospel of Christ.

In Batiffol's view the Judaic notion of inspiration did not at first enter into the selection of the Christian Scriptures. In fact, for the earliest Christians the Gospel of Christ, in the wide sense above noted, was not to be classified with, because transcending, the Old Testament. It was not until about the middle of the second century that under the rubric of *Scripture* the New Testament writings were assimilated to the Old; the authority of the New Testament as the Word preceded and produced its authority as a New Scripture. (Revue Biblique, 1903, 226 sqq.) Monsignor Batiffol's hypothesis has this in common with the views of other recent students of the New Testament Canon, that the idea of a new body of sacred writings became clearer in the Early Church as the faithful advanced in a knowledge of the Faith. But it should be remembered that the inspired character of the New Testament is a Catholic dogma, and must therefore in some way have been revealed to, and taught by, Apostles.-- Assuming that Apostolic authorship is a positive criterion of inspiration, two inspired[6] Epistles of St. Paul have been lost. This appears from I Cor., v, 9, sqq.; II Cor., ii, 4, 5.

3. The formation of the Tetramorph, or Fourfold Gospel

Irenæus, in his work "Against Heresies" (A.D. 182-88), testifies to the existence of a *Tetramorph*, or Quadriform Gospel, given by the Word and unified by one Spirit; to repudiate this Gospel or any part of it, as did the Alogi and Marcionites, was to sin against revelation and the Spirit of God. The saintly Doctor of Lyons explicitly states the names of the four Elements of this Gospel, and repeatedly cites all the Evangelists in a manner parallel to his citations from the Old Testament. From the testimony of St. Irenæus alone there can be no reasonable doubt that the Canon of the Gospel was inalterably fixed in the Catholic Church by the last quarter of the second century. Proofs might be multiplied that our canonical Gospels were then universally recognized in the Church, to the exclusion of any pretended Evangels.

The magisterial statement of Irenæus may be corroborated by the very ancient catalogue known as the Muratorian Canon, and St. Hippolytus, representing Roman tradition; by Tertullian in Africa, by Clement in Alexandria; the works of the Gnostic Valentinus, and the Syrian Tatian's Diatessaron,[7] a blending together of the Evangelists' writings, presuppose the authority enjoyed by the fourfold Gospel towards the middle of the second century. To this period or a little earlier belongs the pseduo-Clementine epistle in which we find, for the first time after II Peter, iii, 16, the word *Scripture* applied to a New Testament book. But it is needless in the present article to array the full force of these and other witnesses, since even rationalistic scholars like Harnack admit the canonicity of the quadriform Gospel between the years 140-175.

But against Harnack we are able to trace the Tetramorph as a sacred collection back to a more remote period. The apocryphal Gospel of St. Peter, dating from about 150, is based on our canonical Evangelists. So with the very ancient Gospel of the Hebrews and Egyptians (see APOCRYPHA). St. Justin Martyr (130-63) in his Apology refers to certain "memoirs of the Apostles, which are called gospels", and which "are read in Christian assemblies together with the writings of the Prophets". The identity of these "memoirs" with our Gospels is established by the certain traces of three, if not all, of them scattered through St. Justin's works; it was not yet the age of explicit quotations. Marcion, the heretic refuted by Justin in a lost polemic, as we know from Tertullian, instituted a criticism of Gospels bearing the names of the Apostles and disciples of the Apostles, and a little earlier (c. 120) Basilides, the Alexandrian leader of a Gnostic sect, wrote a commentary on "the Gospel" which is known by the allusions to it in the Fathers to have comprised the writings of the Four Evangelists.

In our backward search we have come to the sub-Apostolic[8] age, and its important witnesses are divided into Asian, Alexandrian, and Roman:

» St. Ignatius, Bishop of Antioch, and St. Polycarp, of Smyrna, had been disciples of Apostles; they wrote their epistles in the first decade of the second century (100-110). They employ Matthew, Luke, and John. In St. Ignatius we find the first instance of the consecrated term "it is written" applied to a Gospel (Ad Philad., viii, 2). Both these Fathers show not only a personal acquaintance with "the Gospel" and the thirteen Pauline Epistles, but they suppose that their readers are so familiar with them that it would be superfluous to name them. Papias, Bishop of Phrygian Hierapolis, according to Irenæus a disciple of St. John, wrote about A.D. 125. Describing the origin of St. Mark's Gospel, he speaks of Hebrew (Aramaic) Logia, or Sayings of Christ, composed by St. Matthew, which there is reason to believe formed the basis of the canonical Gospel of that name, though the greater part of Catholic writers identify them with the Gospel. As we have only a few fragments of Papias, preserved by Eusebius, it cannot be alleged that he is silent about other parts of the New Testament.

» The so-called Epistle of Barnabas, of uncertain origin, but of highest antiquity, cites a passage from the First Gospel under the formula "it is written". The Didache, or Teaching of the Apostles, an uncanonical work dating from c. 110, implies that "the Gospel" was already a well-known and definite collection.

» St. Clement, Bishop of Rome, and disciple of St. Paul, addressed his Letter to the Corinthian Church c. A.D. 97, and, although it cites no Evangelist explicitly, this epistle contains combinations of texts taken from the three synoptic Gospels, especially from St. Matthew. That Clement does not allude to the Fourth Gospel is quite natural, as it was not composed till about that time.

Thus the patristic testimonies have brought us step by step to a Divine inviolable fourfold Gospel existing in the closing years of the Apostolic Era. Just how the Tetramorph was welded into unity and given to the Church, is a matter of conjecture. But, as Zahn observes, there is good reason to believe that the tradition handed down by Papias, of the approval of St. Mark's Gospel by St. John the Evangelist, reveals that either the latter himself or a college of his disciples added the Fourth Gospel to the Synoptics, and made the group into the compact and unalterable "Gospel", the one in four, whose existence and authority left their clear impress upon all subsequent ecclesiastical literature, and find their conscious formulation in the language of Irenæus.

4. The Pauline Epistles

Parallel to the chain of evidence we have traced for the canonical standing of the Gospels extends one for the thirteen Epistles of St. Paul, forming the other half of the irreducible kernel of the complete New Testament Canon. All the authorities cited for the Gospel Canon show acquaintance with, and recognize, the sacred quality of these letters. St. Irenæus, as acknowledged by the Harnackian critics, employs all the Pauline writings, except the short Philemon, as sacred and canonical. The Muratorian Canon,[9] contemporary with Irenæus, gives the complete list of the thirteen, which, it should be remembered, does not include Hebrews. The heretical Basilides and his disciples quote from this Pauline group in general. The copious extracts from Marcion's works scattered through Irenæus and Tertullian show that he was acquainted with the thirteen as in ecclesiastical use, and selected his *Apostolikon* of six from them. The testimony of Polycarp and Ignatius is again capital in this case. Eight of St. Paul's writings are cited by Polycarp; St. Ignatius of Antioch ranked the Apostles above the Prophets, and must therefore have allowed the written compositions of the former at least an equal rank with those of the latter ("Ad Philadelphios", v). St. Clement of Rome refers to Corinthians as at the head "of the Evangel"; the Muratorian Canon gives the same honour to I Corinthians, so that we may rightfully draw the inference, with Dr. Zahn, that as early as Clement's day St. Paul's Epistles had been collected and formed into a group with a fixed order. Zahn has pointed out confirmatory signs of this in the manner in which Sts. Ignatius and Polycarp employ these Epistles. The tendency of the evidence is to establish the hypothesis that the important Church of Corinth was the first to form a complete collection of St. Paul's writings.

5. The remaining Books

In this formative period the Epistle to the Hebrews did not obtain a firm footing in the Canon of the Universal Church. At Rome it was not yet recognized as canonical, as shown by the Muratorian catalogue of Roman origin; Irenæus probably cites it, but makes no reference to a Pauline origin. Yet it was known at Rome as early as St. Clement, as the latter's epistle attests. The Alexandrian Church admitted it as the work of St. Paul, and canonical. The Montanists favoured it, and the aptness with which vi, 4-8, lent itself to the Montanist and Novatianist rigour was doubtless one reason why it was suspect in the West. Also during this period the excess over the minimal Canon composed of the Gospels and thirteen epistles varied. The seven "Catholic" Epistles (James, Jude, I and II Peter, and the three of John) had not yet been brought into a special group, and, with the possible exception of the three of St. John, remained isolated units, depending for their canonical strength on variable circumstances. But towards the end of the second century the canonical minimum was enlarged and, besides the Gospels and Pauline Epistles, unalterably embraced Acts, I Peter, I John (to which II and III John were probably attached), and Apocalypse. Thus Hebrews, James, Jude, and II Peter remained hovering outside the precincts of universal canonicity, and the controversy about them and the subsequently disputed Apocalypse form the larger part of the remaining history of the Canon of the New Testament

However, at the beginning of the third century the New Testament was formed in the sense that the content of its main divisions, what may be called its essence, was sharply defined and universally received, while *all* the secondary books were recognized in some Churches. A singular exception to the universality of the above-described substance of the New Testament was the Canon of the primitive East Syrian Church, which did not contain any of the Catholic Epistles or Apocalypse.

6. The idea of a New Testament

The question of the principle that dominated the practical canonization of the New Testament Scriptures has already been discussed under paragraph A.2 above. The faithful must have had from the beginning some realization that in the writings of the Apostles and Evangelists they had acquired a new body of Divine Scriptures, a New written Testament destined to stand side by side with the Old. That the Gospel and Epistles were the written Word of God, was fully realized as soon as the fixed collections were formed; but to seize the relation of this new treasure to the old was possible only when the faithful acquired a better knowledge of the faith. In this connection Zahn observes with much truth that the rise of Montanism, with its false prophets, who claimed for their written productions--the self-styled Testament of the Paraclete--the authority of revelation, around the Christian Church to a fuller sense that the age of revelation had expired with the last of the Apostles, and that the circle of sacred Scripture is not extensible beyond the legacy of the Apostolic Era. Montanism began in 156; a generation later, in the works of Irenæus, we discover the firmly-rooted idea of two Testaments, with the same Spirit operating in both. For Tertullian (c. 200) the body of the New Scripture is an *instrumentum* on at least an equal footing and in the same specific class as the *instrumentum* formed by the Law and the Prophets. Clement of Alexandria was the first to apply the word "Testament" to the sacred library of the New Dispensation. A kindred external influence is to be added to Montanism: the need of setting up a barrier, between the genuine inspired literature and the flood of pseudo-Apostolic apocrypha, gave an additional impulse to the idea of a New Testament Canon, and later contributed not a little to the demarcation of its fixed limits.

B. THE PERIOD OF DISCUSSION (A.D. 220-367)

In this stage of the historical development of the Canon of the New Testament we encounter for the first time a consciousness reflected in certain ecclesiastical writers, of the differences between the sacred collections in divers sections of Christendom. This variation is witnessed to, and the discussion stimulated by, two of the most learned men of Christian antiquity,

Origen, and Eusebius of Cæsarea, the ecclesiastical historian. A glance at the Canon as exhibited in the authorities of the African, or Carthaginian, Church, will complete our brief survey of this period of diversity and discussion:-

1. Origen and his school

Origen's travels gave him exceptional opportunities to know the traditions of widely separated portions of the Church and made him very conversant with the discrepant attitudes toward certain parts of the New Testament He divided books with Biblical claims into three classes:

» those universally received;
» those whose Apostolicity was questioned;
» apocryphal works.

In the first class, the *Homologoumena*, stood the Gospels, the thirteen Pauline Epistles, Acts, Apocalypse, I Peter, and I John. The contested writings were Hebrews, II Peter, II and III John, James, Jude, Barnabas, the Shepherd of Hermas, the Didache, and probably the Gospel of the Hebrews. Personally, Origen accepted all of these as Divinely inspired, though viewing contrary opinions with toleration. Origen's authority seems to have given to Hebrews and the disputed Catholic Epistles a firm place in the Alexandrian Canon, their tenure there having been previously insecure, judging from the exegetical work of Clement, and the list in the Codex Claromontanus, which is assigned by competent scholars to an early Alexandrian origin.

2. Eusebius

Eusebius, Bishop of Cæsarea in Palestine, was one of Origen's most eminent disciples, a man of wide erudition. In imitation of his master he divided religious literature into three classes:

» *Homologoumena*, or compositions universally received as sacred, the Four Gospels, thirteen Epistles of St. Paul, Hebrews, Acts, I Peter, I John, and Apocalypse. There is some inconsistency in his classification; for instance, though ranking Hebrews with the books of universal reception, he elsewhere admits it is disputed.
» The second category is composed of the Antilegomena, or contested writings; these in turn are of the superior and inferior sort. The better ones are the Epistles of St. James and St. Jude, II Peter, II and III John; these, like Origen, Eusebius wished to be admitted to the Canon, but was forced to record their uncertain status; the Antilegomena of the inferior sort were Barnabas, the Didache, Gospel of the Hebrews, the Acts of Paul, the Shepherd, the Apocalypse of Peter.
» All the rest are spurious (*notha*).

Eusebius diverged from his Alexandrian master in personally rejecting Apocalypse as an un-Biblical, though compelled to acknowledge its almost universal acceptance. Whence came this unfavourable view of the closing volume of the Christian Testament?--Zahn attributes it to the influence of Lucian of Samosata, one of the founders of the Antioch school of exegesis, and with whose disciples Eusebius had been associated. Lucian himself had acquired his education at Edessa, the metropolis of Eastern Syria, which had, as already remarked, a singularly curtailed Canon. Luician is known to have edited the Scriptures at Antioch, and is supposed to have introduced there the shorter New Testament which later St. John Chrysostom and his followers employed--one in which Apocalypse, II Peter, II and III John, and Jude had no place. It is known that Theodore of Mopsuestia rejected all the Catholic Epistles.

In St. John Chrysostom's ample expositions of the Scriptures there is not a single clear trace of the Apocalypse, in which he seems to implicitly exclude the four smaller Epistles--II Peter, II and III John, and Jude--from the number of the canonical books. Lucian, then, according to Zahn, would have compromised between the Syriac Canon and the Canon of Origen by admitting the three longer Catholic Epistles and keeping out Apocalypse. But after allowing fully for the prestige of the founder of the Antioch school, it is difficult to grant that his personal authority could have sufficed to strike such an important work as Apocalypse from the Canon of a notable Church, where it had previously been received. It is more probable that a reaction against the abuse of the Johannine Apocalypse by the Montanists and Chiliasts--Asia Minor being the nursery of both these errors--led to the elimination of a book whose authority had perhaps been previously suspected. Indeed it is quite reasonable to suppose that its early exclusion from the East Syrian Church was an outer wave of the extreme reactionist movement of the Aloges--also of Asia Minor--who branded Apocalypse and all the Johannine writings as the work of the heretic Cerinthus.

Whatever may have been all the influences ruling the personal Canon of Eusebius, he chose Lucian's text for the fifty copies of the Bible which he furnished to the Church of Constantinople at the order of his imperial patron Constantine; and he incorporated all the Catholic Epistles, but excluded Apocalypse. The latter remained for more than a century banished from the sacred collections as current in Antioch and Constantinople. However, this book kept a minority of Asiatic suffrages, and, as both Lucian and Eusebius had been tainted with Arianism, the approbation of Apocalypse, opposed by them, finally came to be looked upon as a sign of orthodoxy. Eusebius was the first to call attention to important variations in the text of the Gospels, viz., the presence in some copies and the absence in others of the final paragraph of Mark, the passage of the Adulterous Woman, and the Bloody Sweat.

3. The African Church

St. Cyprian, whose Scriptural Canon certainly reflects the contents of the first Latin Bible, received all the books of the New Testament except Hebrews, II Peter, James, and Jude; however, there was already a strong inclination in his environment to admit II Peter as authentic. Jude had been recognized by Tertullian, but, strangely, it had lost its position in the African Church, probably owing to its citation of the apocryphal Henoch. Cyprian's testimony to the non-canonicity of Hebrews and James is confirmed by Commodian, another African writer of the period. A very important witness is the document known as Mommsen's Canon, a manuscript of the tenth century, but whose original has been ascertained to date from West Africa about the year 360. It is a formal catalogue of the sacred books, unmutilated in the New Testament portion, and proves that at its time the books universally acknowledged in the influential Church of Carthage were almost identical with those received by Cyprian a century before. Hebrews, James, and Jude are entirely wanting. The three Epistles of St. John and II Peter appear, but after each stands the note *una sola*, added by an almost contemporary hand, and evidently in protest against the reception of these Antilegomena, which, presumably, had found a place in the official list recently, but whose right to be there was seriously questioned.

C. THE PERIOD OF FIXATION (A.D. 367-405)

1. St. Athanasius

While the influence of Athanasius on the Canon of the Old Testament was negative and exclusive (see *supra*), in that of the New Testament it was trenchantly constructive. In his "Epistola Festalis" (A.D. 367) the illustrious Bishop of Alexandria ranks all of Origen's New Testament Antilegomena, which are identical with the deuteros, boldly inside the Canon, without noticing any of the scruples about them. Thenceforward they were formally and firmly fixed in the Alexandrian Canon. And it is significant of the general trend of ecclesiastical authority that not only were works which formerly enjoyed high standing at broad-minded Alexandria--the Apocalypse of Peter and the Acts of Paul--involved by Athanasius with the apocrypha, but even some that Origen had regarded as inspired--Barnabas, the Shepherd of Hermas, the Didache--were ruthlessly shut out under the same damnatory title.

2. The Roman Church, the Synod under Damasus, and St. Jerome

The Muratorian Canon or Fragment, composed in the Roman Church in the last quarter of the second century, is silent about Hebrews, James,

II Peter; I Peter, indeed, is not mentioned, but must have been omitted by an oversight, since it was universally received at the time. There is evidence that this restricted Canon obtained not only in the African Church, with slight modifications, as we have seen, but also at Rome and in the West generally until the close of the fourth century. The same ancient authority witnesses to the very favourable and perhaps canonical standing enjoyed at Rome by the Apocalypse of Peter and the Shepherd of Hermas. In the middle decades of the fourth century the increased intercourse and exchange of views between the Orient and the Occident led to a better mutual acquaintance regarding Biblical canons and the correction of the catalogue of the Latin Church. It is a singular fact that while the East, mainly through St. Jerome's pen, exerted a disturbing and negative influence on Western opinion regarding the Old Testament, the same influence, through probably the same chief intermediary, made for the completeness and integrity of the New Testament Canon. The West began to realize that the ancient Apostolic Churches of Jerusalem and Antioch, indeed the whole Orient, for more than two centuries had acknowledged Hebrews and James as inspired writings of Apostles, while the venerable Alexandrian Church, supported by the prestige of Athanasius, and the powerful Patriarchate of Constantinople, with the scholarship of Eusebius behind its judgment, had canonized all the disputed Epistles. St. Jerome, a rising light in the Church, though but a simple priest, was summoned by Pope Damasus from the East, where he was pursuing sacred lore, to assist at an eclectic, but not ecumenical, synod at Rome in the year 382. Neither the general council at Constantinople of the preceding year nor that of Nice (365) had considered the question of the Canon. This Roman synod must have devoted itself specially to the matter. The result of its deliberations, presided over, no doubt, by the energetic Damasus himself, has been preserved in the document called "Decretum Gelasii de recipiendis et non recipiendis libris", a compilation partly of the sixth century, but containing much material dating from the two preceding ones. The Damasan catalogue presents the complete and perfect Canon which has been that of the Church Universal ever since. The New Testament portion bears the marks of Jerome's views. St. Jerome, always prepossessed in favour of Oriental positions in matters Biblical, exerted then a happy influence in regard to the New Testament; if he attempted to place any Eastern restriction upon the Canon of the Old Testament his effort failed of any effect. The title of the decree--"Nunc vero de scripturis divinis agendum est quid universalis Catholica recipiat ecclesia, et quid vitare debeat"--proves that the council drew up a list of apocryphal as well as authentic Scriptures. The Shepherd and the false Apocalypse of Peter now received their final blow. "Rome had spoken, and the nations of the West had heard" (Zahn). The works of the Latin Fathers of the period--Jerome, Hilary of Poitiers, Lucifer of Sardina, Philaster of Brescia--manifest the changed attitude toward Hebrews, James, Jude, II Peter, and III John.

3. Fixation in the African and Gallican Churches

It was some little time before the African Church perfectly adjusted its New Testament to the Damasan Canon. Optatus of Mileve (370-85) does not use Hebrews. St. Augustine, while himself receiving the integral Canon, acknowledged that many contested this Epistle. But in the Synod of Hippo (393) the great Doctor's view prevailed, and the correct Canon was adopted. However, it is evident that it found many opponents in Africa, since three councils there at brief intervals--Hippo, Carthage, in 393; Third of Carthage in 397; Carthage in 419--found it necessary to formulate catalogues. The introduction of Hebrews was an especial crux, and a reflection of this is found in the first Carthage list, where the much vexed Epistle, though styled of St. Paul, is still numbered separately from the time-consecrated group of thirteen. The catalogues of Hippo and Carthage are identical with the Catholic Canon of the present. In Gaul some doubts lingered for a time, as we find Pope Innocent I, in 405, sending a list of the Sacred Books to one of its bishops, Exsuperius of Toulouse.

So at the close of the first decade of the fifth century the entire Western Church was in possession of the full Canon of the New Testament In the East, where, with the exception of the Edessene Syrian Church, approximate completeness had long obtained without the aid of formal enactments, opinions were still somewhat divided on the Apocalypse. But for the Catholic Church as a whole the content of the New Testament was definitely fixed, and the discussion closed.

The final process of this Canon's development had been twofold: positive, in the permanent consecration of several writings which had long hovered on the line between canonical and apocryphal; and negative, by the definite elimination of certain privileged apocrypha that had enjoyed here and there a canonical or quasi-canonical standing. In the reception of the disputed books a growing conviction of Apostolic authorship had much to do, but the ultimate criterion had been their recognition as inspired by a great and ancient division of the Catholic Church.

Thus, like Origen, St. Jerome adduces the *testimony of the ancients* and ecclesiastical usage in pleading the cause of the Epistle to the Hebrews (De Viris Illustribus, lix). There is no sign that the Western Church ever positively repudiated any of the New Testament deuteros; not admitted from the beginning, these had slowly advanced towards a complete acceptance there. On the other hand, the apparently formal exclusion of Apocalypse from the sacred catalogue of certain Greek Churches was a transient phase, and supposes its primitive reception. Greek Christianity everywhere, from about the beginning of the sixth century, practically had a complete and pure New Testament canon.

(*See* EPISTLE TO THE HEBREWS; EPISTLES OF ST. PETER; EPISTLE OF JAMES; EPISTLE OF JUDE; EPISTLES OF JOHN; APOCALYPSE.)

D. SUBSEQUENT HISTORY OF THE NEW TESTAMENT CANON

1. To the Protestant Reformation

The New Testament in its canonical aspect has little history between the first years of the fifth and the early part of the sixteenth century. As was natural in ages when ecclesiastical authority had not reached its modern centralization, there were sporadic divergences from the common teaching and tradition. There was no diffused contestation of any book, but here and there attempts by individuals to *add* something to the received collection. In several ancient Latin manuscripts the spurious Epistle to the Laodiceans is found among the canonical letters, and, in a few instances, the apocryphal III Corinthians. The last trace of any Western contradiction within the Church to the Canon of the New Testament reveals a curious transplantation of Oriental doubts concerning the Apocalypse. An act of the Synod of Toledo, held in 633, states that many contest the authority of that book, and orders it to be read in the Churches under pain of excommunication. The opposition in all probability came from the Visigoths, who had recently been converted from Arianism. The Gothic Bible had been made under Oriental auspices at a time when there was still much hostility to Apocalypse in the East.

2. The New Testament and the Council of Trent (1546)

This ecumenical synod had to defend the integrity of the New Testament as well as the Old. Luther[10], basing his action on dogmatic reasons and the judgment of antiquity, had discarded Hebrews, James, Jude, and Apocalypse as altogether uncanonical. Zwingli could not see in Apocalypse a Biblical book. (OEcolampadius[11] placed James, Jude, II Peter, II and III John in an inferior rank. Even a few Catholic scholars of the Renaissance type, notably Erasmus and Cajetan, had thrown some doubts on the canonicity of the above-mentioned Antilegomena. As to whole books, the Protestant doubts were the only ones the Fathers of Trent took cognizance of; there was not the slightest hesitation regarding the authority of any entire document. But the deuterocanonical parts gave the council some concern, viz., the last twelve verses of Mark, the passage about the Bloody Sweat in Luke, and the *Pericope Adulteræ* in John. Cardinal Cajetan had approvingly quoted an unfavourable comment of St. Jerome regarding Mark, xvi, 9-20; Erasmus had rejected the section on the Adulterous Woman as unauthentic. Still, even concerning these no doubt of authenticity was expressed at Trent; the only question was as to the manner of their reception. In the end these portions were received, like the deuterocanonical books, without the slightest distinction. And the clause "cum omnibus suis partibus" regards especially these portions.--For an account of the action of Trent on the Canon, the reader is referred back to the respective section of the article: *The Canon of the Old Testament in the Catholic Church*.[12]

The Tridentine decree defining the Canon affirms the authenticity of the books to which proper names are attached, without however including this in the definition. The order of books follows that of the Bull of Eugenius IV (Council of Florence), except that Acts was moved from a place before Apocalypse to its present position, and Hebrews put at the end of St. Paul's Epistles. The Tridentine order has been retained in the official Vulgate and vernacular Catholic Bibles. The same is to be said of the titles, which as a rule are traditional ones, taken from the Canons of Florence and Carthage. (For the bearing of the Vatican Council [of 1870 AD] on the New Testament, see Appendix A above.)

3. The New Testament Canon outside the [Roman Catholic] Church

The Orthodox Russian and other branches of the Eastern Orthodox Church have a New Testament identical with the Catholic. In Syria the Nestorians possess a Canon almost identical with the final one of the ancient East Syrians; they exclude the four smaller Catholic Epistles and Apocalypse. The Monophysites receive all the books. The Armenians have one apocryphal letter *to* the Corinthians and two *from* the same. The Coptic-Arabic Church include with the canonical Scriptures the Apostolic Constitutions and the Clementine Epistles. The Ethiopic New Testament also contains the so-called "Apostolic Constitutions".

As for Protestantism, the Anglicans and Calvinists always kept the entire New Testament. But for over a century the followers of Luther excluded Hebrews, James, Jude, and Apocalypse, and even went further than their master by rejecting the three remaining deuterocanonicals, II Peter, II and III John. The trend of the seventeenth century Lutheran theologians was to class all these writings as of doubtful, or at least inferior, authority. But gradually the German Protestants familiarized themselves with the idea that the difference between the contested books of the New Testament and the rest was one of degree of certainty as to origin rather than of intrinsic character. The full recognition of these books by the Calvinists and Anglicans made it much more difficult for the Lutherans to exclude the New Testament deuteros than those of the Old. One of their writers of the seventeenth century allowed only a theoretic difference between the two classes, and in 1700 Bossuet could say that all Catholics and Protestants agreed on the New Testament Canon. The only trace of opposition now remaining in German Protestant Bibles is in the order, Hebrews, coming with James, Jude, and Apocalypse at the end; the first not being included with the Pauline writings, while James and Jude are not ranked with the Catholic Epistles.

4. The criterion of inspiration (less correctly known as the criterion of canonicity)

Even those Catholic theologians who defend Apostolicity as a test for the inspiration of the New Testament (see above) admit that it is not exclusive of another criterion, viz., Catholic tradition as manifested in the universal reception of compositions as Divinely inspired, or the ordinary teaching of the Church, or the infallible pronouncements of ecumenical councils. This external guarantee is the sufficient, universal, and ordinary proof of inspiration. The unique quality of the Sacred Books is a revealed dogma. Moreover, by its very nature inspiration eludes human observation and is not self-evident, being essentially superphysical and supernatural. Its sole absolute criterion, therefore, is the Holy inspiring Spirit, witnessing decisively to Itself, not in the subjective experience of individual souls, as Calvin maintained, neither in the doctrinal and spiritual tenor of Holy Writ itself, according to Luther, but through the constituted organ and custodian of Its revelations, the [Roman Catholic] Church. All other evidences fall short of the certainty and finality necessary to compel the absolute assent of faith. (See Franzelin, "De Divinâ Traditione et Scripturâ"; Wiseman, "Lectures on Christian Doctrine", Lecture ii; also INSPIRATION.)

About this page

APA citation. *Reid, G. (1908). Canon of the New Testament. In The Catholic Encyclopedia. New York: Robert Appleton Company. Retrieved April 26, 2010 from New Advent: http://www.newadvent.org/cathen/03274a.htm*

MLA citation. *Reid, George. «Canon of the New Testament.» The Catholic Encyclopedia. Vol. 3. New York: Robert Appleton Company, 1908. 26 Apr. 2010 <http://www.newadvent.org/cathen/03274a.htm>.*

Transcription. *This article was transcribed for New Advent by Ernie Stefanik.*

Ecclesiastical approbation. *Nihil Obstat. November 1, 1908. Remy Lafort, S.T.D., Censor. Imprimatur. +John Cardinal Farley, Archbishop of New York.*

Contact information. *The editor of New Advent is Kevin Knight. My email address is* webmaster@newadvent.org.

* * *

1. See the Bibliography under New Advent, including WWW.NewAdvent.org
2. [Own Note] For Appendix B, I have added numbers to the sub-paragraph headings within the article.
3. Written by George J. Reid. Transcribed by Ernie Stefanik. The Catholic Encyclopedia, Volume III. Published 1908. New York: Robert Appleton Company. (New Advent on the Web).
4. [Own Note] It is interesting that in the earliest years of the Church, the Letter to the Hebrews was not assumed to be one of Paul's, which aligns with the view prevalent today.
5. [Own Note] Entries like this are cross-references to such entries elsewhere in New Advent.
6. [Own Note] It is intriguing that the compilers of the Catholic Encyclopaedia of 1908, based upon the assumption "…that Apostolic authorship is a positive criterion of inspiration…", attach the adjective "inspired" to the two missing epistles. Apostolic authorship being a positive criterion is one thing, for it to be a *sufficient* criterion is surely a separate issue, and I have been inclined to speculate that perhaps Paul had said things in the two missing letters to his problematic congregation in Corinth that many years later he had wished that he had left unsaid or perhaps communicated in a different tone.
7. [Own Note] Cf., Artefact #8, Chapter 11, of Book Two (*The Great Collaboration*) in this collection.
8. [Own Note] The period 100 AD onwards was called the sub-Apostolic age by the Catholic Encyclopaedia of 1908, but is what Raymond E. Brown et al referred to as the post-Apostolic age. Brown reserved the designation sub-Apostolic to the earlier period of AD 67–100. Cf. Section B of Book Four (*The Jigsaw Puzzle Church*) in this collection.
9. [Own Note] cf. Appendix C in this present volume.
10. [Own Note] The ecumenically-insensitive Catholic Encyclopaedia of 1908 had used the designation "pseudo-Reformer" here in referring to Martin Luther.,
11. [Own Note] Johannes Œcolampadius, or Œkolampad (German: Johannes Oekolampad) (1482 – 24 November 1531.
12. Appendix A.

* * *

Appendix C - The Muratorian Fragment

(Two representations)

The **Muratorian Fragment** is the oldest[1] known list of New Testament books. It was discovered by Ludovico Antonio Muratori in a manuscript in the Ambrosian Library in Milan, and published by him in 1740. * It is called a fragment because the beginning of it is missing. Although the manuscript in which it appears was copied during the seventh century, the list itself is dated to about 170 because its author refers to the episcopate of Pius I of Rome (died 157) as recent. He mentions only two epistles of John, without describing them. The Apocalypse of Peter is mentioned as a book which "some of us will not allow to be read in Church." A very helpful and detailed discussion of this document is to be found in Bruce Metzger's *The Canon of the New Testament* (Oxford: Clarendon Press, 1987), pp. 191-201. Below is Metzger's English translation of a critically amended text of the Fragment, from Appendix IV of the same book (pp. 305-7). I include Metzger's footnotes, with their original enumeration, and add some supplementary footnotes of my own. —M.D.M.[2]

---

* Ludovico Antonio Muratori, ed., *Antiquitates Italicae Medii Aevi*, v. 3 (ex typographia Societatis palatinæ, Mediolani, 1740). Reprinted in Bologna, 1965.

* * *

THE MURATORIAN CANON

(First representation)

The following translation usually follows the amended text edited by Hans Lietzmann, *Das Muratorische Fragment und die Monarchianischen Prologue zu den Evangelien* (*Kleine Texte*, i; Bonn, 1902; 2nd ed., Berlin, 1933). Owing to the wretched state of the Latin text, it is sometimes difficult to know what the writer intended; several phrases, therefore, are provided with alternative renderings (enclosed within parentheses). Translational expansions are enclosed within square brackets. The numerals indicate the lines of the original text. For a discussion, see chap. VIII.1 above, where freer renderings are sometimes given in place of the following literalistic translation.

. . . at which nevertheless he was present, and so he placed [them in his narrative].[3] (2) The third book of the Gospel is that according to Luke. (3) Luke, the well-known physician, after the ascension of Christ, (4-5) when Paul had taken with him as one zealous for the law,[4] (6) composed it in his own name, according to [the general] belief.[5] Yet he himself had not (7) seen the Lord in the flesh; and therefore, as he was able to ascertain events, (8) so indeed he begins to tell the story from the birth of John. (9) The fourth of the Gospels is that of John, [one] of the disciples. (10) To his fellow disciples and bishops, who had been urging him [to write], (11) he said, "Fast with me from today to three days, and what (12) will be revealed to each one (13) let us tell it to one another." In the same night it was revealed (14) to Andrew, [one] of the apostles, (15-16) that John should write down all things in his own name while all of them should review it. And so, though various (17) elements[6] may be taught in the individual books of the Gospels, (18) nevertheless this makes no difference to the faith of believers, since by the one sovereign[7] Spirit all things (20) have been declared in all [the Gospels]: concerning the (21) nativity, concerning the passion, concerning the resurrection, (22) concerning life with his disciples, (23) and concerning his twofold coming; (24) the first in lowliness when he was despised, which has taken place, (25) the second glorious in royal power, (26) which is still in the future. What (27) marvel is it then, if John so consistently (28) mentions these particular points also in his Epistles, (29) saying about himself, "What we have seen with our eyes (30) and heard with our ears and our hands (31) have handled, these things we have written to you?[8] (32) For in this way he professes [himself] to be not only an eye-witness and hearer, (33) but also a writer of all the marvellous deeds of the Lord, in their order. (34) Moreover, the acts of all the apostles (35) were written in one book. For "most excellent Theophilus"[9] Luke compiled (36) the individual events that took place in his presence — (37) as he plainly shows by omitting the martyrdom of Peter (38) as well as the departure of Paul from the city [of Rome][10] (39) when he journeyed to Spain. As for the Epistles of (40-1) Paul, they themselves make clear to those desiring to understand, which ones [they are], from what place, or for what reason they were sent. (42) First of all, to the Corinthians, prohibiting their heretical schisms; (43) next,[11] to the Galatians, against circumcision; (44-6) then to the Romans he wrote at length, explaining the order (or, plan) of the Scriptures, and also that Christ is their principle (or, main theme).[12] It is necessary (47) for us to discuss these one by one, since the blessed (48) apostle Paul himself, following the example of his predecessor (49-50) John, writes by name to only seven Churches in the following sequence: To the Corinthians (51) first, to the Ephesians second, to the Philippians third, (52) to the Colossians fourth, to the Galatians fifth, (53) to the Thessalonians sixth, to the Romans (54-5) seventh. It is true that he writes once more to the Corinthians and to the Thessalonians for the sake of admonition, (56-7) yet it is clearly recognizable that there is one Church spread throughout the whole extent of the earth. For John also in the (58) Apocalypse, though he writes to seven Churches, (59-60) nevertheless speaks to all. [Paul also wrote] out of affection and love one to Philemon, one to Titus, and two to Timothy; and these are held sacred (62-3) in the esteem of the Church catholic for the regulation of ecclesiastical discipline. There is current also [an epistle] to (64) the Laodiceans, [and] another to the Alexandrians, [both] forged in Paul's (65) name to [further] the heresy of Marcion,[13] and several others (66) which cannot be received into the catholic Church (67)— for it is not fitting that gall be mixed with honey. (68) Moreover, the epistle of Jude and two of the above-mentioned (or, bearing the name of) John are counted (or, used) in the catholic [Church];[14] and [the book of] Wisdom, (70) written by the friends[15] of Solomon in his honour. (71) We receive only the apocalypses of John and Peter, (72)[16] though some of us are not willing that the latter be read in Church. (73) But Hermas wrote the *Shepherd* (74) very recently,[17] in our times, in the city of Rome, (75) while bishop Pius, his brother, was occupying the [episcopal] chair (76) of the Church of the city of Rome.[18] (77) And therefore it ought indeed to be read; but (78) it cannot be read publicly to the people in Church either among (79) the Prophets, whose number is complete,[19] or among (80) the Apostles, for it is after [their] time. (81) But we accept nothing whatever of Arsinous or Valentinus or Miltiades, (82) who also composed (83) a new book of psalms for Marcion, (84-5) together with Basilides, the Asian founder of the Cataphrygians[20]...

* * *

Latin Text of the Fragment

The Latin text of the fragment, which is believed by most scholars to be a translation from Greek, is full of barbarisms and obscurities. Various scholars have published emended texts, as for example Westcott in his *General Survey of the History of the Canon of the New Testament* (London, 1870). For a critical edition and commentary see S.P. Tregelles, Canon *Muratorianus: The*

Earliest Catalogue of the Books of the New Testament, Edited with Notes and a Facsimile of the MS. in the Ambrosian Library at Milan (Oxford: Clarendon Press, 1867). I give the original text below, without any alteration, and with the original line breaks, as printed in Henry M. Gwatkin, ed., *Selections from Early Writers Illustrative of Church History to the Time of Constantine* (London: MacMillan and co., 1937), pp. 82-88. The horizontal line put over some letters is the scribe's mark of abbreviation.

1. ...quibus tamen interfuit et ita posuit
2. tertio evangelii librum secundo lucan
3. lucas iste medicus post ascensum XPi
4. cum eo paulus quasi ut juris studiosum
5. secundum adsumsisset numeni suo
6. ex opinione conscripset dnm tamen nec ipse
7. vidit in carne et ide prout asequi potuit
8. ita et ad nativitate iohannis incipet dicere.
9. quarti evangeliorum iohannis ex decipolis.
10. cohortantibus condescipulis et eps suis
11. dixit conieiunate mihi odie triduo et quid
12. cuique fuerit revelatum alterutrum
13. nobis ennarremus eadem nocte reve
14. latum andreae ex apostolis ut recognis
15. centibus cuntis iohannis suo nomine
16. cuncta describeret et ideo licet varia sin
17. culis evangeliorum libris principia
18. doceantur nihil tamen differt creden
19. tium fidei cum uno ac principali spu de
20. clarata sint in omnibus omnia de nativi
21. tate de passione de resurrectione
22. de conversatione cum decipulis suis
23. ac de gemino eius adventu
24. primo in humilitate dispectus quod fo
25. it secundum potestate regali ... pre
26. clarum quod foturum est quid ergo
27. mirum si iohannes tam constanter
28. sincula etia in epistulis suis proferam
29. dicens in semeipsu quae vidimus oculis
30. nostris et auribus audivimus et manus
31. nostrae palpaverunt haec scripsimus vobis
32. sic enim non solum visurem sed et auditorem
33. sed et scriptore omnium mirabiliu dni per ordi
34. nem proftetur acta aute omniu apostolorum
35. sub uno libro scribta sunt lucas obtime theofi
36. le comprindit quia sub praesentia eius sincula
37. gerebantur sicuti et semote passione petri
38. evidenter declarat sed et profectione pauli ab ur
39. be ad spania proficiscentis epistulae autem
40. pauli quae a quo loco vel qua ex causa directe

138

41. sint volentibus intellegere ipse declarant
42. primu omnium corintheis scysmae heresis in
43. terdicens deinceps b callaetis circumcisione
44. romanis aute ordine scripturarum sed et
45. principium earum ... esse XPm intimans
46. prolexius scripsit de quibus sincolis neces
47. se est ad nobis disputari cum ipse beatus
48. apostolus paulus sequens prodecessoris sui
49. iohannis ordine non nisi nominati sempte
50. ecclesiis scribat ordine tali a corenthios
51. prima ad efesius seconda ad philippinses ter
52. tia ad colosensis quarta ad calatas quin
53. ta ad tensaolenecinsis sexta ad romanos
54. septima verum corintheis et thesaolecen
55. sibus licet pro correbtione iteretur una
56. tamen per omnem orbem terrae ecclesia
57. deffusa esse denoscitur et iohannis eni in a
58. pocalebsy licet septe eccleseis scribat
59. tamen omnibus dicit veru ad filemonem una
60. et at titu una et ad tymotheu duas pro affec
61. to et dilectione in honore tamen eclesiae ca
62. tholice in ordinatione eclesiastice
63. discepline scificate sunt fertur etiam ad
64. laudecenses alia ad alexandrinos pauli no
65. mine fincte ad heresem marcionis et alia plu
66. ra quae in catholicam eclesiam recepi non
67. potest fel enim cum melle misceri non con
68. cruit epistola sane iude et superscrictio
69. iohannis duas in catholica habentur et sapi
70. entia ab amicis salomonis in honore ipsius
71. scripta apocalapse etiam iohanis et pe
72. tri tantum recipimus quam quidam ex nos
73. tris legi in eclesia nolunt pastorem vero
74. nuperrim e temporibus nostris in urbe
75. roma herma conscripsit sedente cathe
76. tra urbis romae aecclesiae pio eps fratre
77. eius et ideo legi eum quide oportet se pu
78. blicare vero in eclesia populo neque inter
79. profetas completum numero neque inter
80. apostolos in fine temporum potest
81. arsinoi autem seu valentini vel mitiadis [?]
82. nihil in totum recipemus qui etiam novu
83. psalmorum librum marcioni conscripse
84. runt una cum basilide assianom catafry
85. cum constitutorem ...

* * *

The Muratorian Fragment

(Second representation)

The single eighth century manuscript, published by Muratori in 1740, suffers from barbarous spelling. The English translation and the Latin, both the original of Muratori and the restored reading, are taken from Theron in *Evidence of Tradition*, pp. 106-113. The Latin text is thought to be based on an earlier Greek text. If you would like to see a fourth column with Lightfoot's retranslation into Greek, go to the Muratorian Canon in Latin and Greek web page.[21] Underlining represents supralinear strokes, and striked text means that the scribe corrected the letters striked. Since I have not encountered a division into verses, such division is my own.[22]

Latin (Original)	Latin (Restored)	English (Theron)
[1] quibus tamen interfuit et ita posuit. tertio euangelii librum secundo lucan [3] lucas iste medicus [4] post ascensum xri. [5] cum eo paulus quasi ut iuris studiosum [6] secundum adsumsisset numeni suo ex opinione concripset [7] dnm tamen nec ipse d uidit in carne [8] et ide prout asequi potuit. [9] ita et ad natiuitate iohannis incipet dicere,	[1] quibus tamen interfuit et ita posuit. [2] tertium euangelii librum secundum Lucam. [3] Lucas iste medicus [4] post ascensum Christi [5] cum eum Paulus quasi itineris sui socium [6] secum adsumsisset nomine suo ex opinione conscripsit — [7] Dominum tamen nec ipse uidit in carne — [8] et idem prout assequi potuit: [9] ita et a nativitate Iohannis incepit dicere.	[1] ... But he was present among them, and so he put [the facts down in his Gospel.] [2] The third book of the Gospel [is that] according to Luke. [3] Luke, "the" physician, [4] after the ascension of Christ, [5] when Paul had taken him with him as a companion of his traveling, [6] [and after he had made] an investigation, wrote in his own name — [7] but neither did he see the Lord in the flesh — [8] and thus, as he was able to investigate, [9] so he also begins to tell the story [starting] from the nativity of John.
[10] quarti euangeliorum iohannis ex decipolis	[10] quarti euangeliorum Iohannis ex discipulis.	[10] The fourth [book] of the Gospels is that of John [one] of the

[11] cohortantibus condescipulis et eps suis dixit [12] conieiunate mihi. odie triduo [13] et quid cuique fuerit reuelatum alterutrum nobis ennarremus [14] eadem nocte reuelatum andreae ex apostolis ut recogniscentibus cuntis iohannis suo nomine cuncta discriberet	[11] cohortantibus condiscipulis et episcopis suis dixit [12] Conieiunate mihi hodie triduum, [13] et quid cuique fuerit reuelatum alteratrum nobis enarremus. [14] eadem nocte reuelatum Andreae ex apostolis, ut recognoscentibus cunctis, Iohannes suo nomine cuncta describeret.	disciples. [11] When his fellow-disciples and bishops urged [him], he said: [12] "Fast together with me today for three days [13] and, what shall be revealed to each, let us tell [it] to each other." [14] On that same night it was revealed to Andrew, [one] of the Apostles, that, with all of them reviewing [it], John should describe all things in his own name.
[15] et ideo licit uaria sinculis euangeliorum libris principia doceantur [16] nihil tamen differt credentium fidei [17] cum uno ac principali spu declarate sint in omnibus omnia [18] de natiuitate de passione de resurrectione de conuersatione cum decipulis suis [19] ac de gemino eius aduentu primo in humilitate dispectus quod fotu secundum potestate regali preclarum quod foturum est.	[15] et ideo licet varia singulis euangeliorum libris principia doceantur [16] nihil tamen differt credentium fidei, [17] cum uno ac principali spiritu declarata sint in omnibus omnia [18] de natiuitate, de passione, de resurrectione, de conuersatione cum discipulis suis, [19] et de gemino eius aduentu, primum in humilitate despectus, quod fuit, secundum potestate regali praeclarum, quod futurum est.	[15] And so, although different beginnings might be taught in the separate books of the Gospels, [16] nevertheless it makes no difference to the faith of believers, [17] since all things in all [of them] are declared by the one sovereign Spirit — [18] concering [His] nativity, concerning [His] passion, concerning [His] resurrection, concerning [His] walk with His disciples, [19] and concerning His double advent: the first in humility when He was despised, which has been; the second in royal power, glorious, which is to be.
[20] quid ergo mirum si iohannes tam constanter sincula etia in epistulis	[20] quid ergo mirum, si Iohannes tam constanter singula etiam in epistolis	[20] What marvel, therefore, if John so constantly brings

suis proferam dicens in semeipsu [21] quae uidimus oculis nostris et auribus audiuimus et manus nostrae palpauerunt haec scripsimus uobis [22] sic enim non solum uisurem sed & auditorem sed & scriptore omnium mirabiliu dni per ordinem profetetur	suis proferat dicens in semetipso [21] Quae uidimus oculis nostris, et auribus audiuimus, et manus nostrae palpauerunt, haec scripsimus uobis? [22] Sic enim non solum uisorem, sed et auditorem, sed et scriptorem omnium mirabilium Domini per ordinem profitetur.	forward particular [matters] also in his Epistles, saying of himself: [21] "What we have seen with our eyes and have heard with [our] ears and our hands have handled, these things we have written to you." [22] For thus he declares that he was not only an eyewitness and hearer, but also a writer of all the wonderful things of the Lord in order.
[23] acta aute omniu apostolorum sub uno libro scribta sunt [24] lucas obtime theofile conprindit quia sub praesentia eius singula gerebantur [25] sicute et semote passione petri euidenter declarat [26] sed & profectione pauli ab urbe ad spania proficescentis	[23] Acta autem omnium apostolorum sub uno libro scripta sunt. [24] Lucas "optimo Theophilo" comprehendit, quae sub praesentia eius singula gerebantur, [25] sicut et remote passionem Petri evidenter declarat, [26] sed et profectionem Pauli ab urbe ad Spaniam proficiscentis.	[23] The Acts of all the Apostles, however, were written in one volume. [24] Luke described briefly "for" most excellent Theophilus particular [things], which happened in his presence, [25] as he also evidently relates the death of Peter (?) [26] and also Paul's departure from the city as he was proceeding to Spain.
[27] epistulae autem pauli quae a quo loco uel qua ex causa directe sint uolentatibus intellegere ipse declarant [28] primu omnium corintheis scysmae heresis interdicens [29] deinceps b callatis circumcisione [30] romanis aute ornidine	[27] Epistolae autem Pauli, quae, a quo loco, uel qua ex causa directae sint, uolentibus intelligere ipsae declarant. [28] primum omnium Corinthiis schisma haeresis interdicens, [29] deinceps Galatis	[27] The Epistles of Paul themselves, however, show to those, who wish to know, which [they are], from what place, and for what cause they were sent. [28] First of all he wrote to the Corinthians, admonishing against schism of heresy;

scripturarum sed et principium earum osd esse xpm intimans prolexius scripsit	circumcisionem, [30] Romanis autem ordine scripturarum, sed et principium earum esse Christum intimans, prolixius scripsit;	[29] thereupon to the Galatians [admonishing against] circumcision; [30] to the Romans, however, [he wrote] rather lengthily pointing out with a series of Scripture quotations that Christ is their main theme also (?).
[31] de quibus sincolis necesse est ad nobis desputari [32] cum ipse beatus apostolus paulus sequens prodecessuris sui iohannis ordine non nisi nomenati semptae ecclesiis scribat ordine tali [33] a corenthios prima. ad efesius seconda ad philippinses tertia ad colosensis quarta ad calatas quinta ad tensaolenicinsis sexta. ad romanos septima	[31] de quibus singulis necesse est a nobis disputari; [32] cum ipse beatus Apostolus Paulus sequens prodecessoris sui Iohannis ordinem, nonnisi nominatim septem ecclesiis scribat ordine tali: [33] ad Corinthios prima, ad Ephesios secunda, ad Philippenses tertia, ad Colossenses quarta, ad Galatas quinta, ad Thessalonicensibus sexta, ad Romanos septima.	[31] But it is necessary that we have a discussion singly concerning these, [32] since the blessed Apostle Paul himself, imitating the example of his predecessor, John, wrote to seven Churches only by name [and] in this order: [33] The first [Epistle] to the Corinthians, the second to the Ephesians, the third to the Philippians, the fourth to the Colossians, the fifth to the Galatians, the sixth to the Thessalonians, and the seventh to the Romans.
[34] uerum corentheis et thesaolecensibus licet pro correbtione iteretur [35] una tamen per omnem orbem terrae ecclesia deffusa esse denoscitur [36] et iohannis eni in apocalebsy licet septe eccleseis scribat tamen omnibus dicit	[34] uerum Corinthiis, et Thessalonicensibus licet pro correptione iteretur, [35] una tamen per omnem orbem terrae ecclesia diffusa esse denoscitur. [36] et Iohannes enim in Apocalypsi licet septem ecclesiis scribat, tamen omnibus dicit.	[34] But, although he wrote twice to the Corinthians and to the Thessalonians, for reproof (?), [35] nevertheless [it is evident that] one Church is made known to be diffused throughout the whole globe of the earth. [36] For John also,

		though he wrote in the Apocalypse to seven Churches, nevertheless he speaks to them all.
[37] ueru ad filemonem una et at titu una et ad tymotheu duas pro affecto et dilectione [38] in honore tamen eclesiae catholice in ordinatione eclesiastice descepline scificate sunt.	[37] uerum ad Philemonem unam, et ad Titum unam, et ad Timotheum duas pro affectu et dilectione; [38] in honore tamen ecclesiae catholicae in ordinatione ecclesiasticae disciplinae sanctificatae sunt.	[37] But he [wrote] one [letter] to Philemon and one to Titus, but two to Timothy for the sake of affection and love. [38] In honor of the [=Catholic] Church, however, they have been sanctified by an ordination of the ecclesiastical discipline.
[39] Fertur etiam ad laudecenses alia ad alexandrinos pauli nomine fincte ad heresem marcionis [40] et alia plura quae in chatholicam eclesiam recepi non potest fel enim cum melle misceri non concruit	[39] fertur etiam ad Laodicenses, alia ad Alexandrinos, Pauli nomine fictae ad haeresem Marcionis, [40] et alia plura, quae in catholicam ecclesiam recipi non potest; fel enim cum melle misceri non congruit.	[39] There is extant also [an epistle] to the Laodiceans, and another to the Alexandrians, forged in the name of Paul according to the heresy of Marcion. [40] There are also many others which cannot be received in the [=Catholic] Church, for gall cannot be mixed with honey.
[41] epistola sane iude et superscrictio iohannis duas in catholica habentur [42] et sapientia ab amicis salomonis in honore ipsius scripta [43] apocalapse etiam iohanis et petri tantum recipimus quam quidam ex nostris legi in eclesia nolunt [44] pastorem uero	[41] Epistola san Iudae, et superscriptio Iohannis duas in catholica habentur; [42] et Sapientia ab amicis Salomonis in honorem ipsius scripta. [43] apocalypses etiam Iohannis, et Petri, tantum recipimus, quam quidam ex nostris legi in ecclesia nolunt. [44] Pastorem uero	[41] The Epistle of Jude indeed and the two with the superscription "Of John," are accepted in the [=Catholic] [Church] — [42] so also the Wisdom of Solomon written by friends in his honor. [43] We accept only the Apocalypses of John and of Peter, although some of us do not want it to be read in the Church.

nuperrim ettemporibus nostris in urbe roma herma conscripsit sedente cathetra urbis romae aeclesiae pio eps fratrer eius [45] et ideo legi eum quide oportet se puplicare uero in eclesia populo [46] neque inter profetas conpletum numero [47] neque inter apostolos in fine temporum potest.	nuperrime temporibus nostris in Urbe Roma Hermas conscripsit, sedente cathedra Urbis Romae ecclesiae Pio Episcopo fratre eius; [45] et ideo legi eum quidem oportet, se publicare uero in ecclesia populo, [46] neque inter Prophetas, completum numero, [47] neque inter apostolos, in finem temporum potest.	[44] But Hermas composed The Shepherd quite recently in our times in the city of Rome, while his brother, Pius, the bishop, occupied the [episcopal] seat of the city of Rome. [45] And therefore, it should indeed be read, but it cannot be published for the people in the Church, [46] neither among the Prophets, since their number is complete, [47] nor among the Apostles for it is after their time (?).
[48] arsinoi autem seu ualentini. uel mitiadis nihil in totum recipemus. [49] qui etiam nouu psalmorum librum marcioni conscripserunt una cum basilide assianom catafry cum constitutorem....	[48] Arsinoi autem, seu Ualentini, uel Mitiadis nihil in totum recipimus. [49] qui etiam nouum Psalmorum librum Marcioni concripserunt una cum Basilide Assianum Catafrygum constitutorem....	[48] But we accept nothing at all of Arsinoes, or Valentinus, or Metiades (?). [49] Those also [are rejected] who composed a new book of Psalms for Marcion together with Basilides and the Cataphrygians of Asia (?)....

* * *

---

1   Cf. The body of the text where reference is made to this dating being challenged.

2   http://www.bible-researcher.com/muratorian.html
Michael D. Marlowe (editor) http://www.bible-researcher.com/biog.html

3   The meaning may be that Mark arranged the material of his Gospel in the order indicated by Peter, who was participant in the events narrated.

4   The reading of the Fragment, *quasi ut uris studiosum*, "as so to speak, one zealous for (or, learned in) the law," has been variously interpreted and/or emended. For example, Routh took *iuris* as translating του δικαιου, i.e. Luke was studious of righteousness; Buchanan replaced *ut iuris* with *adiutorem*, "assistant"; Bartlet supposed that the translator read νοσου as νομου (Luke was "a student of disease"); Zahn replaced *ut iuris* with *itineris*,

thereby referring to Luke's readiness to accompany Paul on his journeys; Lietzmann conjectured *litteris*, i.e. Luke was well versed as an author. Harnack (*Sitzungsberichte der königlich Preussischen Akademie der Wissenschaften* [1903], p. 213) and Ehrhardt (op. cit.), who retain *iuris studiosus* of the Fragment, have pointed out that in technical language of Roman law this could refer to an assesor or legal expert who served on the staff of a Roman official. Although this title was current prior to the time of Justinian's *Digest* (published in 533) and so was available to the translator of the Fragment, it is anybody's guess what Greek phrase it represented—assuming, of course, that the Canon was drawn up originally in Greek (unfortunately no help is provided in David Magie, *De Romanorum iuris publici sacrisque vocabulis sollemnibus in Graecum sermonem conversis* [Leipzig, 1905]).

It is significant that the Latin text of the Fragment appears to have been a source for Chromace of Aquileia, who in his commentary on Matthew (written between 398 and 407) refers to Luke as follows: *Dominum in carne non vidit, sed quia eruditissimus legis erat quippe qui comes Pauli apostoli* ... (See Joseph Lemarie, "saint Chromace d'Aquilee temoin du Canon de Muratori," *Revue des etudes augustiniennes*, xxiv [1978], pp. 101-2).

5   Here *ex opinione* is taken as the equivalent of εξ ακοης. Others conjecture *ex ordine*, representing καθεξης ("orderly sequence." Luke i.3).

6   Latin, *principia*. —M.D.M.

7   Latin, *principali*. —M.D.M.

8   I John i.1-3.

9   Luke i.3.

10 That is, the city of Rome. This lack of specificity is one indication that the author was a Roman. —M.D.M.

11 The letter "b" in the Latin text before "Galatians" may belong to "Corinthians" (προς Κορινθιους "Β").

12 Latin, *principium*. —M.D.M.

13 Marcion revised Paul's Epistle to the Ephesians and called it the Epistle to the Laodiceans. Nothing is known of the Epistle to the Alexandrians mentioned here. —M.D.M.

14 It may be, as Zahn (*Geschichte*, ii, 66) and others have supposed, that a negative has fallen out of the text here.

15 Tregelles suggests that the Latin translator of this document mistook the Greek *Philonos* "Philo" for *philon* "friends." Many in ancient times thought that the so-called "Wisdom of Solomon" was really written by Philo of Alexandria. —M.D.M.

16 The Apocalypse of Peter describes with some imaginative detail the torments of hell and the blessings of heaven. It was read with respect and used for admonition throughout the Churches in early times. —M.D.M.

17 The Shepherd of Hermas is another work widely read in early times. It is a kind of moral allegory, like Bunyan's Pilgrim's Progress, but more impressive in that it purports to convey a series of divine revelations. —M.D.M.

18 This would be Pius I, bishop of Rome from about 142 to 157. —M.D.M.

19 Perhaps the Fragmentist means that there are three major Prophets and twelve minor Prophets.

20 The few words that follow this are unintelligible, and so the fragment practically ends here. —M.D.M.

21 http://www.earlychristianwritings.com/text/muratorian-greek.html

22 http://www.earlychristianwritings.com/text/muratorian-latin.html

* * *

Appendix D - Evangelicals and the Canon of the New Testament

M. James Sawyer, Ph.D.
Associate Professor of Theology and Church History
Western Seminary
San Jose, CA[1]

Canon Determination for Evangelicals

Over the past two decades American Evangelical scholarship has ably risen to the defence of the doctrine of the inerrancy of the Bible as a touchstone upholding the historic position of the Church of Jesus Christ with reference to its authority. While volumes have been penned discussing the nature of biblical inspiration and the consequent authority of the scripture, it seems curious that in all the bibliological discussions one crucial issue is scarcely mentioned; that issue is the issue of Canon. Apart from R. Laird Harris' *Inspiration and Canonicity of the Bible*, David Dunbar's chapter, "The Biblical Canon" in *Hermeneutics, Authority and Canon,* Geisler and Nix's discussion in their *General Introduction to the Bible* and the recent series of articles in *Christianity Today*,[2] American Evangelicals who affirm the inerrancy of Scripture have had little to say concerning the shape of the Canon. [3] The sixty-six books which compose the Protestant Scriptures are assumed to be the complete written revelation of God to man without further comment or debate.

It has been charged that conservative evangelicalism's reticence to discuss the issue of Canon is due to the fact that it "finds itself imprisoned within a 19th century biblicism *which believes that to question the Canon is to undermine the authority of Scripture.*"[4] Outside the evangelical fold, the question of Canon has been debated for decades with the discussion centering on the nature of Canon itself. Emil Bruner has noted:

The question of Canon has never, in principle, been answered, but is being continually reopened. Just as the Church of the second, third and fourth centuries had the right to decide what was "apostolic" and what was not, on their own responsibilities as believers, so in the same way every Church in every period in the history of the Church possesses the same right and the same duty.[5]

While Bruner may overstate the case, the question he raises is the question of the certainty of historical knowledge. This question has profound implications for the faith.

I would propose that the evangelical approach to Canon determination has historically been the weakest link in its bibliology. This weakness has persisted for several reasons. (1) Canon has not been a pressing issue of debate on the larger theological horizon. (2) It has been *assumed* that the Canon of the New Testament was closed definitively in the fourth century. (3) Apostolicity has been assumed as the controlling issue because of the early mention of this feature by the Fathers. (4) The New Testament Canon has been accepted uncritically because of the theological assumption that through divine providence the early Church was led (infallibly) to its canonical decisions.

In this paper I want to (1) address the question of Canon, (2) look critically at the traditional inerrantist apologetic for the Canon, (3) trace briefly the development of the New Testament Canon up through the Reformation, and (4) propose an alternative determination process.

Evangelical Proposals on Canon Determination

Evangelical understanding of the criteria by which the New Testament books were recognized as canonical follows the basic outline laid down by B. B. Warfield and his fellow Princetonians, Charles and A. A. Hodge over a century ago. These criteria focused exclusively upon the question of apostolicity. The unstated corollary of apostolicity was the conviction that divine providence had led the Church to recognize all and only those books which were apostolic. An examination of Warfield as a principle architect, and of R. Laird Harris and Geisler and Nix as contemporary adherents will demonstrate this outlook.

B. B. Warfield

Warfield echoed the sentiment of the early Church in stressing the primacy of apostolicity in Canon determination.[6] He argued that *apostolicity* was a somewhat wider concept than strictly apostolic authorship, although in the early Church these two issues were often confounded.[7] "The principle of canonicity was not apostolic authorship," contended Warfield, "but *imposition by the apostles as law.*"[8] The practical effect of this subtle distinction is to allow for the inclusion of books such as Mark, Luke, James, Jude and Hebrews which were not actually penned by the apostles, but were, according to tradition, written under apostolic sanction. Warfield asserted that the Canon of Scripture was complete when the last book of the New Testament was penned by the Apostle John circa A.D. 95. From the divine standpoint the Canon of Scripture was complete. However, human acceptance of an individual book of that Canon hinged upon "*authenticating proof* of its apostolicity."[9] The key idea here is the concept of *apostolic law*. Scripture was authoritative because it was written by an apostle who *imposed* his writing upon the Church in the same fashion as Torah was imposed upon Israel.

As he stated,

> We rest our acceptance of the New Testament Scriptures as authoritative thus, not on the fact that they are the product of the revelation-age of the Church, for so are many other books which we do not thus accept; but on the fact *that God's authoritative agents in founding the Church gave them as authoritative to the Church which they founded*.... It is clear that prophetic and apostolic origin is the very essence of the authority of the Scriptures.[10]

The fact that these manuscripts were hand copied coupled with the lack of modern methods of travel made the slow collection of the manuscripts a foregone conclusion.

The problem for the Church today, as Warfield admitted, is that "we cannot at this day hear the apostolic voice in its (a New Testament book's) authorization. Beyond the witness one apostolic book was to bear to another--as Paul in 1 Timothy 5:18 authenticates Luke--and what witness an apostolic book may bear to itself, we cannot appeal at this day to immediate apostolic authorization."[11]

To answer the question of canonicity, Warfield took as a test case the epistle of Second Peter, a book whose canonicity had been repeatedly doubted over the centuries, and proceeded to investigate the provenance of the epistle to prove its canonicity. He asserted that if one demonstrated that the letter was old enough to have been written by an apostle and that the Church had from the beginning held the book to be an authoritative rule of faith, then "the presumption is overwhelming that the Church from the apostolic age held it to be divine only because it had received it from the apostles as divine."[12] Having completed his external proof, Warfield then examined critical objections to Petrine authorship based upon internal evidence to see if indeed the critical objections were valid.. Having dismissed the critical objections,[13] he concluded that the book was genuine and that to question its canonicity is to lead the Church astray into heresy.[14]

Warfield's argument is closely reasoned and convincing. He incisively demolished the arguments of his opponents showing their inadequate basis and contradictory presuppositions. However, even his colleague and friend at Princeton, Francis Landy Patton in eulogizing Warfield, noted that the rationalism of Warfield's system of logic was built upon probability which precluded the absolute certainty of his conclusions.[15]

R. Laird Harris

Harris's (1957,1969) work, *Inspiration and Canonicity of the Bible*, was among the first in recent years to address seriously the question of Canon from an evangelical perspective. Harris follows Warfield closely in insisting upon apostolic authorship as *the* criterion for New Testament canonicity.[16] He goes beyond Warfield by denying that the Reformation principle of the witness of the Spirit is a valid test of canonicity.[17] Harris painstakingly demonstrates that the crucial question for the early Church was, "Was the work written by an apostle?" To answer this question he deduces numerous quotations from the ancient fathers which attest the apostolic authorship of the New Testament books.

To answer the question of the presence of books which make no claim to apostolic authorship, he asserts that such books were written by disciples of the apostles who carefully reproduced their master's teaching. With reference to Mark, Harris notes the ancient tradition connecting the second gospel with the Apostle Peter. ". . . Papias explicitly states that the second Gospel is accepted because of Peter, not because of Mark."[18]

With reference to the book of Hebrews, Harris cites the early traditions which ascribe the work to Paul, noting that the lack of that apostle's characteristic salutation was, according to Pantaenus, due to the fact that Paul was apostle to the Gentiles, rather than the apostle to the Hebrews. He notes, too, the statement of Clement that the epistle had been composed in Hebrew and then translated into Greek by Luke.[19] This early testimony notwithstanding, Harris denies Pauline authorship to the book of Hebrews because the author of the epistle himself claims to be a second generation believer (Heb. 2:3-4). But having said this he asserts that: "No apostle other than Paul is seriously mentioned in connection with the writing of Hebrews."[20]

So committed is Harris to the proposition of apostolic authorship, that having noted the fact that the author himself claims to be a *second generation believer*, not of the apostolic inner circle, he then notes that wherever the epistle was accepted as canonical it was accepted into the Canon only in those places . . . where it was considered to be a genuine work of Paul. Appeal was not made to its antiquity nor to the testimony of the Holy Spirit, nor to any other auxiliary reason. Authorship was what was decisive.[21]

Harris recognizes the dilemma in which this position places him. If the book is not Pauline in *authorship*, should it be excised from the canon? His previous judgment notwithstanding, he proposes that the book *was* written by Paul employing Barnabas as his amanuensis.[22] "This would at once explain the unquestioned acceptance (no other anonymous work was so accepted), variation in style from Paul's, the anonymity where the details of authorship were not known and only the style problem appeared, and the double tradition of authorship in other circles."[23]

While he seriously proposes the Paul-Barnabas authorship of Hebrews, he recognizes that this cannot be proved beyond the shadow of a doubt, and allows that there may have been some other amanuensis. Even so the basic thrust of the argument remains the same. Apostolicity in the strict sense remains the governing criterion for acceptance into the Canon.

Geisler and Nix

Geisler and Nix in their *General Introduction to the Bible*[24] evidence a widening of the very narrow position adopted by Harris. Taking a different starting point than Warfield and Harris, they assert that canonicity is determined by God. Humans do not determine Canon, they merely discover the already existent Canon which God has given. The key concept in the discovery of canonicity was the recognition of a book's inspiration by God.[25] In addition, canonicity is seen as being inexorably linked to authenticity. While Harris made apostolicity the *sole* criterion for the Church's subjective determination of the already existent objective Canon, Geisler and Nix propose five principles which guided the ancient Church in its discovery of Canon. It should be noted that these five principles involve assumption on their part. There is no documentation from patristic sources that these principles were consciously employed.

The first of these principles is that of *authority*. Specifically, this criterion looks at the book itself and asks the question, "Does it have a self-vindicating authority that commands attention as it communicates?"[26] Many books were either rejected or doubted because the voice of God was not heard clearly in the book.

The second test for canonicity was that of the *prophetic* nature of the book. Whereas the former test looked at the book itself, this test looked at authorship. ". . . A book was judged as to whether or not it was genuinely written by the stated author who was a spokesman in the mainstream of redemptive revelation, either a prophet (whether in Old or New Testament times) or an apostle."[27] This criterion evidences a loosening of the principle of apostolicity which Harris asserts, since Geisler and Nix would include New Testament prophets (presumably Mark, Luke, James, Jude, the author of Hebrews, etc.). By this test all pseudonymous writings written under false pretenses and forgeries are to be rejected.[28]

The third test for canonicity which Geisler and Nix contend was operational in the early Church was that of *authenticity*. (By authenticity they mean authenticity of doctrine rather than authorship.) This test would compare the teachings of any book vying for entrance into the Canon with the doctrine of the already accepted books. Since truth cannot contradict truth, if the book under consideration was found to be at variance with the rest of the Canon it would automatically be rejected as non-canonical.

The fourth test was one of power. "Does the book come with the *power* of God?" Since the Word of God was living and active and it was profitable for edification, if a book did not accomplish this goal it was rejected.[29]

The fifth and final test was its *reception*: Was it generally accepted by the orthodox Church? This they admit "is rather a confirmation, and does serve the obvious purpose of *making final* the decision and availability of the books."[30]

Weaknesses of the Evangelical View

Whether the criterion be inspiration, apostolicity or something else, I believe that we must acknowledge the *a posteriori* nature of the methods of Canon determination which have been proposed. Ridderbos has well noted:

> As their artificiality indicates, these arguments are a posteriori in character. To hold that the Church was led to accept these writings by such *criteria*, in fact speak here of a *criteria canonicitais* is to go too far. It is rather clear that we have to do with more or less successful attempts to *cover* with arguments what had already been fixed for a long time and for the fixation of which, such reasoning or such criteria had never been employed.[31]

>> ...the Church did not begin by making formal decisions as to what was valid as Canon, nor did it begin by setting specific criteria of canonicity.[32]

Brevard Childs concurs in this assessment noting: "It is hard to escape the impression that the later expositions of the criteria of canonicity were, in large part, after-the-fact explanations of the Church's experience of faith in Jesus Christ which were evoked by the continued use of certain books."[33] The real problem of these *a posteriori* explanations is that they inject another level of Canon into the discussion. As Ridderbos contended:

> Every attempt to find an a posteriori element to justify the Canon, whether sought in the authority of its doctrine or in the consensus of the Church that gradually developed goes beyond the Canon itself, and thereby posits a Canon above the Canon which comes in conflict with the nature of Canon itself.[34]

The questions of inspiration and apostolicity must be briefly addressed. Geisler and Nix, as noted above, make inspiration a criterion for canonicity. While I do not dispute the truth of this statement, I contend that it is inadequate and does not solve the problem. The concept of writing under inspiration was common (albeit not universal) in the ancient Church.[35] Clement makes this claim for his epistle to the Corinthians.[36] Even Eusebius makes the claim for his life of Constantine.[37] Yet, neither Clement nor Eusebius claim that their writings have the authority of Scripture. My point here is not to argue that Clement or Eusebius were or were not inspired, but that the criterion of inspiration for canonicity was not *consciously* employed by the ancient Church.[38] With reference to the claim of apostolicity, I believe we must admit that the apostles wrote more documents than have been preserved for us (e.g. 3 Corinthians; Laodiceans) which evidently bore the full weight of their apostolic authority. While we may argue that these documents were not inspired and were therefore not preserved, from a strictly logical point of view, we merely beg the question. Thus, while either of these two criteria alone or both together can contribute to our assurance as to the shape of the New Testament Canon, they fail to fully answer the question at hand.

If we insist upon apostolicity as *the* means by which we are assured that our twenty-seven book Canon is in fact the Canon of Jesus Christ, as did Warfield and Harris, we *ultimately* are forced to rely upon the "assured results of higher criticism" for the certainty of our Scriptures. Since even as Warfield noted, "We cannot this day hear the apostolic voice in its authorization. . . ." Ridderbos, I believe rightly, contends:

> ...an historical judgement cannot be the final and sole ground for the acceptance of the New Testament as canonical by the Church. To do so would mean that the Church would base its faith on the results of historical investigation.[39]

The Development of the New Testament Canon

Discussions of Canon tend to develop in one of two directions depending upon the definition of Canon adopted by the theologian. Warfield and Geisler and Nix adopt a *material* definition and stress the objective existence of a God-given standard, which exists by virtue of its divine inspiration. In this sense, Canon emphasizes the inherent authority of the writing. The second type of discussion, taking its clue from the original usage of the term "canon," stresses the *formal* development of the Canon in the sense of a completed list, an authoritative collection, a closed collection, if you will, to which nothing can be added.[40] These discussions view the formal recognition process and usually see the Church in some sense as giving its official approval to the collection.[41]

The common evangelical view of the development of the New Testament Canon sees the Canon as having arisen gradually and through usage rather than through conciliar pronouncement *which vested the books of the New Testament with some kind of authority*. Athanasius' festal letter (A.D. 367) is generally viewed as the document which fixed the Canon in the East, and the decision of the Council of Carthage in the West is viewed as having fixed the Latin Canon. Youngblood summarizes this position in his recent *Christianity Today* article,

> The earliest known recognition of the 27 books of the New Testament as alone canonical, to which nothing is to be added and from which nothing is to be subtracted, is the list preserved by Athanasius (A.D. 367). The Synod of Hippo (A.D. 393) and the Third Synod of Carthage (A.D. 397) duly acquiesced, again probably under the influence of the redoubtable Augustine.[42]

The closing of the two canons and their amalgamation into one are historical watersheds that it would be presumptuous to disturb.[43]

Evangelicals insist upon the primacy of the written documents of Scripture over and against all human authority. However, in so doing we tend to overlook the fact that other authority did in fact exist in the ancient Church, particularly the authority of Jesus Christ and His apostles. We often fail to appreciate that the Church was founded not upon the apostolic documents, but rather the apostolic doctrine. The Church existed at least a decade before the earliest book of the New Testament was penned, and possibly as long as six decades until it was completed. But during this period it was not without authority. Its standard, its Canon, was ultimately Jesus Christ Himself,[44] and mediately His apostles. Even in the immediate post-apostolic[45] period we find a great stress on apostolic *tradition* along side a written New Testament Canon.[46]

As the apostles died, this living stream of tradition grew fainter. The written documents became progressively more important to the on-going life of the Church. The question of competing authorities in the sense of written and oral tradition subsided. However, even as late as the mid-second century we find an emphasis on oral tradition which stands *in some way* parallel to the written gospels as authoritative.[47]

The concept of an authoritative Christian tradition can be traced back into the New Testament itself. On numerous occasions Paul speaks of the chain of receiving and delivering a body of teaching.[48] It is therefore not surprising to see in this early period both written works and oral tradition existing side by side in some sort of authoritative fashion.[49]

Without doubt, the earliest Bible for the Church consisted of the Old Testament Scriptures, interpreted Christologically. Additionally, in the New Testament itself we find at least one case of some New Testament books being placed on a par with the Old Testament.[50] This probably indicates that even at this early date the writings of the apostles were viewed in some circles as being on a par with the Old Testament.[51] However, as Bruce has noted:

> ...such hints would not necessarily indicate a new corpus of sacred scripture: if Paul's letters are reckoned along with "the other scriptures" in 2 Peter 3:16, that might in itself imply their addition to the Old Testament writings, perhaps in kind of an appendix, rather than the emergence of a new and distinct Canon.[52]

The earliest solid evidence we find of a New Testament Canon, in the sense of an authoritative collection of writings comes not from the hand of the orthodox Church with its apostolic tradition, but from the second century heretic, Marcion.[53] It was in part this heretical threat which impelled the Church to come to grips with the extent of its authoritative writings. The earliest evidence we possess of a canonical collection of books by the ancient Church is the Muratorian Canon, dated in the mid to late second century.[54]

Another factor which affected the formation of the New Testament Canon was theological. The Montanist movement, with its claim to a continuing prophetic revelation, relied heavily upon the Apocalypse.[55] This provoked a reaction particularly by the orthodox Church of Syria, which from this point forward, rejected the Apocalypse, although it had earlier looked upon the book with favour. Evidently, this was a situation where the apostolic *tradition* was looked to in adjudging the heterodox nature of the Montanist position. In an attempt to discredit this position, parts of the ancient Church were not averse to denying books it had previously approved, in order to cut the ground out from under the heterodox.

Yet another factor which must be considered in the canonization of the New Testament is the phenomenon of Tatian's Diatesseron. Tatian, a pupil of Justin Martyr, took the four canonical gospels and from them composed a harmony. This work supplanted the canonical gospels in the Syrian Church well into the fifth century, at which time the hierarchy made a concerted effort to stamp out the work and restore the four canonical gospels to their rightful place within the Canon.[56]

The Festal letter of Athanasius (c. A.D. 367) is well known as the first list to contain all and only the present twenty-seven book New Testament Canon. Thirty years later the Synod of Carthage, under the influence of the great Augustine, reached a similar conclusion. Youngblood gives the common Protestant evaluation of these pronouncements:

> Thus led (as we believe) by divine Providence, scholars during the latter half of the fourth century settled for all time the limits of the New Testament Canon. The 27 books of Matthew through Revelation constitute that New Testament, which possesses divine authority equal to that of the Old.[57]

The problem with such a sweeping assertion is that it does not fit the historical facts. First, the synods of Hippo and Carthage were not ecumenical councils, but local assemblies whose decisions held sway only in the local sees.[58] The Festal letter of Athanasius, to be sure, gives us the judgment of a key figure of the ancient Church, but it did not bind even the Eastern Church.[59] The ancient Church *never* reached a conscious and binding decision as to the extent of Canon. Proof of this fact can be seen in the canons of the various Churches of the empire.

While the Canon in the West proved to be relatively stable from the late fourth century, the Canon in the oriental Churches varied, sometimes widely. The Syriac Church at the beginning of the fifth century employed only the *Diatesseron* (in place of the four gospels),[60] Acts, and the Pauline epistles.[61] During the fifth century the *Peshitta* [62]was produced and became the standard Syriac version. In it the *Diatesseron* was replaced by the four gospels, 3 Corinthians was removed and three Catholic epistles, James, 1 Peter and 1 John were included. The Apocalypse and the other Catholic epistles were excluded, making a twenty-two book Canon. The remaining books did not make their way into the Syriac Canon until the late sixth century with the appearance of the Harclean Syriac Version.[63] While the Syrian Church recognized an abbreviated Canon, the Ethiopic Church recognized the twenty-seven books of the New Testament plus *The Shepherd of Hermas, 1 & 2 Clement* and eight books of the *Apostolic Constitutions.*[64]

Even in the West the Canon was not closed as tightly as commonly believed. A case in point is the apocryphal *Epistle to the Laodiceans*. In the tenth century, Alfric, later Archbishop of Canterbury, lists the work as among the canonical Pauline epistles. Westcott observes that the history of this epistle "forms one of the most interesting episodes in the literary history of the Bible."[65] He notes that from the sixth century onward *Laodiceans* occurs frequently in Latin manuscripts, including many which were prepared for Church use. So common was the epistle in the Medieval period, it passed into several vernacular translations, including the Bohemian Bible as late as 1488. It also occurred in the Albigensian Version of Lyons, and while not translated by Wycliffe personally, it was added to several manuscripts of his translation of the New Testament.[66]

On the eve of the Reformation, it was not only Luther who had problems with the extent of the New Testament Canon. Doubts were being expressed even by some of the loyal sons of the Church. Luther's opponent at Augsburg, Cardinal Cajetan, following Jerome, expressed doubts concerning the canonicity of Hebrews, James, 2 and 3 John, and Jude. Of the latter three he states: "They are of less authority than those which are certainly Holy Scripture."[67] Erasmus likewise expressed doubts concerning Revelation as well as the apostolicity of James, Hebrews and 2 Peter. It was only as the Protestant Reformation progressed, and Luther's willingness to excise books from the Canon threatened Rome that, at Trent, the Roman Catholic Church hardened its consensus stand on the extent of the New Testament Canon into a conciliar pronouncement.[68]

The point of this survey has been to demonstrate that the New Testament Canon was not closed in the fourth century. Debates continued concerning the fringe books of the Canon until the Reformation. During the Reformation, both the Reformed and Catholic Churches independently asserted the twenty-seven book New Testament Canon. Youngblood asserts that the Canon was closed by providence and we have no right to question that closure. I believe Youngblood errs at this point. The problem I find with his assertion is that it is an extra-biblical pronouncement to which, apparently, the theological equivalent of canonical authority is being given.[69] While I believe that divine providence did superintend the collection of the New Testament Canon, we cannot equate providence with the belief of the majority. If this were true, we should all be Roman Catholic today! As Klyne Snodgrass has asserted, "Providence is not enough."[70] Rather than focus solely upon the external criteria of apostolicity, inspiration or providence for our assurance that our present twenty-seven book NT Canon is indeed the Canon of Jesus Christ I believe that there is a better way for us to approach the problem. This way is not new but a return to and recognition of the Reformers' doctrine of the witness of the Spirit and the self-authenticating nature of Scripture

The Autopistie *of Scripture and the Witness of the Spirit*

Discomfort with the traditional conservative Evangelical apologetic for the Canon is not new. A century ago this became a central focus of Charles Briggs' attack on the Princetonian bibliology.[71] More recently, Ridderbos has argued that the common apologetic for Canon ultimately leads a person to one of two alternatives, a certainty based upon what amounts to the assured results of higher criticism, or the infallibility of the Church.[72] For the evangelical Protestant neither of these alternatives is ultimately satisfying.

Ridderbos and Briggs both build their rationale for Canon recognition upon the Reformers, arguing that the *autopistie* of the writings themselves objectively, and the witness of the Spirit subjectively form the proper matrix through which we should view the shape of the Canon.[73] Shifting the means of our certainty of the form of the Canon from the objective external criterion of apostolicity alone should in no way imply down-playing the importance of this factor as a *ground* of Canon. Rather as Warfield and Ridderbos both have noted, no book of the New Testament *as we possess it* contains a certificate of authentication as to its apostolic origin. That is, from our perspective, separated by nearly two millennia from the autographs, we cannot rely upon such means as the known signature of the apostle Paul to assure a book's authenticity. Hence, we cannot use apostolicity as the means by which we are *ultimately* assured of the shape of the Canon. The same can be said for the criterion of prophetic authorship, unless we merely beg the question and assert that the book itself is evidence that its author was a prophet.

I believe that the starting point of canonicity must be a recognition that at the most basic level it is the risen Lord Himself who is ultimately the Canon of His Church.[74] As Ridderbos has observed:

The very ground or basis for the recognition of the Canon is therefore, in principle, redemptive-historical, i.e. Christological. For Christ himself is not only the Canon in which God comes to the world, but Christ establishes the Canon and gives it its concrete historical form.[75]

It then follows that it is also Christ who causes His Church to accept the Canon and to recognize it by means of the witness of the Holy Spirit. With this proposition I believe most evangelical Protestants would agree. However, this does not relieve us of the responsibility of examining the history of the Canon, nor does it give us the right to identify absolutely the Canon of Jesus Christ with the Canon of the Church. As Ridderbos has said, ". . . the absoluteness of the Canon cannot be separated from the relativity of history."[76] In short, we confess that our Lord has given us an objective standard of authority, for our purposes today that consists of the written documents. But we also recognize that, due to sinfulness, insensitivity or misunderstanding, it is possible for us subjectively to fail to recognize properly the objective Canon Christ has given. We may include a book which does not belong, or exclude a book which does belong.

How then are we to determine what properly belongs to the canon? Is it "every man for himself"? I believe that Charles Briggs has proposed a viable method for us to consider today. Following the Reformers, he proposed a threefold program for Canon determination, built upon the "rock of the Reformation principle of the Sacred Scriptures."[77] The first principle in Canon determination was the testimony of the Church. By examining tradition and the early written documents, he contended that *probable* evidence could be presented to men that the Scriptures "recognized as of divine authority and canonical by such general consent are indeed what they claim to be."[78]

With reference to the Protestant Canon this evidence was, he believed, unanimous. This evidence was not determinative, however. It was only "probable." It was the evidence of general consent, although given under the leading of the Spirit. It was from this general consent that conciliar pronouncements were made. It did not, however, settle the issue, since divine authority could not be derived from ecclesiastical pronouncement or consensus. The second and next higher level of evidence was that of the character of the Scriptures themselves. This is the Reformers' doctrine of the *autopistie* of the Scriptures. Their character was pure and holy, having a beauty, harmony and majesty. The Scriptures also breathed piety and devotion to God; they revealed redemption and satisfied the spiritual longing within the soul of man. All these features served to convince that the Scriptures were indeed the very Word of God. As Briggs stated, "If men are not won by the holy character of the biblical books, it must be because for some reason their eyes have been withheld from seeing it."[79] It is in light of this concept that we should understand the Syriac Church's rejection of the Apocalypse and Luther's rejection of the book of James. In both cases there was a pressing theological reason which kept them from seeing the divine fingerprints upon specific books of the New Testament. In a very real sense it was their zeal for the truth of the apostolic faith/gospel which blinded them.[80]

The third and highest principle of Canon determination was that of the witness of the Spirit. He stated, "The Spirit of God bears witness by and with the particular writing . . . , in the heart of the believer, removing every doubt and assuring the soul of its possession of the truth of God."[81]

Briggs saw the witness of the Spirit as threefold. As noted earlier, the Spirit bore witness to the particular writing. Secondly, the Spirit bore witness "by and with the several writings in such a manner as to assure the believer"[82] that they were each a part of the one divine revelation. This argument was cumulative. As one recognized one book as divine, it became easier to recognize the same marks in another of the same character.[83] A systematic study of the Scriptures yielded a conviction of the fact that the Canon was an organic whole. The Holy Spirit illumined the mind and heart to perceive this organic whole and thus gave certainty to the essential place of each writing in the Word of God.[84]

Third, the Spirit bore witness "to the Church as an organized body of believers, through their free consent in their various communities and countries to the unity and variety of the . . . Scriptures as the complete and perfect Canon. "[85] This line of evidence was a reworking of the historical argument but strengthening it with the "vital argument of the divine evidence."[86] Whereas before, the Church testimony was external and formal, whenever the believer came to recognize the Holy Spirit as the guiding force in the Church in both the formation and recognition of the Canon, "then we may know that the testimony of the Church is the testimony of divine Spirit speaking through the Church."[87]

Focusing on the principle of the witness of the Spirit for assurance in canonical questions introduced a subjectivity factor which rendered the question of Canon, in the absolute sense, undefinable.[88] While the Reformers did attempt in their creeds to define the limits of Canon, Briggs contended that in so doing they betrayed their own principle of Canon determination. If Scripture was self-evidencing, then that evidence that God was the Author was to the individual.[89] In addition, doctrinal definition, in order to be binding upon the Church, had to be held by consensus of the whole Church. Both the Reformed Churches and the Roman Catholic Church represented but a fraction of the Church catholic, hence, they could not give definitive pronouncement to Canon questions.[90] He held that the question of Canon must then be regarded as open to this day in the subjective sense. An individual believer was thus free to doubt the canonicity of a particular book without the fear of being charged with heresy.[91]

Summarizing Briggs' method of Canon determination: first, the logical order began with the human testimony as probable evidence to the divine origin of Scripture. This testimony brought the individual to esteem the Scriptures highly. Next, when he turned to the pages of Scripture itself, they exerted an influence upon his soul. Finally, the divine testimony convinced him of the extent of the truth of God, at which point he shared in the consensus of the Church.[92]

Conclusion

The question of the Canon of the New Testament is clearly not as simple as it appears in survey texts and popular presentations. Among evangelicals, theories of Canon determination have tended to stress external criteria for assurance that the Scripture we possess today is in fact the whole extent of the Revelation which God has given to the believer. While I do not believe this is totally invalid, I have suggested weaknesses in this approach if by it we want to build absolute assurance.

Earlier I used the phrase "the assured results of higher criticism" to describe our apologetic for our New Testament Canon. I use the phrase advisedly, not hyperbolically, for it is indeed literary criticism upon which we engage when we seek to explore the provenance of a document. I use this phrase also to bring to mind the arrogant reconstructionist claims of the nineteenth century concerning the nature of Scripture. As we have watched archaeologists' shovels undercut these "assured results" we have rejoiced that the historic faith of the Church in its scriptures has been vindicated again and again. Yet, American evangelicals have forsaken their Reformation heritage and slipped into the same type of rationalism regarding the Canon as that for which we castigate liberals of a bygone era. My point here is that we as Evangelical Christians are by definition, people of *faith*. I believe that when we attempt to build our rationale for our New Testament Canon solely upon rational ground we betray the faith principle.

The individual's ultimate assurance that the Scripture he has received is indeed the Word of God must be grounded upon something more (but not less) than historical investigation. Scripture as the Word of God brings with it its own witness, the Holy Spirit, who alone can give certainty and assurance.

The Canon of the New Testament was not closed historically by the early Church. Rather, its extent was debated until the Reformation. Even then, it was closed in a sectarian fashion. Therefore the question must be asked, is it then heresy for a person to question or reject a book of the present Canon? There have been repeated re-evaluations of the Church's Canon. This happened during the initial sifting period. It happened again during the Renaissance and Reformation period, and it is beginning to happen again now. In such instances the fringe books of the Canon have been repeatedly questioned. If an individual believer should come to question or reject a book or books of the accepted Canon, should that person be regarded as a heretic, or accepted as a brother whose opinions are not necessarily endorsed?

* * *

1   Sawyer, 2004, https://Bible.org/article/evangelicals-and-canon-new-testament. [Own Note] The original paper is not dated, and one gets the sense from the dates of many of Sawyer's references that it may have been written quite some time prior to 2004.
2   The February 5, 1988 issue of *Christianity Today* included five brief articles covering different issues and perspectives on the subject of canon; Ronald Youngblood, "The Process; How We Got Our Bible," Richard B. Gaffin, Jr., "The New Testament: How Do We Know for Sure?"; Klyne Snodgrass, "Providence Is Not Enough"; David G. Dunbar, "Why The Canon Still Rumbles"; Kenneth S. Kantzer, "Confidence in the Face of Confusion."
3   Throughout this paper the term "conservative Evangelical" will be employed in the restricted sense of one who affirms the inerrancy of Scripture. More latitudinal Evangelicals have recently published significant works on the NT canon. Bruce Metzger's *The Canon of The New Testament* (Oxford: Clarendon, 1987) is the most significant of these.
4   Richard Lyon Morgan, "Let's be Honest About the Canon, " *The Christian Century* 84 (May 31, 1967), 717.84 (May 31, 1967), 717 (italics added). This confounding of the questions of inspiration and canonicity occurs on both the conservative and liberal side of the theological spectrum. One need only remember that some of those who do not profess evangelical convictions attempt to prove that Luther did not hold to inerrancy since he questioned books on the fringes of the canon.
5   Ibid.
6   F.F. Bruce discusses surveys the concept of apostolicity in the early Church and documents numerous mentions of this factor as being a primary criterion in Canon determination. He also mentions other issues related to apostolicity which were mentioned by some patristic writers as offering evidence that a book was indeed canonical.(The Canon of Scripture [Downers Grove: InterVarsity Press, 1988], 256-269, especially 256-258]. R. Laird Harris, surveying the same material insists that the sole criterion was apostolic authorship. Harris (Canonicity) (1957, 1969), p.219-245, especially 244-245.)
7   B. B. Warfield, "The Formation of the Canon of The New Testament," *The Inspiration and Authority of the Bible* (Philadelphia: Presbyterian and Reformed, 1970), 415.
8   Ibid.
9   Ibid., (italics added).
10 B. B. Warfield, "Review of A. W. Deickhoff, *Das Gepredigte Wort und die Heilge Schrift* and *Das Wort Gottes*," *The Presbyterian Review* 10 (1890):506.
11 B.B. Warfield, "The Canonicity of Second Peter," in *The Selected Shorter Writings Of B.B.Warfield-II*,(edited by John Meeter) (Philadelphia: Presbyterian and Reformed, 1976), 48-49.
12 Ibid., 49.
13 The internal objections Warfield dealt with were six. [1] Peter's name was frequently forged in the ancient Church . [2] The external support of 2 Peter is insufficient. [3] The

epistle has plainly borrowed largely from Jude, which by some was judged unworthy of an apostle , while others held this to be a proof that 2 Peter belongs to the second century, on the ground of the assumed ungenuineness of Jude. [4] The author exhibits too great a desire to make himself out to be Peter. [5] The author betrays that he wrote in a later time by numerous anachronisms. [6] The style of 2 Peter is too divergent from that of 1 Peter to have been written by the same individual. In typical style, Warfield concluded:

The state of the argument, then , really is this: a mountain mass of presumption in favor of the genuineness and canonicity of 2 Peter, to be raised and overturned only by a very strong lever of rebutting evidence; a pitible show of rebutting evidence offered as a lever. It is doubtless true that we can move the world if proper lever and fulcrum be given. But if the lever is a common quarryman's tool and the fulcrum thin air! Then woe to the man who wields it. What can such rebutting evidence as we have here injure, except his own cause? (Ibid., 74-75)

14   Ibid., 79.

15   F. L. Patton, "Benjamin Breckinridge Warfield," *The Princeton Theological Review* 19 (1921), 369-91. Norman Kraus rightly observes concerning Warfield's use of reason,

His "evidence," on his own admission, did not amount to demonstration, and yet he sought to escape the logical consequences of this admission by claiming that "probable" evidence though different in kind from "demonstrable evidence" is nonetheless objective, rational, and capable of establishing certainty of conviction. Thus he claimed that the probable evidence which he had produced was of such a quantity and quality as to overwhelmingly establish the rational ground for and force mental assent to the message and authority of Scripture. But in the final analysis, he was unable to close the gap between probability and absolute certainty with a rational demonstration of mathematical quality. . . And as long as the gap between probability and demonstration remains, there also remains the necessity of a subjective and volitional response to the appeal of truth before there can be certainty *(The Principle of Authority in the Theology of B. B. Warfield, William Adams Brown, and Gerald Birney Smith,* [Ann Arbor Mi: University Microfilms (Drew University Ph.D. dissertation) 1961], 270). [Italics added]

Warfield has frequently been criticized on this point by friend and foe alike. See C. Van Til's introduction to Warfield's *Inspiration and Authority of the Bible* (Nutley, NJ: Presbyterian and Reformed) 3-68; J. J. Makarian, *The Calvinistic Concept of Biblical Revelation in the Theology of Benjamin Breckinridge Warfield,* (Ann Arbor, MI: University Microfilms [Drew University Ph.D. dissertation] 1963), 75; William Livingston, *The Princeton Apologetic as Exemplified by the Work of Benjamin Breckinridge Warfield and J. Gresham Machen: A study in American Theology, 1880-1930* [Yale University, Ph.D. dissertation] 1963.

16   This corresponds to the requirement of prophetic authorship as the requirement for canonicity of an Old Testament book.

17   Harris (Canonicity) (1957,1969), p.287-289. Of the *fides divina* Warfield had stated, ." . . that the inspired Scriptures as such may be determined for faith, there is need, besides the witness of the Holy Ghost, of an external criterion." ("Review of A. W. Deickhoff, *Das Gepredigte Wort und die Heilige Schrift und Das Wort Gottes,"* *The Presbyterian Review* 10 [1890]:507). While he did not deny the principle of the witness of the Spirit, he did reduce it to a sanctified rationalism.

18   Harris (Canonicity) (1957,1969), p.239-240. Similar evidence is adduced from Justin. Harris concludes concerning the authorship:

It appears that Mark and Luke were not mere second-generation disciples who followed their masters in time and wrote what they pleased, but were disciples who followed the teachings of their masters in such a way that they presented their masters' teachings, and their production had their masters' authority. . . We are reminded of Tertullian's use of the phrase "apostolic men," referring to Mark and Luke. In both cases it should be noted that these are not mere companions of the apostles but are, as it were, assistants, understudies, who reproduced their masters' teachings. . . Quite clearly Mark and Luke are not authoritative in their own right; rather they are authoritative because of their adherence to their apostolic masters. (Ibid.)

Elsewhere, Harris cites the tradition coming from Clement of Alexandria that Mark began his composition before the death of Peter. He even notes Eusebius' claim that Peter approved of the finished work. While he recognizes that the accuracy of this tradition cannot be verified, his inclusion of the tradition with pointed emphasis seems to indicate that he at least thinks the tradition may be accurate (262). But should the tradition not be accurate, and it be demonstrated that Mark composed his gospel following Peter's death (as other patristic writers indicate) and supplemented Peter's teaching with reference to the already composed Gospel of Matthew, Mark could still be seen as preserving his master's teaching (263).

As he turns our attention to the books of the antilegomena where the question of apostolicity becomes more acute, Harris goes to great lengths to demonstrate the possibility that the books in question were written by members of the original inner circle of the Twelve. With reference to James and Jude, Harris notes the tradition of two Jameses and two Judes in the apostolic Church.

. . . Comparison of John 19:25 with Mark 15:40 indicates that the two Marys, sisters, were at the Cross, and one is variously called the mother of James and the wife of Cleopas. It appears that Cleopas is to be identified with Alphaeus, the father of James and Jude. So if there were half brothers of Jesus called James and Jude, they would have been cousins of the apostolic brothers James and Jude (261).

The Roman Catholic Church holds that there was only one pair of brothers, hence the apostolic pair is seen by Catholics as the authors of the books bearing their names. While the usual Protestant position is that Our Lord had biological brothers, Harris notes: "We should remember that according to the usual Protestant view, these Epistles, if genuine, may very well be apostolic, written by the sons of Alphaeus" (262). However, should it be demonstrated the books were penned by the half brothers of Christ, "it may yet be inferred that the half brothers of Christ, like Paul, were also inducted into the apostolic office as those born out of due season" (263). He concludes his discussion noting, "We at least do not have enough information to deny the apostolic authorship of these two Epistles." (Ibid.) At this point Harris begs the question at hand.

19 Ibid., 264.
20 Ibid., 266.
21 Ibid., 268.
22 Ibid., 270.
23 Ibid.
24 Norman Geisler and William Nix, *A General Introduction to the Bible* (Chicago: Moody Press, 1968).
25 Ibid., 133.
26 Ibid., 138. This criterion is akin to the Reformed doctrine of the *autopistie* of Scripture.

27 Ibid., 139.
28 Ibid., 140. Geisler and Nix are careful to point out that pseudonymity adopted as a *literary device* would not exclude a book from the canon. The case in point here would be the book of Ecclesiastes in which many understand the author to have written autobiographically as though he were Solomon. Such a device would in their view be allowable since it involved no moral deception.
29 Ibid., 142.
30 Ibid., 143. Italics original.
31 Herman Ridderbos, *The Authority of the New Testament Scriptures,* (Philadelphia: Presbyterian & Reformed Publishing Co., 1963), 46-47.
32 Ibid., 44.
33 Brevard S. Childs, *The New Testament as Canon: an Introduction,* (Philadelphia: Fortress Press, 1984), 33.
34 Ridderbos, 39.
35 For a more detailed discussion of the concept of "inspiration" or writing under the leading or influence of the Holy Spirit in the ancient Church see Bruce, Canon of Scripture , 266-267. This is not to imply the term theopneustos was so employed by the patristic writers. Warfield has demonstrated that this term was early an epithet for Scripture while later it broadened to mean something approaching divine. (Inspiration and Authority, 272-276)
36 1 Clement 63:2; 59:1. Clement does not use the Pauline term *theopneustos* but does state variously, ." . . the things we have written through the Holy Spirit." (63:2) and "to the words which have been spoken by Him (Jesus Christ) through us."(59:1).
37 Life of Constantine 1.11.2. Here Eusebius speaks of the inspiring aid of the heavenly Word as he writes. For a fuller discussion of the concept of inspiration in the early Church see Sundberg, "The Bible Canon and the Christian Doctrine of Inspiration," Interp 29 (1975):365-370.
38 See Thomas A. Hoffman, "Inspiration, Normativeness, Canonicity, and the Unique Sacred Character of the Bible," *CBQ* 44 (1982), 457-58.
39 Ridderbos, 36. He also notes that the judgment of the early Church is an insufficient ground for accepting a book as canonical: " . . . it is equally obvious that, a posteriori *the historical judgment of the Church* as to what is and is not apostolic can never be the final basis for the acceptance of the New Testament as holy and canonical."(35).
40 Bruce Metzger notes that the term Canon had both a material and a formal sense:
. . . ecclesiastical writers during the first three centuries used the word *kanon* to refer to what was for Christianity an inner law and binding norm of belief ("rule of faith" and/or "rule of truth"). From the fourth century onward the word also came to be used in connection with the sacred writings of the Old and New Testaments . . . . according to Zahn and Souter, the formal meaning of Canon as "a list" was primary, for otherwise it would be difficult to explain the use of the verb *kanonizein* (`to include in a canon") when it is applied to particular books and to the books collectively. *The Canon of the New Testament* (Oxford: Clarendon Press, 1987), 293.
41 The question of whether the Canon is a "collection of authoritative books" or an "authoritative collection of books" hinges on what definition of Canon one adopts. If one argues that the individual writings are canonical because of their divine inspiration, then he would logically see the Canon as a collection of authoritative books. If on the other hand, one views the Canon in the sense of a completed list to which nothing can be added, he would tend to see the Canon as an authoritative collection. However, I believe that at

this point to be consistent one would have to admit that the authority of the *collection* is imposed by ecclesiastical authority.

42   Youngblood, 27.

43   Ibid., 28.

44   This is readily apparent within the pages of Scripture. Jesus Himself constantly taught "as one who had authority." This in distinction to the normal rabbinic tradition. Christ on numerous occasions declared, "You have heard it said . . . but I tell you." In the epistles of the apostles, a word of the Lord was enough to settle a matter. (e.g. 1 Cor 7:10-11, with reference to marriage and divorce; 1 Cor 11:23ff, with reference to conduct in worship) additionally, sayings of the Lord, not found in the canonical gospels are cited as authoritative (canonical) (Acts 20:35 also cf. 1 Thess 5:22).

45   [Own Note] What Sawyer refers to here as the post-Apostolic period, Raymond E. Brown et al referred to as the sub-Apostolic (AD 67–100). Cf. Section B of Book Four (*The Jigsaw Puzzle Church*) in this collection.

46   In the New Testament itself we find on occasion the preference for a personal visit over a letter. In Gal 4 Paul declares his desire to be with the Galatians. In other places we find this same mentality (e.g. 1 Thess 3). On other occasions a letter was preferable to a personal visit e.g., 1 Cor. See F.F. Bruce, "some Thoughts on the Development of the New Testament Canon" *Bulletin of the John Rylands Library* 65 (1983), 39.

47   Cf. 2 Pet 1:19-21. There was a problem in knowing how to sort out which tradition was genuine and which was spurious. The answer, proposed by Papias, was that a tradition which was traceable to the apostles themselves was regarded as genuine. Eusebius quotes Papias as declaring:

But I shall not hesitate to put down for you along with my interpretation whatsoever things I have at any time learned carefully from the elders and carefully remembered, guaranteeing their truth. For I did not, like the multitude, take pleasure in those that speak much, but in those that teach the truth; not in those that relate strange commandments, but in those who deliver the commandments given by the Lord to faith and springing to truth itself. If then any one came, who had been a follower of the elders,--what Andrew or what Peter said, or what was said by Philip, or by Thomas, or by James, or by John, or by Matthew, or by any other of the disciples of the Lord, and what things Aristion and the Presbyter John, the disciples of the Lord say. For I did not think that what was to be gotten out of books would profit me as much as what came from the living and abiding voice (Eusebius, *Ecclesiastical History*, III. 39. 4).

Theo Donner objects to the interpretation of Papias' words which would make him downplay the importance of the written Scripture. He insists that Papias was "relying on oral tradition only for his commentary on the words of the Lord, not for the actual content of the words" ("some Thoughts on the History of the New Testament Canon, " *Themelios* 7 (1981-82), 25). McGiffert notes that Papias' statement should not be interpreted to mean that Papias' faith was in oral tradition as opposed to written tradition, but that the oral tradition supplemented the written tradition (*NPNF*, I, 171, n. 5). In his following discussion of Papias, Eusebius notes that Papias preserved heretofore unwritten tradition of the words of Christ on the authority of Aristion and John the elder (172). The point here is that at this period the two, written and oral tradition existed side by side.

48   e.g. 2 Tim 2:2; 1 Cor. 11:23. Kistemaker notes:

Tradition is governed by apostolic authority, which finds its origin in Christ. Behind the tradition recorded in the New Testament stands Jesus Christ. He is the first link in the chain of tradition. The apostles transmitted this tradition through sound teaching. "What you (Timothy) have heard from me, keep as the pattern of sound teaching," says Paul in 2 Timothy 1:13. The

Apostolic deposit was kept by way of faithful teachers. At first they taught by word of mouth, and as time progressed they taught by means of the written page. *JETS* 20, 6.

49 Ibid.

50 In 2 Pet 3:16 the apostle makes reference to the ignorant and unstable who twist the letters of Paul "to their own destruction as they do the rest of Scripture." The second occurrence (disputed by some) is 1 Timothy 5:18 where Paul coordinates a quotation from Deut 25:4 (Do not muzzle the ox while he is treading out the grain) with a citation from Luke 10:7 (The laborer deserves his wages.), citing both as Scripture.

51 In a recent study on p^{46} Young Kyu Kim has argued on calligraphic grounds that the papyrus, which contains a majority of eight of the Pauline epistles plus the book of Hebrews should be dated during the late first century reign of Domitian ("Paleographic Dating of p46 to the Later First Century," *Biblica* 69 [1988], 254.). If correct this would argue even more strongly for the authority of the apostolic writings in the early Church.

52 F. F. Bruce, "some Thoughts on the Development of the New Testament Canon" *Bulletin of the John Rylands Library* 65 (1983), 39.

53 Marcion's anti-Jewish theological *a priori* caused him to reject all the gospels except a mutilated form of Luke, (which he attributed to Paul), and ten of Paul's epistles.

54 A fragment, it evidently originally included the four gospels, thirteen Pauline epistles, Jude, two letters of John, Wisdom, and the Apocalypses of John and Peter (Bruce, "some Thoughts," p. 57). Sundberg has asserted that the Muratorian Canon is not an early western Canon, but a fourth century eastern production. If correct, this would remove a key piece of evidence from the puzzle of how the Canon came to be formed ("The Bible Canon and the Christian Doctrine of Inspiration," *Interpretation* 29 [1975], 362. See also "The Making of the New Testament Canon, " *Interpreters One Volume Commentary on the Bible*, [Nashville: Abingdon, 1971], 1223.) F. F. Bruce has denied the validity of Sundberg's analysis of the provenance of the document on linguistic grounds ("some Thoughts," pp. 57-59). Metzger (Canon of The New Testament, 193), Childs (The New Testament as Canon, 238) and Edward Ferguson ("Canon Muratori; Date and Provenance" Studia Patristica, 18 [1982], 677-683) all concur with this evaluation.

55 For a fuller discussion of Montanism's influence in the formation of the Canon see Metzger, *The Canon of the New Testament*, 99-106.

56 J.A. Lamb, "The Place of the Bible in the Liturgy" in *The Cambridge History of the Bible* vol. I (Cambridge: Cambridge University Press) 567. Yet another factor which affected the collection of the books into a coherent collection was the introduction of the codex as it replaced the scroll. Bruce notes, "The nearly simultaneous popularization of the codex and the publication of the fourfold gospel may have been coincidental; on the other hand, one of the two may have had some influence on the other" (Bruce, 49).

57 Ronald Youngblood, "The Process, How We Got Our Bible," *Christianity Today,* February 5, 1988, 27.

58 Augustine, writing in A.D.397 the same year as the third council of Carthage and after the synod of Hippo gave his criteria for canonicity.

Accordingly, among the canonical Scriptures he will judge according to the following standard: to prefer those that are received by all the catholic Churches to those which some do not receive. Among those again which are not received by all, he will prefer such as have sanction of the greater number and those of greater authority, to such as are held by the smaller number and those of lesser authority. If, however, he shall find that some books are held by the greater number, and others by the Churches of greater authority, . . . I think that in such a case the authority on the two sides is to be looked upon as equal. (*On Christian Doctrine* II. 12)

It is significant that Augustine makes no appeal to any council, only to consensus. Bruce notes that it was not a councilliar pronouncement which fixed the Canon in the West. Rather, it was the prestige of Augustine and Jerome. (*Canon of the New Testament*, 231)

59 Bruce notes that while there was a basic unity of content in the East, their canons still reflected a diversity for centuries after Athanasius. (*The Canon of Scripture* [Downers Grove: IVP, 1988],215)

60 [Own Note] cf. Artefact #8 in Chapter 11 of Book Two (The Great Collaboration) in this collection.

61 The Catholic epistles and the Apocalypse were omitted. Hebrews, viewed as Pauline, was accepted, while Philemon, was either unknown or rejected. The fourth century Syrian fathers included 3 Corinthians as canonical (W. G. Kummel, *Introduction to the New Testament* 14th revised ed., translated by A. J. Mattill [Nashville: Abingdon, 1966], 353).

62 [Own Note] cf. Artefact #15 in Chapter 20 of Book Two (The Great Collaboration) in this collection.

63 Ibid.

64 Ibid. The Ethiopic version is dated as early as the fourth century by some. Others would attribute it to the seventh century (Bruce Metzger, *The Text of the New Testament* (New York: Oxford University Press, 1968), 84.

65 B. F. Wescott, *A General Survey of the History of the Canon of the New Testament*, (3rd ed., London: MacMillian, 1870), 426.

66 Ibid., 429. C.f. Metzger, Canon of the New Testament, 238-240.

67 Ibid., 443.

68 It is significant that the early Lutheran Confessions did not contain a list of the canonical writings.

69 See Ridderbos, 39.

70 Klyne Snodgrass, "Providence Is Not Enough," *Christianity Today*, February 5, 1988, 33.

71 See this writer's Th.D. dissertation, *Charles Augustus Briggs and Tensions in Late Nineteenth Century American Theology*, Dallas Theological Seminary, 1987, 214-227. While Briggs' name is infamous as a convicted heretic and he did indeed deny the inerrancy of Scripture, his doctrine of Canon was never challenged as being heterodox., even by his greatest theological foe B.B. Warfield.

72 David G. Dunbar has objected that Ridderbos too easily lumps Protestant appeals to divine providence in guiding the Church's recognition of the Canon together with Roman Catholic claims of ecclesiastical infallibility. To be sure, there is a formal similarity, but materially there is a great difference in the theological program here at work. . . ("The Biblical Canon, " *Hermeneutics, Authority and Canon,* [Grand Rapids: Zondervan, 1986], 355). I would agree that there is a difference between an appeal to an infallible Pope or hierarchy and to consensus. However, the question still remains if indeed the "leading of the Lord" does not ultimately vest some kind of infallible authority in the consensus of the Church.

73 F.F. Bruce, *The Canon of the Scripture* (Downers Grove: IVP, 1988), asserts apostolicity as a valid objective criterion for determining canonicity, but goes on to assert the "self authenticating authority"(276-277) of the New Testament books. This criterion is akin if not identical to Briggs' *autopistie* of te Scripture.

74 It might be objected here that the earliest Church did have a written Canon, that of the Old Testament. While this is true, it was the OT interpreted Christologically by the Lord Himself and His Apostles. Thus, the risen Jesus Christ was the standard, the Canon, by which even the OT was measured.

75 Ridderbos, 40.
76 Ibid., 41.
77 Charles A. Briggs, *General Introduction to the Study of Holy Scripture* (New York: Charles Scribners & Sons, 1899), 163.
78 Ibid.
79 Ibid.
80 See Geoffrey Wainwright, "The New Testament as Canon", *SJT* 28, 554. Cf. also R. Grant, *JSNT* 16, 39.
81 Briggs, *General Introduction*, 163.
82 Ibid.
83 This factor became very important for Calvin in his discussion of the canonicity of 2 Peter. He saw in the epistle nothing that was in conflict with the other Scriptures which he did accept. This became significant in his acceptance of the epistle as canonical despite reservations concerning its style.

For Calvin properly would have us understand not only that such books were accepted by the Church from ancient times but also that they contain nothing which is in conflict with the remainder of Scripture, which was never contested in any way. Is not an important truth to be found, with respects (sic) to the limitations of the Canon, in the statement: *Sacra Scriptura sui ipsius interpres?* (Ridderbos, 51).

84 Briggs, *General Introduction*, 163.
85 Ibid., 166.
86 Ibid.
87 Ibid., 167
88 Ibid., 142-144. Even John Warwick Montgomery has noted, "*absolute* certainty, both in science and theology, rests only with the data (for the former, natural phenomena; for the latter, scriptural affirmations)." ("The Theologian's Craft," *CTM* 37 [1966]: 82 n.72, quoted by Dunbar, "Biblical Canon, " 360.) Dunbar admits that "the shape and limits of the Canon are not scriptural affirmations. Therefore . . . we cannot claim *absolute* empirical certainty for our canonical model" (p. 360). This is not to deny that from a practical perspective some theological formulations attain a "certain" status.
89 Briggs, 142-144.
90 Ibid., 146.
91 Briggs was not here arguing for himself personally. His writings evidence no doubt that the extent of the Canon includes the entire Protestant canon. In fact, he indicated doubt whether several of the apocryphal books ought not be reevaluated and included in the Canon (64).

Ridderbos has noted, (44)

There was never any discussion of the canonicity of the majority of the New Testament writings. The Church never regarded these writings as being anything else except the authoritative witness to the great period of redemption.

92 Ibid.

* * *

Appendix E - Apostolic Succession: An Orthodox Essay

Taught by the Apostles

What is the truth about Jesus? Ask those who knew his earliest followers, said Irenaeus.

by Fr. John Behr. From Issue 96: The Gnostics Hunger for Secret Knowledge. (2007)

"**The Church**," wrote Irenaeus, "having received this preaching and this faith, although scattered throughout the whole world, yet, as if occupying but one house, carefully preserves it. She also believed these points [of doctrine] just as if she had but one soul, and one and the same heart, and she proclaims them, and teaches them, and hands them down, with perfect harmony, as if she possessed one mouth."

From the beginning, Christians have been urged to hold on to "the faith delivered once for all to the saints" (Jude 3). Yet also from the beginning, some people had begun to misunderstand or misinterpret that faith. After the eyewitnesses and apostles passed away, believers could no longer go for answers to those who had laid the foundations of the Church. In every great city, different teachers and leaders claimed to represent true Christianity, each asserting that they maintained the true faith, each appealing to a body of apostolic writings.

To support their doctrines, some Gnostics were claiming a succession of teachers going back to an apostle. In the face of such authoritative-sounding claims, how could Christians know that what the Gnostics taught was wrong and what their own pastor taught was right? Whom could they trust?

Despite these contending claims, even the pagan doctor Galen (129-216?) recognized that there was such a thing as "the Great Church," which was clearly distinct from the multitude of sects. Irenaeus of Lyons was the first Christian leader to write a confident statement of the faith of "the Great Church" and explain why it could be trusted. He considered three things to be inextricably linked: Scripture (both the Old Testament and the apostolic writings), the tradition of the apostles' teaching (the Rule of Faith), and the leadership of the Church.

Passing on the true faith

Today we tend to think of apostolic succession in terms of the laying on of hands: The Church confers an office on a consecrated bishop, who can thereby trace his authority back to the apostles. Roman Catholic, Eastern Orthodox, and Anglican Churches each claim their own unbroken line of ordained leaders. Most Protestants deny the importance of a continuous succession of bishops altogether.

But in the second century, apostolic succession meant something more simple. Two main concerns were at stake: What is the true faith? And how has it been passed on from the apostles to us?

This faith, according to Irenaeus, is found in the Scriptures and summarized in the Rule of Faith. The proof that this is the true faith is that the "Great Church" could point to a visible succession of teachers, presbyters, and bishops who taught the same things throughout the world: This is the teaching common to all the apostles and the Churches founded by them. The leaders of many of these Churches had been taught by the apostles themselves, or disciples of the apostles, and they "neither taught nor knew of anything like what these [heretics] rave about."

This was an important defence of orthodox Christianity against the Gnostic teachers. If the apostles were going to entrust the truth about Jesus to anyone, Irenaeus argued, they would have entrusted it to the same people to whom they entrusted the Churches. They would not have charged some with caring for their flock and then secretly told hidden mysteries to others. In contrast to the Gnostics' secret succession, the Great Church had a succession of teaching that was universal and public—and therefore more trustworthy.

As an example, Irenaeus pointed to the Christian communities in Rome (at that time there were many house Churches, each with its own leaders, not one Church with a single bishop), and in particular the community led by Eleutherius. He listed 12 successive leaders, from the apostles down to Eleutherius, to show that the apostolic teaching had been passed on continuously. He especially noted Clement, one of the first leaders, who had known the apostles and recorded their teaching in a letter that was earlier than any of the Gnostics' texts. "By this succession," Irenaeus wrote, "the ecclesiastical tradition from the apostles, and the preaching of the truth, have come down to us. And this is the most abundant proof that there is one and the same vivifying faith, which has been preserved in the Church from the apostles until now, and handed down in truth."

In later centuries, some Churches began trying to construct similar lists of succession to defend their own authenticity or authority, but this was not Irenaeus's main concern. He was not defending the authority of particular people; he was trying to defend the true faith against heresy by showing that the apostles' message about Jesus had been faithfully preserved in the Churches, and therefore could be trusted. Succession for him did not primarily mean handing down an office; it was the public expression of the continuity of the true faith.

The whole Church

The Roman Church had developed a unique importance in the ancient world; it had been founded by both Peter and Paul, had given generously to Christians in other places, and had preserved the true faith. But Irenaeus pointed out that apostolic succession could also be seen in other cities like Ephesus where the apostles had founded a Church. His own teacher Polycarp in Smyrna had known the apostles and died "having always taught the things which he had learned from the apostles, and which the Church has handed down, and which alone are true."

Those Churches or leaders who could show apostolic succession were not above criticism. Irenaeus had no qualms about writing to bishop Victor, Eleutherius' successor in Rome, and telling him that he was wrong not to respect the Easter practices of Asia Minor Christians. Succession of leadership was not a guarantee of truth, but a powerful witness to the truth that is the common inheritance of all who belong to the Great Church, all who carry on the teachings of the apostles—wherever they may be.

The success of the Great Church—and the weakening of the Gnostics and other sects—did not depend, as some recent popular books have claimed, upon the patriarchal power of authoritarian bishops. At this point in time, bishops and other Christian teachers had no worldly power, no property, and no ability to call upon the political authorities for help. Their power lay in being able to offer Christians a coherent, persuasive picture of the truth handed down from the beginning.

Fr. John Behr is dean and professor of patristics at St. Vladimir's Orthodox Theological Seminary.

Copyright © 2007 by the author or Christianity Today International/Christian History & Biography magazine.

For reprint information on Christian History & Biography, Issue 96, Fall 2007, Vol. XXVII, No. 4, Page 33, please see:
http://www.ctlibrary.com/ch/2007/issue96/10.31.html

✷ ✷ ✷

Appendix F - Vatican II: Dogmatic Constitution on Divine Revelation[1]

(Vatican II, Dei Verbum, 18th November 1965)

PREFACE

1. Hearing the Word of God with reverence and proclaiming it with faith, the sacred synod takes its direction from these words of St. John: "We announce to you the eternal life which dwelt with the Father and was made visible to us. What we have seen and heard we announce to you, so that you may have fellowship with us and our common fellowship be with the Father and His Son Jesus Christ" (1 John 1:2-3). Therefore, following in the footsteps of the Council of Trent and of the First Vatican Council, this present council wishes to set forth authentic doctrine on divine revelation and how it is handed on, so that by hearing the message of salvation the whole world may believe, by believing it may hope, and by hoping it may love. (1)

CHAPTER I
DIVINE REVELATION ITSELF[2]

2. In His goodness and wisdom God chose to reveal Himself and to make known to us the hidden purpose of His will (see Eph. 1:9) by which through Christ, the Word made flesh, man might in the Holy Spirit have access to the Father and come to share in the divine nature (see Eph. 2:18; 2 Peter 1:4). Through this revelation, therefore, the invisible God (see Col. 1;15, 1 Tim. 1:17) out of the abundance of His love speaks to men as friends (see Ex. 33:11; John 15:14-15) and lives among them (see Bar. 3:38), so that He may invite and take them into fellowship with Himself. This plan of revelation is realized by deeds and words having an inner unity: the deeds wrought by God in the history of salvation manifest and confirm the teaching and realities signified by the words, while the words proclaim the deeds and clarify the mystery contained in them. By this revelation then, the deepest truth about God and the salvation of

man shines out for our sake in Christ, who is both the mediator and the fullness of all revelation. (2)

3. God, who through the Word creates all things (see John 1:3) and keeps them in existence, gives men an enduring witness to Himself in created realities (see Rom. 1:19-20). Planning to make known the way of heavenly salvation, He went further and from the start manifested Himself to our first parents. Then after their fall His promise of redemption aroused in them the hope of being saved (see Gen. 3:15) and from that time on He ceaselessly kept the human race in His care, to give eternal life to those who perseveringly do good in search of salvation (see Rom. 2:6-7). Then, at the time He had appointed He called Abraham in order to make of him a great nation (see Gen. 12:2). Through the patriarchs, and after them through Moses and the prophets, He taught this people to acknowledge Himself the one living and true God, provident father and just judge, and to wait for the Saviour promised by Him, and in this manner prepared the way for the Gospel down through the centuries.

4. Then, after speaking in many and varied ways through the prophets, "now at last in these days God has spoken to us in His Son" (Heb. 1:1-2). For He sent His Son, the eternal Word, who enlightens all men, so that He might dwell among men and tell them of the innermost being of God (see John 1:1-18). Jesus Christ, therefore, the Word made flesh, was sent as "a man to men." (3) He "speaks the words of God" (John 3;34), and completes the work of salvation which His Father gave Him to do (see John 5:36; John 17:4). To see Jesus is to see His Father (John 14:9). For this reason Jesus perfected revelation by fulfilling it through his whole work of making Himself present and manifesting Himself: through His words and deeds, His signs and wonders, but especially through His death and glorious resurrection from the dead and final sending of the Spirit of truth. Moreover He confirmed with divine testimony what revelation proclaimed, that God is with us to free us from the darkness of sin and death, and to raise us up to life eternal.

The Christian dispensation, therefore, as the new and definitive covenant, will never pass away and we now await no further new public revelation before the glorious manifestation of our Lord Jesus Christ (see 1 Tim. 6:14 and Tit. 2:13).

5. "The obedience of faith" (Rom. 13:26; see 1:5; 2 Cor 10:5-6) "is to be given to God who reveals, an obedience by which man commits his whole self freely to God, offering the full submission of intellect and will to God who reveals," (4) and freely assenting to the truth revealed by Him. To make this act of faith, the grace of God and the interior help of the Holy Spirit must precede and assist, moving the heart and turning it to God, opening the eyes of the mind and giving "joy and ease to everyone in as-

senting to the truth and believing it." (5) To bring about an ever deeper understanding of revelation the same Holy Spirit constantly brings faith to completion by His gifts.

6. Through divine revelation, God chose to show forth and communicate Himself and the eternal decisions of His will regarding the salvation of men. That is to say, He chose to share with them those divine treasures which totally transcend the understanding of the human mind. (6)

As a sacred synod has affirmed, God, the beginning and end of all things, can be known with certainty from created reality by the light of human reason (see Rom. 1:20); but teaches that it is through His revelation that those religious truths which are by their nature accessible to human reason can be known by all men with ease, with solid certitude and with no trace of error, even in this present state of the human race. (7)

CHAPTER II

THE TRANSMISSION [HANDING ON] OF DIVINE REVELATION

7. In His gracious goodness, God has seen to it that what He had revealed for the salvation of all nations would abide perpetually in its full integrity and be handed on to all generations. Therefore Christ the Lord in whom the full revelation of the supreme God is brought to completion (see 2Cor. 1:20; 3:13-4:6), commissioned the Apostles to preach to all men that Gospel which is the source of all saving truth and moral teaching, (1) and to impart to them heavenly gifts. This Gospel had been promised in former times through the prophets, and Christ Himself had fulfilled it and promulgated it with His lips. This commission was faithfully fulfilled by the Apostles who, by their oral preaching, by example, and by observances handed on what they had received from the lips of Christ, from living with Him, and from what He did, or what they had learned through the prompting of the Holy Spirit. The commission was fulfilled, too, by those Apostles and apostolic men who under the inspiration of the same Holy Spirit committed the message of salvation to writing. (2)

But in order to keep the Gospel forever whole and alive within the Church, the Apostles left bishops as their successors, "handing over" to them "the authority to teach in their own place."(3) This Sacred Tradition, therefore, and Sacred Scripture of both the Old and New Testaments are like a mirror in which the pilgrim Church on earth looks at God, from whom she has received everything, until she is brought finally to see Him as He is, face to face (see 1 John 3:2).

8. And so the apostolic preaching, which is expressed in a special way in the inspired books, was to be preserved by an unending succession of preachers until the end of time. Therefore the Apostles, handing on what they themselves had received, warn the faithful to hold fast to the traditions which they have learned either by word of mouth or by letter (see 2 Thess. 2:15), and to fight in defense of the faith handed on once and for all (see Jude 1:3) (4) Now what was handed on by the Apostles includes everything which contributes toward the holiness of life and increase in faith of the peoples of God; and so the Church, in her teaching, life and worship, perpetuates and hands on to all generations all that she herself is, all that she believes.

This Tradition which comes from the Apostles develop in the Church with the help of the Holy Spirit. (5) For there is a growth in the understanding of the realities and the words which have been handed down. This happens through the contemplation and study made by believers, who treasure these things in their hearts (see Luke, 2:19, 51) through a penetrating understanding of the spiritual realities which they experience, and through the preaching of those who have received through Episcopal succession the sure gift of truth. For as the centuries succeed one another, the Church constantly moves forward toward the fullness of divine truth until the words of God reach their complete fulfillment in her.

The words of the holy fathers witness to the presence of this living Tradition, whose wealth is poured into the practice and life of the believing and praying Church. Through the same Tradition the Church's full canon of the sacred books is known, and the sacred writings themselves are more profoundly understood and unceasingly made active in her; and thus God, who spoke of old, uninterruptedly converses with the bride of His beloved Son; and the Holy Spirit, through whom the living voice of the Gospel resounds in the Church, and through her, in the world, leads unto all truth those who believe and makes the word of Christ dwell abundantly in them (see Col. 3:16).

9. Hence there exists a close connection and communication between Sacred Tradition and Sacred Scripture. For both of them, flowing from the same divine wellspring, in a certain way merge into a unity and tend toward the same end. For Sacred Scripture is the Word of God inasmuch as it is consigned to writing under the inspiration of the divine Spirit, while Sacred Tradition takes the Word of God entrusted by Christ the Lord and the Holy Spirit to the Apostles, and hands it on to their successors in its full purity, so that led by the light of the Spirit of truth, they may in proclaiming it preserve this Word of God faithfully, explain it, and make it more widely known. Consequently it is not from Sacred Scripture alone

that the Church draws her certainty about everything which has been revealed. Therefore both Sacred Tradition and Sacred Scripture are to be accepted and venerated with the same sense of loyalty and reverence.(6)

10. Sacred Tradition and Sacred Scripture form one sacred deposit of the Word of God, committed to the Church. Holding fast to this deposit the entire holy people united with their shepherds remain always steadfast in the teaching of the Apostles, in the common life, in the breaking of the bread and in prayers (see Acts 2, 42, Greek text), so that holding to, practicing and professing the heritage of the faith, it becomes on the part of the bishops and faithful a single common effort. (7)

But the task of authentically interpreting the Word of God, whether written or handed on, (8) has been entrusted exclusively to the living teaching office [Magisterium] of the Church, (9) whose authority is exercised in the name of Jesus Christ. This teaching office is not above the Word of God, but serves it, teaching only what has been handed on, listening to it devoutly, guarding it scrupulously and explaining it faithfully in accord with a divine commission and with the help of the Holy Spirit, it draws from this one deposit of faith everything which it presents for belief as divinely revealed.

It is clear, therefore, that Sacred Tradition, Sacred Scripture and the teaching authority of the Church, in accord with God's most wise design, are so linked and joined together that one cannot stand without the others, and that all together and each in its own way under the action of the one Holy Spirit contribute effectively to the salvation of souls.

CHAPTER III

SACRED SCRIPTURE: ITS DIVINE INSPIRATION AND ITS INTERPRETATION

11. Those divinely revealed realities which are contained and presented in Sacred Scripture have been committed to writing under the inspiration of the Holy Spirit. For holy mother Church, relying on the belief of the Apostles (see John 20:31; 2 Tim. 3:16; 2 Peter 1:19-20, 3:15-16), holds that the books of both the Old and New Testaments in their entirety, with all their parts, are sacred and canonical because written under the inspiration of the Holy Spirit, they have God as their author and have been handed on as such to the Church herself.(1) In composing the sacred books, God chose men and while employed by Him (2) they made use of their powers and abilities, so that with Him acting in them and through them, (3) they, as true authors, consigned to writing everything and only those things which He wanted. (4)

Therefore, since everything asserted by the inspired authors or sacred writers must be held to be asserted by the Holy Spirit, it follows that the books of Scripture must be acknowledged as teaching solidly, faithfully and without error that truth which God wanted put into sacred writings (5) for the sake of salvation. Therefore "all Scripture is divinely inspired and has its use for teaching the truth and refuting error, for reformation of manners and discipline in right living, so that the man who belongs to God may be efficient and equipped for good work of every kind" (2 Tim. 3:16-17, Greek text).

12. However, since God speaks in Sacred Scripture through men in human fashion, (6) the interpreter of Sacred Scripture, in order to see clearly what God wanted to communicate to us, should carefully investigate what meaning the sacred writers really intended, and what God wanted to manifest by means of their words.

To search out the intention of the sacred writers, attention should be given, among other things, to "literary forms." For truth is set forth and expressed differently in texts which are variously historical, prophetic, poetic, or of other forms of discourse. The interpreter must investigate what meaning the sacred writer intended to express and actually expressed in particular circumstances by using contemporary literary forms in accordance with the situation of his own time and culture. (7) For the correct understanding of what the sacred author wanted to assert, due attention must be paid to the customary and characteristic styles of feeling, speaking and narrating which prevailed at the time of the sacred writer, and to the patterns men normally employed at that period in their everyday dealings with one another. (8)

But, since Holy Scripture must be read and interpreted in the sacred spirit in which it was written, (9) no less serious attention must be given to the content and unity of the whole of Scripture if the meaning of the sacred texts is to be correctly worked out. The living Tradition of the whole Church must be taken into account along with the harmony which exists between elements of the faith. It is the task of exegetes to work according to these rules toward a better understanding and explanation of the meaning of Sacred Scripture, so that through preparatory study the judgment of the Church may mature. For all of what has been said about the way of interpreting Scripture is subject finally to the judgment of the Church, which carries out the divine commission and ministry of guarding and interpreting the Word of God. (10)

13. In Sacred Scripture, therefore, while the truth and holiness of God always remains intact, the marvellous "condescension" of eternal wisdom is clearly shown, "that we may learn the gentle kindness of God, which words cannot express, and how far He has gone in adapting His lan-

guage with thoughtful concern for our weak human nature." (11) For the words of God, expressed in human language, have been made like human discourse, just as the word of the eternal Father, when He took to Himself the flesh of human weakness, was in every way made like men.

CHAPTER IV
THE OLD TESTAMENT

14. In carefully planning and preparing the salvation of the whole human race the God of infinite love, by a special dispensation, chose for Himself a people to whom He would entrust His promises. First He entered into a covenant with Abraham (see Gen. 15:18) and, through Moses, with the people of Israel (see Ex. 24:8). To this people which He had acquired for Himself, He so manifested Himself through words and deeds as the one true and living God that Israel came to know by experience the ways of God with men. Then too, when God Himself spoke to them through the mouth of the prophets, Israel daily gained a deeper and clearer understanding of His ways and made them more widely known among the nations (see Ps. 21:29; 95:1-3; Is. 2:1-5; Jer. 3:17). The plan of salvation foretold by the sacred authors, recounted and explained by them, is found as the true Word of God in the books of the Old Testament: these books, therefore, written under divine inspiration, remain permanently valuable. "For all that was written for our instruction, so that by steadfastness and the encouragement of the Scriptures we might have hope" (Rom. 15:4).

15. The principal purpose to which the plan of the old covenant was directed was to prepare for the coming of Christ, the redeemer of all and of the messianic kingdom, to announce this coming by prophecy (see Luke 24:44; John 5:39; 1 Peter 1:10), and to indicate its meaning through various types (see 1 Cor. 10:12). Now the books of the Old Testament, in accordance with the state of mankind before the time of salvation established by Christ, reveal to all men the knowledge of God and of man and the ways in which God, just and merciful, deals with men. These books, though they also contain some things which are incomplete and temporary, nevertheless show us true divine pedagogy. (1) These same books, then, give expression to a lively sense of God, contain a store of sublime teachings about God, sound wisdom about human life, and a wonderful treasury of prayers, and in them the mystery of our salvation is present in a hidden way. Christians should receive them with reverence.

16. God, the inspirer and author of both Testaments, wisely arranged that the New Testament be hidden in the Old and the Old be made manifest in the New. (2) For, though Christ established the new covenant in His

blood (see Luke 22:20; 1 Cor. 11:25), still the books of the Old Testament with all their parts, caught up into the proclamation of the Gospel, (3) acquire and show forth their full meaning in the New Testament (see Matt. 5:17; Luke 24:27; Rom. 16:25-26; 2 Cor. 14:16) and in turn shed light on it and explain it.

CHAPTER V

THE NEW TESTAMENT

17. The Word of God, which is the power of God for the salvation of all who believe (see Rom. 1:16), is set forth and shows its power in a most excellent way in the writings of the New Testament. For when the fullness of time arrived (see Gal. 4:4), the Word was made flesh and dwelt among us in His fullness of graces and truth (see John 1:14). Christ established the kingdom of God on earth, manifested His Father and Himself by deeds and words, and completed His work by His death, resurrection and glorious Ascension and by the sending of the Holy Spirit. Having been lifted up from the earth, He draws all men to Himself (see John 12:32, Greek text), He who alone has the words of eternal life (see John 6:68). This mystery had not been manifested to other generations as it was now revealed to His holy Apostles and prophets in the Holy Spirit (see Eph. 3:4-6, Greek text), so that they might preach the Gospel, stir up faith in Jesus, Christ and Lord, and gather together the Church. Now the writings of the New Testament stand as a perpetual and divine witness to these realities.

18. It is common knowledge that among all the Scriptures, even those of the New Testament, the Gospels have a special pre-eminence, and rightly so, for they are the principal witness for the life and teaching of the incarnate Word, our saviour.

    The Church has always and everywhere held and continues to hold that the four Gospels are of apostolic origin. For what the Apostles preached in fulfillment of the commission of Christ, afterwards they themselves and apostolic men, under the inspiration of the divine Spirit, handed on to us in writing: the foundation of faith, namely, the fourfold Gospel, according to Matthew, Mark, Luke and John.(1)

19. Holy Mother Church has firmly and with absolute constancy held, and continues to hold, that the four Gospels just named, whose historical character the Church unhesitatingly asserts, faithfully hand on what Jesus Christ, while living among men, really did and taught for their eternal salvation until the day He was taken up into heaven (see Acts 1:1). Indeed, after the Ascension of the Lord the Apostles handed on to their hearers what He had said and done. This they did with that clearer

understanding which they enjoyed (3) after they had been instructed by the glorious events of Christ's life and taught by the light of the Spirit of truth. (2) The sacred authors wrote the four Gospels, selecting some things from the many which had been handed on by word of mouth or in writing, reducing some of them to a synthesis, explaining some things in view of the situation of their churches and preserving the form of proclamation but always in such fashion that they told us the honest truth about Jesus.(4) For their intention in writing was that either from their own memory and recollections, or from the witness of those who "themselves from the beginning were eyewitnesses and ministers of the Word" we might know "the truth" concerning those matters about which we have been instructed (see Luke 1:2-4).

20. Besides the four Gospels, the canon of the New Testament also contains the epistles of St. Paul and other apostolic writings, composed under the inspiration of the Holy Spirit, by which, according to the wise plan of God, those matters which concern Christ the Lord are confirmed, His true teaching is more and more fully stated, the saving power of the divine work of Christ is preached, the story is told of the beginnings of the Church and its marvellous growth, and its glorious fulfillment is foretold.

    For the Lord Jesus was with His apostles as He had promised (see Matt. 28:20) and sent them the advocate Spirit who would lead them into the fullness of truth (see John 16:13).

CHAPTER VI
SACRED SCRIPTURE IN THE LIFE OF THE CHURCH

21. The Church has always venerated the divine Scriptures just as she venerates the Body of the Lord, since, especially in the sacred liturgy, she unceasingly receives and offers to the faithful the bread of life from the table both of God's Word and of Christ's Body. She has always maintained them, and continues to do so, together with Sacred Tradition, as the supreme rule of faith, since, as inspired by God and committed once and for all to writing, they impart the Word of God Himself without change, and make the voice of the Holy Spirit resound in the words of the prophets and Apostles. Therefore, like the Christian religion itself, all the preaching of the Church must be nourished and regulated by Sacred Scripture. For in the sacred books, the Father who is in heaven meets His children with great love and speaks with them; and the force and power in the Word of God is so great that it stands as the support and energy of the Church, the strength of faith for her sons, the food of the soul, the pure and everlasting source of spiritual life. Consequently these words are perfectly applicable to Sacred Scripture: "For the word of God is liv-

ing and active" (Heb. 4:12) and "it has power to build you up and give you your heritage among all those who are sanctified" (Acts 20:32; see 1 Thess. 2:13).

22. Easy access to Sacred Scripture should be provided for all the Christian faithful. That is why the Church from the very beginning accepted as her own that very ancient Greek translation of the Old Testament which is called the Septuagint; and she has always given a place of honour to other Eastern translations and Latin ones especially the Latin translation known as the vulgate. But since the Word of God should be accessible at all times, the Church by her authority and with maternal concern sees to it that suitable and correct translations are made into different languages, especially from the original texts of the sacred books. And should the opportunity arise and the Church authorities approve, if these translations are produced in cooperation with the separated brethren as well, all Christians will be able to use them.

23. The bride of the incarnate Word, the Church taught by the Holy Spirit, is concerned to move ahead toward a deeper understanding of the Sacred Scriptures so that she may increasingly feed her sons with the divine words. Therefore, she also encourages the study of the holy Fathers of both East and West and of sacred liturgies. Catholic exegetes then and other students of sacred theology, working diligently together and using appropriate means, should devote their energies, under the watchful care of the sacred teaching office of the Church, to an exploration and exposition of the divine writings. This should be so done that as many ministers of the divine word as possible will be able effectively to provide the nourishment of the Scriptures for the people of God, to enlighten their minds, strengthen their wills, and set men's hearts on fire with the love of God. (1) The sacred synod encourages the sons of the Church and Biblical scholars to continue energetically, following the mind of the Church, with the work they have so well begun, with a constant renewal of vigour. (2)

24. Sacred theology rests on the written Word of God, together with Sacred Tradition, as its primary and perpetual foundation. By scrutinizing in the light of faith all truth stored up in the mystery of Christ, theology is most powerfully strengthened and constantly rejuvenated by that word. For the Sacred Scriptures contain the Word of God and since they are inspired, really are the Word of God; and so the study of the sacred page is, as it were, the soul of sacred theology. (3) By the same word of Scripture the ministry of the word also, that is, pastoral preaching, Catechetics and all Christian instruction, in which the liturgical homily must hold the foremost place, is nourished in a healthy way and flourishes in a holy way.

25. Therefore, all the clergy must hold fast to the Sacred Scriptures through diligent sacred reading and careful study, especially the priests of Christ and others, such as deacons and catechists who are legitimately active in the ministry of the word. This is to be done so that none of them will become "an empty preacher of the Word of God outwardly, who is not a listener to it inwardly" (4) since they must share the abundant wealth of the divine word with the faithful committed to them, especially in the sacred liturgy. The sacred synod also earnestly and especially urges all the Christian faithful, especially Religious, to learn by frequent reading of the divine Scriptures the "excellent knowledge of Jesus Christ" (Phil. 3:8). "For ignorance of the Scriptures is ignorance of Christ."(5) Therefore, they should gladly put themselves in touch with the sacred text itself, whether it be through the liturgy, rich in the divine word, or through devotional reading, or through instructions suitable for the purpose and other aids which, in our time, with approval and active support of the shepherds of the Church, are commendably spread everywhere. And let them remember that prayer should accompany the reading of Sacred Scripture, so that God and man may talk together; for "we speak to Him when we pray; we hear Him when we read the divine saying." (6)

    It devolves on sacred bishops "who have the apostolic teaching"(7) to give the faithful entrusted to them suitable instruction in the right use of the divine books, especially the New Testament and above all the Gospels. This can be done through translations of the sacred texts, which are to be provided with the necessary and really adequate explanations so that the children of the Church may safely and profitably become conversant with the Sacred Scriptures and be penetrated with their spirit.

    Furthermore, editions of the Sacred Scriptures, provided with suitable footnotes, should be prepared also for the use of non-Christians and adapted to their situation. Both pastors of souls and Christians generally should see to the wise distribution of these in one way or another.

26. In this way, therefore, through the reading and study of the sacred books "the word of God may spread rapidly and be glorified" (2 Thess. 3:1) and the treasure of revelation, entrusted to the Church, may more and more fill the hearts of men. Just as the life of the Church is strengthened through more frequent celebration of the Eucharistic mystery, similar we may hope for a new stimulus for the life of the Spirit from a growing reverence for the Word of God, which "lasts forever" (Is. 40:8; see 1 Peter 1:23-25).

* * *

NOTES

Preface

Article 1:

1. cf. St. Augustine, "De Catechizandis Rudibus," C.IV 8: PL. 40, 316.

Chapter I

Article 2:

2. cf. Matt. 11:27; John 1:14 and 17; 14:6; 17:1-3; 2 Cor 3:16 and 4, 6; Eph. 1, 3-14.

Article 4:

3. Epistle to Diognetus, c. VII, 4: Funk, Apostolic Fathers, I, p. 403.

Article 5:

4. First Vatican Council, Dogmatic Constitution on the Catholic Faith, Chap. 3, "On Faith:" Denzinger 1789 (3008).

5. Second Council of Orange, Canon 7: Denzinger 180 (377); First Vatican Council, loc. cit.: Denzinger 1791 (3010).

Article 6:

6. First Vatican Council, Dogmatic Constitution on the Catholic Faith, Chap. 2, "On Revelation:" Denzinger 1786 (3005).

7. Ibid: Denzinger 1785 and 1786 (3004 and 3005).

Chapter II

Article 7:

1. cf. Matt. 28:19-20, and Mark 16:15; Council of Trent, session IV, Decree on Scriptural Canons: Denzinger 783 (1501).

2. cf. Council of Trent, loc. cit.; First Vatican Council, session III, Dogmatic Constitution on the Catholic Faith, Chap. 2, "On revelation:" Denzinger 1787 (3005).

3. St. Irenaeus, "Against Heretics" III, 3, 1: PG 7, 848; Harvey, 2, p. 9.

Article 8:

4. cf. Second Council of Nicea: Denzinger 303 (602); Fourth Council of Constance, session X, Canon 1: Denzinger 336 (650-652).

5. cf. First Vatican Council, Dogmatic Constitution on the Catholic Faith, Chap. 4, "On Faith and Reason:" Denzinger 1800 (3020).

Article 9:

6. cf. Council of Trent, session IV, loc. cit.: Denzinger 783 (1501).

Article 10:

7. cf. Pius XII, apostolic constitution, "Munificentissimus Deus," Nov. 1, 1950: A.A.S. 42 (1950) p. 756; Collected Writings of St. Cyprian, Letter 66, 8: Hartel, III, B, p. 733: "The Church [is] people united with the priest and the pastor together with his flock."

8. cf. First Vatican Council, Dogmatic Constitution on the Catholic Faith, Chap. 3 "On Faith:" Denzinger 1792 (3011).

9. cf. Pius XII, encyclical "Humani Generis," Aug. 12, 1950: A.A.S. 42 (1950) pp. 568-69: Denzinger 2314 (3886).

Chapter III

Article 11:

1. cf. First Vatican Council, Dogmatic Constitution on the Catholic Faith, Chap. 2 "On

Revelation:" Denzinger 1787 (3006); Biblical Commission, Decree of June 18,1915: Denzinger 2180 (3629): EB 420; Holy Office, Epistle of Dec. 22, 1923: EB 499.

2. cf. Pius XII, encyclical "Divino Afflante Spiritu," Sept. 30, 1943: A.A.S. 35 (1943) p. 314; Enchiridion Bible. (EB) 556.

3. "In" and "for" man: cf. Heb. 1, and 4, 7; ("in"): 2 Sm. 23,2; Matt.1:22 and various places; ("for"): First Vatican Council, Schema on Catholic Doctrine, note 9: Coll. Lac. VII, 522.

4. Leo XIII, encyclical "Providentissimus Deus," Nov. 18, 1893: Denzinger 1952 (3293); EB 125.

5. cf. St. Augustine, "Gen. ad Litt." 2, 9, 20:PL 34, 270-271; Epistle 82, 3: PL 33, 277: CSEL 34, 2, p. 354. St. Thomas, "On Truth," Q. 12, A. 2, C.Council of Trent, session IV, Scriptural Canons: Denzinger 783 (1501). Leo XIII, encyclical "Providentissimus Deus:" EB 121, 124, 126-127. Pius XII, encyclical "Divino Afflante Spiritu:" EB 539.

Article 12:

6. St. Augustine, "City of God," XVII, 6, 2: PL 41, 537: CSEL. XL, 2, 228.

7. St. Augustine, "On Christian Doctrine" III, 18, 26; PL 34, 75-76.

8. Pius XII, loc. cit. Denziger 2294 (3829-3830); EB 557-562.

9. cf. Benedict XV, encyclical "Spiritus Paraclitus" Sept. 15, 1920:EB 469. St. Jerome, "In Galatians' 5, 19-20: PL 26, 417 A.

10. cf. First Vatican Council, Dogmatic Constitution on the Catholic Faith, Chapter 2, "On Revelation:" Denziger 1788 (3007).

Article 13:

11. St. John Chrysostom "In Genesis" 3, 8 (Homily 17, 1): PG 53, 134; "Attemperatio" [in English "Suitable adjustment"] in Greek "synkatabasis."

Chapter IV

Article 15:

1. Pius XI, encyclical 'Mit Brennender Sorge," March 14, 1937: A.A.S. 29 (1937) p. 51.

Article 16:

2. St. Augustine, "Quest. in Hept." 2,73: PL 34,623.

3. St. Irenaeus, "Against Heretics" III, 21,3: PG 7,950; (Same as 25,1: Harvey 2, p. 115). St. Cyril of Jerusalem, "Catech." 4,35; PG 33,497. Theodore of Mopsuestia, "In Soph." 1,4-6: PG 66, 452D-453A.

Chapter V

Article 18:

1. cf. St. Irenaeus, "Against Heretics" III, 11; 8: PG 7,885, Sagnard Edition, p. 194.

Article 19:

(Due to the necessities of translation, footnote 2 follows footnote 3 in text of Article 19.)

2. cf. John 14:26; 16:13.

3. John 2:22; 12:16; cf. 14:26; 16:12-13; 7:39.

4. cf. instruction "Holy Mother Church" edited by Pontifical Consilium for Promotion of Bible Studies; A.A.S. 56 (1964) p. 715.

Chapter VI

Article 23:

1. cf. Pius XII, encyclical "Divino Afflante Spiritu:" EB 551, 553, 567. Pontifical Biblical Commission, Instruction on Proper Teaching of Sacred Scripture in Seminaries and

Religious Colleges, May 13, 1950: A.A.S. 42 (1950) pp. 495-505.

2. cf. Pius XII, ibid: EB 569.

Article 24:

3. cf. Leo XIII, encyclical "Providentissmus Deus:" EB 114; Benedict XV, encyclical "Spiritus Paraclitus:" EB 483.

Article 25:

4. St. Augustine Sermons, 179,1: PL 38,966.

5. St. Jerome, Commentary on Isaiah, Prol.: PL 24,17. cf. Benedict XV, encyclical "Spiritus Paraclitus:" EB 475-480; Pius XII, encyclical "Divino Afflante Spiritu:" EB 544.

6. St. Ambrose, On the Duties of Ministers I, 20,88: PL l6,50.

7. St. Irenaeus, "Against Heretics" IV, 32,1: PG 7, 1071; (Same as 49,2) Harvey, 2, p. 255.

* * *

---

1   [Own Note] The Notes [in the form (n)] which constitute an integral part of the *Dogmatic Constitution on Divine Revelation* are here embedded within the document exactly as they are reflected within the document on the Vatican's Website. http://www.vatican.va/archive/hist_councils/ii_vatican_council/documents/vat-ii_const_19651118_dei-verbum_en.html#top

2   [Own Note] In the use of Chapter headings as well as some terminology (such as Sacred Tradition), the conventions followed here sometimes reflect Austin Flannery's edition, [Flannery (Vatican II), pp.750-765].

* * *

The Collection:
One of us - An overview

Book One:

The Dependent God [*God's journey in our journey*]

Book One acts as an introduction to the intersecting journey of God who became One-of-us, and it sets the scene for the topics addressed in the other six books. However, in its own right, Book One does deal with specific issues not covered elsewhere, particularly with regard to covenantal sustainability 'techniques' that God first manifested through Israel, as well as issues of 'Language' and of 'the Oral word' relating to the revelation of God.

* * *

Book Two:

The Great Collaboration [*The journey with God's Written Word*]

This book deals with three topics:

Firstly, it explores the variety of ancient manuscript types which constitute the Bible, illustrating this topic by a study of 21 specific manuscripts embracing both the Old Testament (OT) and the New Testament (NT).

Secondly, it includes a comprehensive 'Case Study' of every piece of manuscript evidence in the NT which undergirds the historical reliability of the Resurrection of Jesus. This evidence is based upon the 1432[1] distinct manuscripts which undergird today's accepted NT Greek text. Inter alia, this study demonstrates the great value to be extracted from the differences as well as from the agreements between the mss. in question.

Thirdly, Book Two concludes with three chapters which face head-on the controversial topics of the inspiration, authorship, and 'inerrancy' of biblical texts.

* * *

Book Three:

Soiling the Hands [*The journey of the Canon of Scripture*]

This, the shortest of the books, plunges us right into the heart of one of our two main topics: the nature of authority, including the authority of God's Word and the authority of the Church.

* * *

Book Four:

The Jigsaw Puzzle Church [*The journey of the Apostolic (AD 33-67) and Sub-Apostolic Church (AD 67-100)*]

This book is a book of two parts:

The first part is a study of the emerging roles of leadership in the churches during the era when they had effectively little or no written New Testament (AD 33-67), and the intriguing relationships between the office-bearing roles of the early churches and those of the office-bearers in pre-Christian Jewish and Gentile mutual benefit societies and organizations.

The second part is a study of how the churches survived in the decades immediately following the deaths (around the year AD 67) of the core of the original apostolic leadership. [This second part depends upon, and draws heavily from, Raymond E. Brown's seminal work, "The Churches the Apostles left behind", but the material is re-worked and expanded upon, and located within the overall journey being aimed for in this collection].

* * *

Books Five, Six, and Seven, are a trilogy on the Eucharist; with distinct domains, as follows:

Book Five:

The Act of Sustainable Covenant [*The Framework & Theology of the Eucharist*]

The sub-title captures the essence of it, but it is worth mentioning that the notion of 'cotemporaneousness', and of certain dynamic characteristics of the Eucharist, feature prominently in this particular work, which is an 'as is' study. As such, while Scripture does of course feature here, the full relationship between the Eucharist and Scripture is addressed separately in Book Seven.

* * *

Book Six:

The Worship of All Nations [*The Cotemporaneous Eucharist of Bishop John Moore (Nigeria 2010), Moél Caích (Ireland 793 AD), & Polycarp (Smyrna 155 AD)*]

This book includes a detailed Eucharistic-journey through the so-called Stowe Missal, which originates from around the year 793 AD, and how it reflects both the same broad framework and the detailed characteristics of Eucharistic liturgies in every century back to the sub-apostolic age, just as it does equally with the Eucharist of the twenty-first century. Such time-resilience is thus a further manifestation of the sustainable covenant expressed in the Eucharist of every age and in every place.

* * *

Book Seven:

From Bruised Reeds to Patmos Island [*The length, breadth, and depth of Scripture in the Eucharist*]

As the sub-title suggests, this is a full treatise on the relationship between the Eucharist and Scripture, made up of the following five sections:

A. Three chapters on The Eucharist and the Synoptic Gospels.

B. The Eucharist in Pauline Theology, (subtitled, "Who do you think you are?").

C. The Act of Sustainable Covenant – The Institution of the Eucharist.

The sixteen chapters in this section include a study of fifteen different insights into the Institution of the Eucharist derived from Scripture when viewed through the prism of The Eucharist Prayer.

D. The Eucharist in Johannine Theology, (subtitled: "As" - Union with the Son as the Son is One with the Father).

E. The Eucharist in Hebrews and Revelation, (subtitled, Eternal worship here and now).

Book Seven concludes with

F. A personal perspective on The Marriage Supper of the Lamb, and

G. A short personal Postscript: *"God's journey in our journey."*

* * *

[Hopefully, one can see from these brief descriptions of the different books why a person can pick up any one of them and start reading it without any sense of loss over having not (yet!) read the other six.]

* * *

Bibliography

For abbreviations to references to journals and other such academic sources, and other various abbreviations, see the key in *The Jerome Biblical Commentary*., Raymond E. Brown SS. Joseph A Fitzmyer SJ, and Roland E. Murphy O.Carm (Editors) (1968). Prentice-Hall Inc. Englewood Cliffs, New Jersey, USA. [Ancient and Modern Publications, Serials, Institutions, pp. xxvii-xxxvi.]

* * *

Abbott-Smith - G. Abbott-Smith, *A Manual Greek Lexicon of the New Testament*. (1921 edition published again in 1991) T&T Clark Ltd, 59 George Street, Edinburgh.

(The) African Bible

(The) African Bible (NAB) (2005) - St Paul Communications/Daughters of St Paul, P.O. Box 49026, Nairobi, Kenya.

Anglican Bishops and Other Clergy of the Anglican Church (1871) - *A Commentary and a Revision of the Translation of the Holy Bible* (Ten Volumes 1871-1881). John Murray, Albemarle Street, London.

Note: All references to the individual commentaries on the Biblical texts and to the various introductions to the individual books and to the associated Critical Notes are given under the names of the individual scholars/commentators.

Benedict XVI - (Jesus of Nazareth – Part One)
Joseph Ratzinger, Pope Benedict XVI. - Jesus of Nazareth [*From the Baptism in the Jordan to the Transfiguration*] (2007). Bloomsbury Publishing PLC, 36 Soho Square, London W1D 3QY

Benedict XVI - (Jesus of Nazareth – Part Two)
Joseph Ratzinger, Pope Benedict XVI - Jesus of Nazareth - Part Two [*Holy Week From the Entrance into Jerusalem to the Resurrection*] (2011). Ignatius Press, San Francisco, USA.

Benedict XVI - (Jesus of Nazareth – *The Infancy Narratives*)
Joseph Ratzinger, Pope Benedict XVI - *Jesus of Nazareth - The Infancy Narratives*) (2012). Image, Random House Inc. New York

Brown [Apocrypha] Raymond E. Brown, S.S - *Apocrypha; Dead Sea Scrolls; Other Jewish Literature* in *The Jerome Biblical Commentary*., Raymond E. Brown SS. Joseph A Fitzmyer SJ, and Roland E. Murphy O.Carm (Editors) (1968). Prentice-Hall Inc. Englewood Cliffs, New Jersey, USA.

Bruce [Canon] - F. F. Bruce (1988) *The Canon of Scripture*. InterVarsity Press, P.O. Box 1400, Downers Grove, IL, USA 60515-1426

Cassidy (1995) - Michael Cassidy, *A Witness For Ever.* Hodder and Stoughton, A Division of Hodder Headline PLC, 338 Euston Road, London NW1 3BH

(The) Catechism of the Catholic Church, [CCC] (1995, Revised Edition 2001), Paulines Publications Africa, PO Box 49026, 00100 GPO, Nairobi, Kenya.

OR: Web versions such as http://www.vatican.va/archive/

NOTE: The numbering system for the CCC is the same for the hard copy text as it is for

Web version, as far as Parts, Sections, Chapters, Articles, Paragraphs, etc, are concerned. However, on occasion, footnotes do not align, and where this is the case, it is the Web version from the Vatican website that has been referenced in this little project.

(The) Catholic Encyclopaedia: [See New Advent: http://www.newadvent.org/cathen/

CCC. - (The) Catechism of the Catholic Church, above.

Cwiekowski SS (1988) Frederick J. Cwiekowski, *The Beginnings of the Church*. Paulist Press, 997 Macarthur Boulevard, Mahwah, New Jersey 07430. USA

(The) Daily Missal (2004) - Paulines Publications Africa, www.paulinesafrica.org

Dillon & Fitzmyer (Acts)
Richard J. Dillon and Joseph A. Fitzmyer, S.J. (1968) - *Acts of the Apostles* in *The Jerome Biblical Commentary*. Raymond E. Brown SS. Joseph A Fitzmyer SJ, and Roland E. Murphy O.Carm (Editors) (1968). Prentice-Hall Inc. Englewood Cliffs, New Jersey, USA

Fitzmyer [Galatians]
Joseph A. Fitzmyer, S.J. (1968) - *The Letter to the Galatians* in *The Jerome Biblical Commentary*. Raymond E. Brown SS. Joseph A Fitzmyer SJ, and Roland E. Murphy O.Carm (Editors) (1968). Prentice-Hall Inc. Englewood Cliffs, New Jersey, USA.

Fitzmyer [Life of Paul]
Joseph A. Fitzmyer, S.J. (1968) - *A Life of Paul* in *The Jerome Biblical Commentary*. Raymond E. Brown SS. Joseph A Fitzmyer SJ, and Roland E. Murphy O.Carm (Editors) (1968). Prentice-Hall Inc. Englewood Cliffs, New Jersey, USA.

Flannery [Vatican II]
Austin P. Flannery OP (Ed.) (1975) - *The Documents of Vatican II*. Pillar Books, Pyramid Communications, Inc. 919 Third Avenue, New York, 10022, USA.
[Also at: www.vatican.va/archive/hist_councils/ii_vatican_council/c].

Grudem   Wayne Grudem - *The GIFT of Prophecy - in the New Testament and Today*, (1988, 1992), Kingsway Publications Ltd, 1 St. Anne's Road, Eastbourne, E. Sussex BN21 3UN. England

JB   The New Jerusalem Bible (Readers Edition) (1990). Bantam Doubleday Dell Publishing Group, Inc. 666 Fifth Avenue, New York, New York 10103.

Jerome (1968) - Raymond E. Brown SS. Joseph A Fitzmyer SJ, and Roland E. Murphy O.Carm (Editors) (1968) *The Jerome Biblical Commentary*. Prentice-Hall Inc. Englewood Cliffs, New Jersey, USA.
Note: All references to the individual commentaries on the Biblical texts and to the various Topical Articles in The Jerome Biblical Commentary include the commentary or topical article number (digits from 1 to 80) and the paragraph number within the commentary/topical article, as well as the page number; e.g. 77:111, p 755.

Johnson [Intellectuals]
Paul Johnson (1988) - *Intellectuals* George Weidenfeld & Nicolson, Ltd. 91 Clapham High Street, London SW4 7TA, UK

Johnson [Papacy]
Paul Johnson (1997) - *The Papacy*. Weidenfeld and Nicolson, The Orion Publishing Group Ltd, Orion House, 5 Upper Saint Martin's Lane, London WC2H 9EA

Keegan   John Keegan (2002) *Churchill*. Phoenix - an imprint of Orion Books, Ltd, Orion House, 5 Upper St Martin's Lane, London WC2H 9EA, UK. (First published by Weidenfeld & Nicolson).

KJV (=AV)   The King James Bible

Lloyd-Jones [Authority]
: Dr. D. Martyn Lloyd Jones (1958) - *Authority – The Authority of Jesus Christ; The Authority of the Scriptures; The Authority of the Holy Spirit.* The Banner of Truth Trust, 3 Murrayfield Road, Edinburgh EH12 6EL.

LXX *The Septuagint Version of the Old Testament.* With an English Translation, and with Various Readings and Critical Notes. (My edition undated). Samuel Bagster and Sons, 15, Paternoster Row, London.

LXX Septuagint Website in Greek and English:
http://www.ellopos.net/elpenor/greek-texts/septuagint/default.asp

Merton (The New Man)
: Thomas Merton (1962) - *The New Man.* Burns & Oates, Wellwood, North Farm Road, Tunbridge Wells, Kent TN2 3DR, England

Morphew: Dr. Derek Morphew - *Breakthrough – Discovering the Kingdom.* (1991, 2007) Vineyard Publishing International, PO Box 53286, Kenilworth, Cape Town, South Africa.

Mounce   William D. Mounce (1993) - *The Analytical Lexicon to the Greek New Testament.* Zondervan Publishing House, Academic and Professional Books, Grand Rapids, Michigan 49530.

NAB See: (The) African Bible (above)

New Advent - The CD-ROM of the Catholic Encyclopaedia, The Church Fathers, Summa Theologica, and The Bible. Published by St. Ignatius Press (Edition 2.1). Cf. WWW. NewAdvent.org and http://www.ignatius.com

New Advent - Multilingual Bible:
: This Bible appears in three languages side-by-side: Greek, English and Latin. The **Greek** Old Testament comes from the Septuagint, and the New Testament is the Westcott-Hort edition, modified for standardized spelling. The **English** comes from the Douay-Rheims translation, modified by New Advent editors to make it clearer to the modern reader. (The unmodified Douay-Rheims is also present) The **Latin** is the Clementine Vulgate. (The **notes** are taken from Bishop Richard Challoner's commentary on the Holy Bible).

NIV F. C. Thompson (1983) - *Thompson Chain-Reference Bible.* (NIV). The Zondervan Corporation, Grand Rapids, Michigan, 49506, USA.

NKJV - The New King James Bible

O'Loughlin (Celtic Theology) Thomas O'Loughlin (2003) - *Celtic Theology – Humanity, World and God in Early Irish Writings.* Continuum, The Tower Building, 11 York road, London SE1 7NX.

Peterson Eugene H. Peterson (1996) - *The Message – New Testament with Psalms and Proverbs.* NavPress, P.O. Box 35001, Colorado Springs, CO 80935

Psalms: *The Revised Grail Psalms* Copyright © 2010, Conception Abbey/The Grail, admin. by GIA Publications, Inc., www.giamusic.com

Rahner [Dictionary]
: Karl Rahner & Herbert Vorgrimler (1968) - *Theological Dictionary.* Herder and Herder, 232 Madison Avenue, New York, N.Y. 10016

Ratzinger - For references to Ratzinger as Pope Benedict XVI, see there.

Rawlings [1978] Maurice Rawlings, MD. (1978) - *Beyond Death's Door.* Bantam Books, 1540 Broadway, New York, 10036

Rawlings [1993] Maurice Rawlings, MD. (1993) - *To Hell and Back.* Thomas Nelson, Inc. Nashville, Tennessee, USA.

Rawlinson - George Rawlinson MA, (1872), Kings Books I and II in *A Commentary and a Revision of the Translation of the Holy Bible* (Ten Volumes 1871-1881). John Murray, Albemarle Street, London.

Renwick & Harman
A.M. Renwick & A.M. Harman (2005) - *The Story of the Church* (Third Edition). Inter-Varsity Press 38 De Montfort Street, Leicester LE1 7GP, England.

Richards Lawrence O. Richards (1987) - *Richard's Complete Bible Handbook*. Word Publishing, Dallas, USA.

Sawyer   M. James Sawyer, Ph.D. - *Evangelicals and the Canon of the New Testament*. [A paper by Sawyer when he was Associate Professor of Theology and Church History at Western Seminary, San Jose, CA., dated as June 3rd 2004 on https://Bible.org/article/evangelicals-and-canon-new-testament].

Septuagint (LXX) - *The Septuagint Version of The Old Testament*. (Greek Text, with an English Translation, and with Various Readings and Critical Notes). Samuel Bagster and Sons, 15, Paternoster Row; (undated).

Stanley & Brown (Aspects of New Testament Thought)
David M. Stanley SJ, & Raymond E. Brown SS. *Aspects of New Testament Thought* in *The Jerome Biblical Commentary*., Raymond E. Brown SS. Joseph A Fitzmyer SJ, and Roland E. Murphy O.Carm (Editors) (1968). Prentice-Hall Inc. Englewood Cliffs, New Jersey, USA.

Thompson - F. C. Thompson (1983) *Thompson Chain-Reference Bible*. (NIV). The Zondervan Corporation, Grand Rapids, Michigan, 49506, USA.

Turro & Brown (Canonicity)
James C. Turro & Raymond E. Brown, S.S. *Canonicity* in *The Jerome Biblical Commentary*., Raymond E. Brown SS. Joseph A Fitzmyer SJ, and Roland E. Murphy O.Carm (Editors) (1968). Prentice-Hall Inc. Englewood Cliffs, New Jersey, USA.

UBS United Bible Societies. *The Greek New Testament*. Third Edition. (1983). Edited by Kurt Aland, Matthew Black, Carlo M. Martini, Bruce M. Metzger, and Allen Wikgren. German Bible Society, P. O. Box 810340, 7000 Stuttgart 80, Germany

Vatican II [Documents]
Refer either to the hardcopy reference above [Austin P. Flannery OP (Ed.) (1975) - *The Documents of Vatican II*] Or to the Vatican Website which contains all of the Council Documents: [www.vatican.va/archive/hist_councils/ii_vatican_council/c].

Venter (Reconciliation)
Alexander Venter (2004). *Doing Reconciliation. Racism ,reconciliation and transformation in the Church and World*. Vineyard International Publishing, PO Box 53286, Kenilworth 7745, Cape Town, South Africa.

Vidmar - John Vidmar, OP. (2005) *The Catholic Church Through the Ages*. Paulist Press, New Jersey 07430

Wright (The Last Word)
N.T. Wright - *The Last Word: Beyond the Bible Wars to a New Understanding of the Authority of Scripture* (2005) HarperCollins Publishers, 10 East 53rd Street, New York, NY 10022.

* * *

WEBSITES:

http://www.archive.org/
http://www.catholicculture.org
http://www.gcatholic.com
http://www.law.umkc.edu/faculty/projects/ftrials/wilde/wilde.htm
http://www.robotwisdom.com/jaj/ulysses/ [The Internet Ulysses by James Joyce, edited by Jorn Barger, updated Feb2001]
http://www.isos.dias.ie/ [Stowe Missal, Royal Irish Academy].
http://www.vatican.va
http://www.vatican.va/archive/hist_councils/ii_vatican_council/
WWW.NewAdvent.org
http://www.ignatius.com
http://www.scborromeo.org/ccc
LXX Septuagint Website in Greek and English:
http://www.ellopos.net/elpenor/greek-texts/septuagint/default.asp
http://www.earlyChurchtexts.com/
http://www.bible-researcher.com/muratorian.html
http://www.earlychristianwritings.com/text/muratorian-greek.html
http://www.earlychristianwritings.com/text/muratorian-latin.html

* * *

---

1   mss. "manuscripts". Where the number (1432) comes from is all explained in Book Two, Chapter 23.

* * *

Also by Michael Mahony

Book One, "The Dependent God", acts as an introduction to the intersecting journey of God who became One-of-us, and it sets the scene for the topics addressed in the other six books. However, in its own right, Book One does deal with specific issues not covered elsewhere, particularly with regard to covenantal sustainability 'techniques' that God first manifested through Israel, as well as issues of 'Language' and of 'the Oral word' relating to the revelation of God.

"The Dependent God" may be obtained at
www.sacatholiconline.org

Also by Michael Mahony

In Book Two, "The Great Collaboration", Michael Mahony explores the variety of ancient manuscript types which constitute the Bible, illustrating this topic by a study of 21 specific manuscripts embracing both the Old Testament (OT) and the New Testament (NT). This is followed by a comprehensive 'Case Study' of every piece of manuscript evidence in the NT which undergirds the historical reliability of the Resurrection of Jesus. This evidence is based upon the 1432 distinct manuscripts which underpin today's accepted NT Greek text. The book concludes with three chapters which face the controversial topics of the inspiration, authorship, and 'inerrancy' of biblical texts head-on.

Order your copy at www.sacatholiconline.org

Also by Michael Mahony

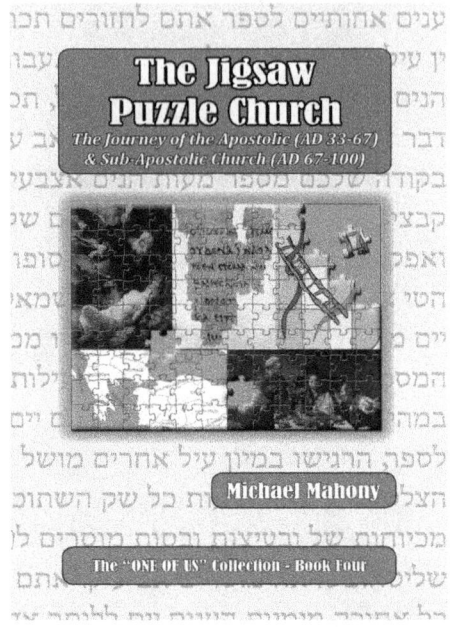

In *The Jigsaw Puzzle Church*, Book Four of the "One of Us" Collection, Michael Mahony takes us upon a journey alongside the extraordinary variety of early Christian communities which emerged in the years immediately following the Resurrection of Jesus. During this time the Church had effectively no written New Testament Scriptures (AD 33-67) or virtually no leadership by the original Apostles (AD 67-100). In this, the fourth book in the collection, the author draws heavily from seminal works by Edwin Hatch in the 19th Century and by Raymond E. Brown in the 20th in order to identify how these communities survived and emerged as The Church in the 2nd Century.

Order your print or ebook copy at www.sacatholiconline.org
or at www.amazon.com and www.amazon.co.uk

Michael Mahony Also Wrote:

    With Book Five of this collection, Michael Mahony introduces his Trilogy on the Eucharist. His objectives in this present volume include exposing a wider Christian audience to the Framework and Theology of the Eucharist, and to the role which the Eucharist plays in God's plan to sustain the Church over time, not least in our present age of "The Runaway Church". At the same time, he challenges Catholic readers to take a fresh look at the much neglected Concluding Rites of the Eucharist, claiming that the link therein between the Eucharist and the Kerygma is central to achieving the purposes of the New Evangelisation, particularly with regard to the laity's role in such evangelisation.

    Order your copy at www.sacatholiconline.org

Michael Mahony Also Wrote:

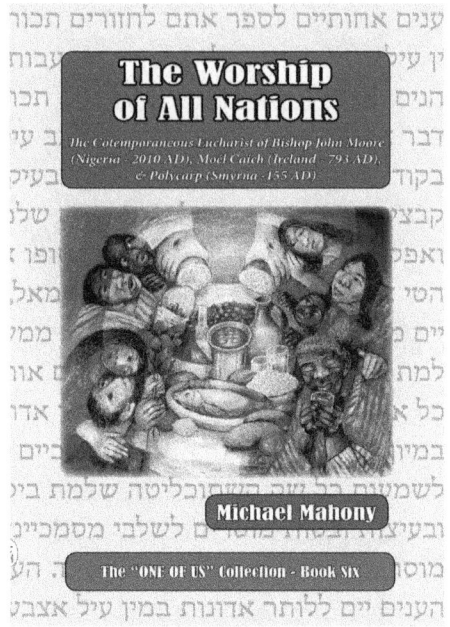

The Eucharist is the great Act of Sustainable Covenant, and here in his sixth book, The Worship of All Nations, Michael Mahony demonstrates that the Eucharist in every age and in every place manifests a consistent theology, incorporating both in its Architecture (Shape) and in its detailed contents, certain essential characteristics of this Jesus-given act of divine worship. He does so by taking us upon a journey through a particular Eucharistic missal originating from the year 793 AD, and he shows how it parallels Eucharistic liturgies from every century right back to the sub-apostolic age, just as it is does with the Eucharist of the twenty-first century as celebrated today in Bauchi, Northern Nigeria (and in New York, Cairo, Tokyo, Tel Aviv, Calcutta, Kiev, Soweto, Hobart and Reykjavik...)

Order your copy at www.sacatholiconline.org

Also by Michael Mahony:

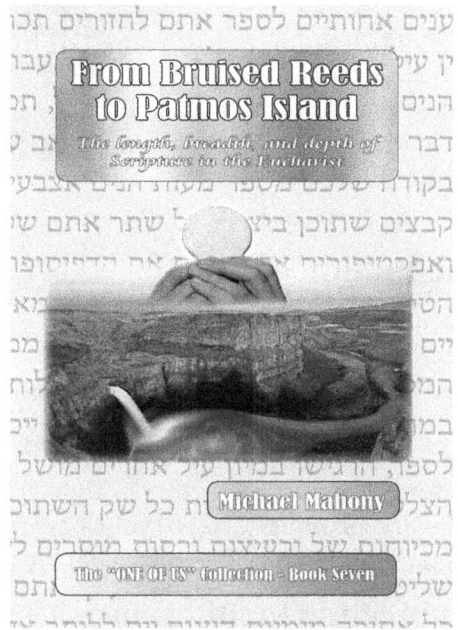

Any person who participates daily in the Mass of the Catholic Church will, over the 2 & 3 year Lectionary cycle, hear, pray, and acclaim Scripture passages from every single book of the Bible, both OT and NT. But in addition, the length, breadth, and depth of Scripture which permeates both the Architecture of the Eucharist and the thousands of prayers expressed in its Liturgy is a topic which Michael Mahony takes up in the final book of his trilogy on the Eucharist, From Bruised Reeds to Patmos Island. In doing so, he challenges and recalibrates the term, "A Bible-believing Church," and draws upon seminal research by Cistercian Abbot Emeritus, Fr. Denis Farkasfalvy, to explore the symbiotic relationship between the Eucharist and Scripture in a refreshingly new way, one which throws surprising light upon the provenance of NT texts.

Order your copy at www.sacatholiconline.org

What is SA Catholic Online Books?

SA Catholic Online Books is a specialised publishing facilitator, with the objective of assisting Catholic authors to get their books published, either in print form or in eBook form, or both.

These are some of our services:

Publishing Facilitation

Our publishing facilitation services include proofreading, editing, typesetting, layout & cover design, to print-ready material. We also facilitate paperback printing locally and internationally.

Ebook Services - Creation & Conversions

We create fully interactive eBooks from: (1) Your Manuscript as a Word document; (2) The Pre-print material of your new print book (Adobe Indesign files), and (3) the PDFs of your previously printed book.

Specialised Publishing Facilitation

Specialised publishing services include: the reproduction and re-publishing of old, out-of-print books, books for private consumption, children's books, magazines and newsletters.

Print Book Sales on Major Online Platforms

Thanks to our partnership with Print On Demand, we can now offer your books for sale on a print-on-demand basis on Takealot in South Africa! We also sell your print books internationally on Amazon!

eBook Sales in our own eBookstore

We have set up our own eBooks sales platform to provide an eBook outlet for South African independent and self-published authors. We also continue to offer eBook sales internationally on Amazon.

Chapbook Publishing Services

Chapbooks are the ideal entry level publishing solution for first-time writers. See our affordable publishing packages for your story, fictional short story or collection of poetry at Write-On Chapbooks

For more information, go to www.sacatholiconline.org

www.ingramcontent.com/pod-product-compliance
Lightning Source LLC
Chambersburg PA
CBHW070548050426
42450CB00011B/2770